MW00491040

Casenote® *Legal Briefs*

CONTRACTS

Keyed to Courses Using

Crandall and Whaley's
Cases, Problems, and Materials on Contracts
Sixth Edition

This publication is designed to provide accurate and authoritative information in regard to the subject matter covered. It is sold with the understanding that the publisher is not engaged in rendering legal, accounting, or other professional services. If legal advice or other expert assistance is required, the services of a competent professional person should be sought.

— From a Declaration of Principles adopted jointly by a Committee of the American Bar Association and a Committee of Publishers and Associates

Copyright © 2012 CCH Incorporated.

Published by Wolters Kluwer Law & Business in New York.

Wolters Kluwer Law & Business serves customers worldwide with CCH, Aspen Publishers, and Kluwer Law International products. (www.wolterskluwerlb.com)

No part of this publication may be reproduced or transmitted in any form or by any means, electronic or mechanical, including photocopy, recording, or utilized by any information storage and retrieval system, without written permission from the publisher. For information about permissions or to request permissions online, visit us at wolterskluwerlb.com or a written request may be faxed to our permissions department at 212-771-0803.

To contact Customer Service, e-mail customer.service@wolterskluwer.com, call 1-800-234-1660, fax 1-800-901-9075, or mail correspondence to:

Wolters Kluwer Law & Business
Attn: Order Department
P.O. Box 990
Frederick, MD 21705

Printed in the United States of America.

1 2 3 4 5 6 7 8 9 0

ISBN 978-1-4548-0803-9

About Wolters Kluwer Law & Business

Wolters Kluwer Law & Business is a leading global provider of intelligent information and digital solutions for legal and business professionals in key specialty areas, and respected educational resources for professors and law students. Wolters Kluwer Law & Business connects legal and business professionals as well as those in the education market with timely, specialized authoritative content and information-enabled solutions to support success through productivity, accuracy and mobility.

Serving customers worldwide, Wolters Kluwer Law & Business products include those under the Aspen Publishers, CCH, Kluwer Law International, Loislaw, Best Case, ftwilliam.com and MediRegs family of products.

CCH products have been a trusted resource since 1913, and are highly regarded resources for legal, securities, antitrust and trade regulation, government contracting, banking, pension, payroll, employment and labor, and healthcare reimbursement and compliance professionals.

Aspen Publishers products provide essential information to attorneys, business professionals and law students. Written by preeminent authorities, the product line offers analytical and practical information in a range of specialty practice areas from securities law and intellectual property to mergers and acquisitions and pension/benefits. Aspen's trusted legal education resources provide professors and students with high-quality, up-to-date and effective resources for successful instruction and study in all areas of the law.

Kluwer Law International products provide the global business community with reliable international legal information in English. Legal practitioners, corporate counsel and business executives around the world rely on Kluwer Law journals, looseleafs, books, and electronic products for comprehensive information in many areas of international legal practice.

Loislaw is a comprehensive online legal research product providing legal content to law firm practitioners of various specializations. Loislaw provides attorneys with the ability to quickly and efficiently find the necessary legal information they need, when and where they need it, by facilitating access to primary law as well as state-specific law, records, forms and treatises.

Best Case Solutions is the leading bankruptcy software product to the bankruptcy industry. It provides software and workflow tools to flawlessly streamline petition preparation and the electronic filing process, while timely incorporating ever-changing court requirements.

ftwilliam.com offers employee benefits professionals the highest quality plan documents (retirement, welfare and non-qualified) and government forms (5500/PBGC, 1099 and IRS) software at highly competitive prices.

MediRegs products provide integrated health care compliance content and software solutions for professionals in healthcare, higher education and life sciences, including professionals in accounting, law and consulting.

Wolters Kluwer Law & Business, a division of Wolters Kluwer, is headquartered in New York. Wolters Kluwer is a market-leading global information services company focused on professionals.

Format for the Casenote® Legal Brief

Nature of Case: This section identifies the form of action (e.g., breach of contract, negligence, battery), the type of proceeding (e.g., demurrer, appeal from trial court's jury instructions), or the relief sought (e.g., damages, injunction, criminal sanctions).

Fact Summary: This is included to refresh your memory and can be used as a quick reminder of the facts.

Rule of Law: Summarizes the general principle of law that the case illustrates. It may be used for instant recall of the court's holding and for classroom discussion or home review.

Facts: This section contains all relevant facts of the case, including the contentions of the parties and the lower court holdings. It is written in a logical order to give the student a clear understanding of the case. The plaintiff and defendant are identified by their proper names throughout and are always labeled with a (P) or (D).

Palsgraf v. Long Island R.R. Co.

Injured bystander (P) v. Railroad company (D)

N.Y. Ct. App., 248 N.Y. 339, 162 N.E. 99 (1928).

NATURE OF CASE: Appeal from judgment affirming verdict for plaintiff seeking damages for personal injury.

FACT SUMMARY: Helen Palsgraf (P) was injured on R.R.'s (D) train platform when R.R.'s (D) guard helped a passenger aboard a moving train, causing his package to fall on the tracks. The package contained fireworks which exploded, creating a shock that tipped a scale onto Palsgraf (P).

🏛 RULE OF LAW
The risk reasonably to be perceived defines the duty to be obeyed.

FACTS: Helen Palsgraf (P) purchased a ticket to Rockaway Beach from R.R. (D) and was waiting on the train platform. As she waited, two men ran to catch a train that was pulling out from the platform. The first man jumped aboard, but the second man, who appeared as if he might fall, was helped aboard by the guard on the train who had kept the door open so they could jump aboard. A guard on the platform also helped by pushing him onto the train. The man was carrying a package wrapped in newspaper. In the process, the man dropped his package, which fell on the tracks. The package contained fireworks and exploded. The shock of the explosion was apparently of great enough strength to tip over some scales at the other end of the platform, which fell on Palsgraf (P) and injured her. A jury awarded her damages, and R.R. (D) appealed.

ISSUE: Does the risk reasonably to be perceived define the duty to be obeyed?

HOLDING AND DECISION: (Cardozo, C.J.) Yes. The risk reasonably to be perceived defines the duty to be obeyed. If there is no foreseeable hazard to the injured party as the result of a seemingly innocent act, the act does not become a tort because it happened to be a wrong as to another. If the wrong was not willful, the plaintiff must show that the act as to her had such great and apparent possibilities of danger as to entitle her to protection. Negligence in the abstract is not enough upon which to base liability. Negligence is a relative concept, evolving out of the common law doctrine of trespass on the case. To establish liability, the defendant must owe a legal duty of reasonable care to the injured party. A cause of action in tort will lie where harm, though unintended, could have been averted or avoided by observance of such a duty. The scope of the duty is limited by the range of danger that a reasonable person could foresee. In this case, there was nothing to suggest from the appearance of the parcel or otherwise that the parcel contained fireworks. The guard could not reasonably have had any warning of a threat to Palsgraf (P), and R.R. (D) therefore cannot be held liable. Judgment is reversed in favor of R.R. (D).

DISSENT: (Andrews, J.) The concept that there is no negligence unless R.R. (D) owes a legal duty to take care as to Palsgraf (P) herself is too narrow. Everyone owes to the world at large the duty of refraining from those acts that may unreasonably threaten the safety of others. If the guard's action was negligent as to those nearby, it was also negligent as to those outside what might be termed the "danger zone." For Palsgraf (P) to recover, R.R.'s (D) negligence must have been the proximate cause of her injury, a question of fact for the jury.

▶ ANALYSIS

The majority defined the limit of the defendant's liability in terms of the danger that a reasonable person in defendant's situation would have perceived. The dissent argued that the limitation should not be placed on liability, but rather on damages. Judge Andrews suggested that only injuries that would not have happened but for R.R.'s (D) negligence should be compensable. Both the majority and dissent recognized the policy-driven need to limit liability for negligent acts, seeking, in the words of Judge Andrews, to define a framework "that will be practical and in keeping with the general understanding of mankind." The Restatement (Second) of Torts has accepted Judge Cardozo's view.

━━

Quicknotes

FORESEEABILITY A reasonable expectation that change is the probable result of certain acts or omissions.

NEGLIGENCE Conduct falling below the standard of care that a reasonable person would demonstrate under similar conditions.

PROXIMATE CAUSE The natural sequence of events without which an injury would not have been sustained.

━━

Party ID: Quick identification of the relationship between the parties.

Concurrence/Dissent: All concurrences and dissents are briefed whenever they are included by the casebook editor.

Analysis: This last paragraph gives you a broad understanding of where the case "fits in" with other cases in the section of the book and with the entire course. It is a hornbook-style discussion indicating whether the case is a majority or minority opinion and comparing the principal case with other cases in the casebook. It may also provide analysis from restatements, uniform codes, and law review articles. The analysis will prove to be invaluable to classroom discussion.

Issue: The issue is a concise question that brings out the essence of the opinion as it relates to the section of the casebook in which the case appears. Both substantive and procedural issues are included if relevant to the decision.

Holding and Decision: This section offers a clear and in-depth discussion of the rule of the case and the court's rationale. It is written in easy-to-understand language and answers the issue presented by applying the law to the facts of the case. When relevant, it includes a thorough discussion of the exceptions to the case as listed by the court, any major cites to the other cases on point, and the names of the judges who wrote the decisions.

Quicknotes: Conveniently defines legal terms found in the case and summarizes the nature of any statutes, codes, or rules referred to in the text.

Wolters Kluwer Law & Business is proud to offer *Casenote® Legal Briefs*—continuing thirty years of publishing America's best-selling legal briefs.

Casenote® Legal Briefs are designed to help you save time when briefing assigned cases. Organized under convenient headings, they show you how to abstract the basic facts and holdings from the text of the actual opinions handed down by the courts. Used as part of a rigorous study regimen, they can help you spend more time analyzing and critiquing points of law than on copying bits and pieces of judicial opinions into your notebook or outline.

Casenote® Legal Briefs should never be used as a substitute for assigned casebook readings. They work best when read as a follow-up to reviewing the underlying opinions themselves. Students who try to avoid reading and digesting the judicial opinions in their casebooks or online sources will end up short-changing themselves in the long run. The ability to absorb, critique, and restate the dynamic and complex elements of case law decisions is crucial to your success in law school and beyond. It cannot be developed vicariously.

Casenote® Legal Briefs represents but one of the many offerings in Legal Education's Study Aid Timeline, which includes:

- *Casenote® Legal Briefs*
- *Emanuel® Law Outlines*
- *Examples & Explanations* Series
- *Emanuel® Law in a Flash* Flash Cards
- *Emanuel® CrunchTime®* Series
- *Siegel's Essay and Multiple-Choice Questions and Answers* Series

Each of these series is designed to provide you with easy-to-understand explanations of complex points of law. Each volume offers guidance on the principles of legal analysis and, consulted regularly, will hone your ability to spot relevant issues. We have titles that will help you prepare for class, prepare for your exams, and enhance your general comprehension of the law along the way.

To find out more about Wolters Kluwer Law & Business' study aid publications, visit us online at *www. wolterskluwerlb.com* or email us at *legaledu@ wolterskluwer.com*. We'll be happy to assist you.

How to Brief a Case

A. Decide on a Format and Stick to It

Structure is essential to a good brief. It enables you to arrange systematically the related parts that are scattered throughout most cases, thus making manageable and understandable what might otherwise seem to be an endless and unfathomable sea of information. There are, of course, an unlimited number of formats that can be utilized. However, it is best to find one that suits your needs and stick to it. Consistency breeds both efficiency and the security that when called upon you will know where to look in your brief for the information you are asked to give.

Any format, as long as it presents the essential elements of a case in an organized fashion, can be used. Experience, however, has led *Casenote® Legal Briefs* to develop and utilize the following format because of its logical flow and universal applicability.

NATURE OF CASE: This is a brief statement of the legal character and procedural status of the case (e.g., "Appeal of a burglary conviction").

There are many different alternatives open to a litigant dissatisfied with a court ruling. The key to determining which one has been used is to discover *who is asking this court for what.*

This first entry in the brief should be kept as *short as possible.* Use the court's terminology if you understand it. But since jurisdictions vary as to the titles of pleadings, the best entry is the one that addresses who wants what in this proceeding, not the one that sounds most like the court's language.

RULE OF LAW: A statement of the general principle of law that the case illustrates (e.g., "An acceptance that varies any term of the offer is considered a rejection and counteroffer").

Determining the rule of law of a case is a procedure similar to determining the issue of the case. Avoid being fooled by red herrings; there may be a few rules of law mentioned in the case excerpt, but usually only one is *the* rule with which the casebook editor is concerned. The techniques used to locate the issue, described below, may also be utilized to find the rule of law. Generally, your best guide is simply the chapter heading. It is a clue to the point the casebook editor seeks to make and should be kept in mind when reading every case in the respective section.

FACTS: A synopsis of only the essential facts of the case, i.e., those bearing upon or leading up to the issue.

The facts entry should be a short statement of the events and transactions that led one party to initiate legal proceedings against another in the first place. While some cases conveniently state the salient facts at the beginning of the decision, in other instances they will have to be culled from hiding places throughout the text, even from concurring and dissenting opinions. Some of the "facts" will often be in dispute and should be so noted. Conflicting evidence may be briefly pointed up. "Hard" facts must be included. Both must be *relevant* in order to be listed in the facts entry. It is impossible to tell what is relevant until the entire case is read, as the ultimate determination of the rights and liabilities of the parties may turn on something buried deep in the opinion.

Generally, the facts entry should not be longer than three to five *short* sentences.

It is often helpful to identify the role played by a party in a given context. For example, in a construction contract case the identification of a party as the "contractor" or "builder" alleviates the need to tell that that party was the one who was supposed to have built the house.

It is always helpful, and a good general practice, to identify the "plaintiff" and the "defendant." This may seem elementary and uncomplicated, but, especially in view of the creative editing practiced by some casebook editors, it is sometimes a difficult or even impossible task. Bear in mind that the *party presently* seeking something from this court may not be the plaintiff, and that sometimes only the cross-claim of a defendant is treated in the excerpt. Confusing or misaligning the parties can ruin your analysis and understanding of the case.

ISSUE: A statement of the general legal question answered by or illustrated in the case. For clarity, the issue is best put in the form of a question capable of a "yes" or "no" answer. In reality, the issue is simply the Rule of Law put in the form of a question (e.g., "May an offer be accepted by performance?").

The major problem presented in discerning what is *the* issue in the case is that an opinion usually purports to raise and answer several questions. However, except for rare cases, only one such question is really the issue in the case. Collateral issues not necessary to the resolution of the matter in controversy are handled by the court by language known as *"obiter dictum"* or merely *"dictum."* While dicta may be included later in the brief, they have no place under the issue heading.

To find the issue, ask *who wants what* and then go on to ask *why did that party succeed or fail in getting it.* Once this is determined, the "why" should be turned into a question.

The complexity of the issues in the cases will vary, but in all cases a single-sentence question should sum up the issue. *In a few cases,* there will be two, or even more rarely, three issues of equal importance to the resolution of the case. Each should be expressed in a single-sentence question.

Since many issues are resolved by a court in coming to a final disposition of a case, the casebook editor will reproduce the portion of the opinion containing the issue or issues most relevant to the area of law under scrutiny. A noted law professor gave this advice: "Close the book; look at the title on the cover." Chances are, if it is Property, you need not concern yourself with whether, for example, the federal government's treatment of the plaintiff's land really raises a federal question sufficient to support jurisdiction on this ground in federal court.

The same rule applies to chapter headings designating sub-areas within the subjects. They tip you off as to what the text is designed to teach. The cases are arranged in a casebook to show a progression or development of the law, so that the preceding cases may also help.

It is also most important to remember to *read the notes and questions* at the end of a case to determine what the editors wanted you to have gleaned from it.

HOLDING AND DECISION: This section should succinctly explain the rationale of the court in arriving at its decision. In capsulizing the "reasoning" of the court, it should always include an application of the general rule or rules of law to the specific facts of the case. Hidden justifications come to light in this entry: the reasons for the state of the law, the public policies, the biases and prejudices, those considerations that influence the justices' thinking and, ultimately, the outcome of the case. At the end, there should be a short indication of the disposition or procedural resolution of the case (e.g., "Decision of the trial court for Mr. Smith (P) reversed").

The foregoing format is designed to help you "digest" the reams of case material with which you will be faced in your law school career. Once mastered by practice, it will place at your fingertips the information the authors of your casebooks have sought to impart to you in case-by-case illustration and analysis.

B. Be as Economical as Possible in Briefing Cases

Once armed with a format that encourages succinctness, it is as important to be economical with regard to the time spent on the actual reading of the case as it is to be economical in the writing of the brief itself. This does not mean "skimming" a case. Rather, it means reading the case with an "eye" trained to recognize into which "section" of your brief a particular passage or line fits and having a system for quickly and precisely marking the case so that the passages fitting any one particular part of

the brief can be easily identified and brought together in a concise and accurate manner when the brief is actually written.

It is of no use to simply repeat everything in the opinion of the court; record only enough information to trigger your recollection of what the court said. Nevertheless, an accurate statement of the "law of the case," i.e., the legal principle applied to the facts, is absolutely essential to class preparation and to learning the law under the case method.

To that end, it is important to develop a "shorthand" that you can use to make marginal notations. These notations will tell you at a glance in which section of the brief you will be placing that particular passage or portion of the opinion.

Some students prefer to underline all the salient portions of the opinion (with a pencil or colored underliner marker), making marginal notations as they go along. Others prefer the color-coded method of underlining, utilizing different colors of markers to underline the salient portions of the case, each separate color being used to represent a different section of the brief. For example, blue underlining could be used for passages relating to the rule of law, yellow for those relating to the issue, and green for those relating to the holding and decision, etc. While it has its advocates, the color-coded method can be confusing and time-consuming (all that time spent on changing colored markers). Furthermore, it can interfere with the continuity and concentration many students deem essential to the reading of a case for maximum comprehension. In the end, however, it is a matter of personal preference and style. Just remember, whatever method you use, underlining must be used sparingly or its value is lost.

If you take the marginal notation route, an efficient and easy method is to go along underlining the key portions of the case and placing in the margin alongside them the following "markers" to indicate where a particular passage or line "belongs" in the brief you will write:

N   (NATURE OF CASE)
RL (RULE OF LAW)
I   (ISSUE)
HL (HOLDING AND DECISION, relates to the RULE OF LAW behind the decision)
HR (HOLDING AND DECISION, gives the RATIONALE or reasoning behind the decision)
HA (HOLDING AND DECISION, APPLIES the general principle(s) of law to the facts of the case to arrive at the decision)

Remember that a particular passage may well contain information necessary to more than one part of your brief, in which case you simply note that in the margin. If you are using the color-coded underlining method instead of marginal notation, simply make asterisks or checks in the margin next to the passage in question in the colors that indicate the additional sections of the brief where it might be utilized.

The economy of utilizing "shorthand" in marking cases for briefing can be maintained in the actual brief writing process itself by utilizing "law student shorthand" within the brief. There are many commonly used words and phrases for which abbreviations can be substituted in your briefs (and in your class notes also). You can develop abbreviations that are personal to you and which will save you a lot of time. A reference list of briefing abbreviations can be found on page xii of this book.

C. Use Both the Briefing Process and the Brief as a Learning Tool

Now that you have a format and the tools for briefing cases efficiently, the most important thing is to make the time spent in briefing profitable to you and to make the most advantageous use of the briefs you create. Of course, the briefs are invaluable for classroom reference when you are called upon to explain or analyze a particular

case. However, they are also useful in reviewing for exams. A quick glance at the fact summary should bring the case to mind, and a rereading of the rule of law should enable you to go over the underlying legal concept in your mind, how it was applied in that particular case, and how it might apply in other factual settings.

As to the value to be derived from engaging in the briefing process itself, there is an immediate benefit that arises from being forced to sift through the essential facts and reasoning from the court's opinion and to succinctly express them in your own words in your brief. The process ensures that you understand the case and the point that it illustrates, and that means you will be ready to absorb further analysis and information brought forth in class. It also ensures you will have something to say when called upon in class. The briefing process helps develop a mental agility for getting to the *gist* of a case and for identifying, expounding on, and applying the legal concepts and issues found there. The briefing process is the mental process on which you must rely in taking law school examinations; it is also the mental process upon which a lawyer relies in serving his clients and in making his living.

Abbreviations for Briefs

Table of Cases

Intent to Contract: Offer and Acceptance

Quick Reference Rules of Law

Lucy v. Zehmer

Farmer (P) v. Seller of farm (D)

Va. Sup. Ct., 196 Va. 493, 84 S.E.2d 516 (1954).

NATURE OF CASE: Appeal from dismissal of action for specific performance of a land sale contract.

FACT SUMMARY: Zehmer (D) failed to sell Lucy (P) a tract of land on the grounds that Zehmer (D) was joking when he signed the contract and never intended to sell.

🏛 RULE OF LAW
If a person's words and acts, judged by a reasonable standard, manifest an intention to agree, it is immaterial what may be the real but unexpressed state of his mind.

FACTS: One night in Zehmer's (D) restaurant, Lucy (P) offered Zehmer (D) $50,000 for his farm. On the back of a restaurant bill, Zehmer (D) wrote up a contract stating he would sell the land to Lucy (P), but Lucy (P) made him draft a new contract using the term "we agree to sell," as Zehmer's (D) wife had to sign off as well. Zehmer (D) then had his wife (D) sign the agreement. Lucy (P) offered $5.00 on the spot to make the transaction official, but Zehmer (D) refused to take the money. The following Monday, Lucy (P) hired an attorney, made inquiries into the title of the land, and then contacted Zehmer (D) regarding the closing of the deal. Zehmer (D) replied by mail, stating that he never intended to sell the land and would not do so. Lucy (P) sued Zehmer (D) for specific performance. The trial court ruled that Lucy (P) had not established his right to specific performance and dismissed the suit. Lucy (P) appealed.

ISSUE: If a person's words and acts, judged by a reasonable standard, manifest an intention to agree, is it immaterial what may be the real but unexpressed state of his mind?

HOLDING AND DECISION: (Buchanan, J.) Yes. If a person's words and acts, judged by a reasonable standard, manifest an intention to agree, it is immaterial what may be the real but unexpressed state of his mind. A person cannot assert that he was joking when his conduct and words would lead a reasonable person to believe that he intended to enter into a binding agreement. Here, Zehmer (D) claimed the contract was entered into purely as a joke and that everyone had been drinking so much that they could not have intended otherwise. The evidence, however, indicated that the parties were not so intoxicated as to be unable to enter into a binding agreement, as they were capable of understanding what they were doing. Moreover, even though Zehmer (D) claims he never intended to sell, as it was all in jest, his actions and words prove otherwise. He drafted two specific agreements, discussed the terms with Lucy (P) for over thirty minutes, and had his wife sign off on the document. These actions would lead any reasonable man to believe that a binding contract was being entered into. Zehmer's (D) unexpressed intentions are immaterial since his words and actions evidenced intent to sell the land to Lucy (P). Reversed and remanded.

▌ *ANALYSIS*

This case highlights the need for parties to clearly articulate their intentions before entering into a contract. A debate has arisen as to whether an objective or subjective standard of assent should be used to determine the intentions of the parties. Generally, the objective (outward manifestation) standard is used today.

■■■

Quicknotes

INTENT The existence of a particular state of mind whereby an individual seeks to achieve a particular result by his action.

REASONABLE PERSON A hypothetical person whose judgment represents the standard to which society requires its members to act in their private affairs and in their dealings with others.

SPECIFIC PERFORMANCE An equitable remedy, whereby the court requires the parties to perform their obligations pursuant to a contract.

■■■

Stepp v. Freeman

Employee (P) v. Co-employee (D)

Ohio Ct. App., 119 Ohio App. 3d 68, 694 N.E.2d 792 (1997).

NATURE OF CASE: Appeal from an opinion in favor of the plaintiff on his equitable estoppel and breach of implied contract claims.

FACT SUMMARY: Due to an argument between Stepp (P) and Freeman (D), Freeman (D) failed to include Stepp (P) in a group lottery purchasing pool. Stepp (P) commenced this cause of action alleging breach of express contract, breach of implied contract, and equitable estoppel. The court found for Stepp (P) on his equitable estoppel and breach of implied contract claims. Freeman (D) appealed.

> ## 🏛 RULE OF LAW
> In an implied-in-fact contract, assent is demonstrated by the surrounding circumstances, including the conduct and declarations of the parties.

FACTS: Freeman (D) ran an employee pool to purchase lottery tickets. Stepp (P) had been a member of this pool for five years and had the formal role of copying all the tickets purchased for members of the group. The group was limited to 20 members and no new member could enter unless an existing member voluntarily left the group and expressed this desire to Freeman (D). On March 3, 1993, the group won the $8 million lottery jackpot. One week prior to this, Freeman (D) and Stepp (P) had a serious work-related dispute. Though Freeman (D) generally reminded group members when it was time to contribute to the pool or gave them the option of deciding for themselves whether they would drop out of the group, Freeman (D) neither reminded Stepp (P) to contribute to this pool nor allowed him to decide on his status before considering him dropped from the group. Freeman (D) paid for the extra ticket and no one took Stepp's (P) place in the group. Stepp (P) was not allowed to share in the proceeds of this win and commenced this action for breach express contract, breach of implied contract, and equitable estoppel.

ISSUE: Did Stepp (P) prove all of the elements of an implied-in-fact contract?

HOLDING AND DECISION: (Young, J.) Yes. There was an implied-in-fact contract that Stepp (P) would pay his share and perform his role within the group-purchasing pool when he was informed that the group was playing the lottery. We can imply this from the facts and circumstances surrounding this case: Stepp (P) had been a member of this group for five years, had never failed to contribute his share, had a formal role in the group and had been reminded that his money was due in the past. Freeman (D) failed to inform Stepp (P) that the group was playing the lottery and

thus breached this implied-in-fact contract. Further, Freeman (D) breached the implied-in-fact agreement that none of the twenty members would be dropped from the group unless they expressed a desire to leave the group when he dropped Stepp (P) without consulting him. Judgment affirmed.

▶ ANALYSIS

Stepp demonstrates that an express contract differs from an implied-in-fact contract in one material way—how assent is manifested.

■══■

Quicknotes

BREACH The violation of an obligation imposed pursuant to contract or law, by acting or failing to act.

EQUITABLE ESTOPPEL A doctrine that precludes a person from asserting a right to which he or she was entitled due to his or her action, conduct or failing to act, causing another party to justifiably rely on such conduct to his or her detriment.

IMPLIED CONTRACT An agreement between parties that may be inferred from their general course of conduct.

■══■

PFT Roberson, Inc. v. Volvo Trucks North America, Inc.

Trucking fleet (P) v. Truck supplier (D)

420 F.3d 728 (7th Cir. 2005).

NATURE OF CASE: Appeal of jury award.

FACT SUMMARY: A company tried to enforce as a contract an email giving the status of a contract negotiation.

🏛 RULE OF LAW
The agreement between parties on any particular term of a contract under negotiation does not give rise to a jury question as to whether there is a contract on that term alone.

FACTS: PFT Roberson, Inc. (Roberson) (P) operates a fleet of trucks and trailers. Freightliner supplies and repairs Roberson's (P) trucks. When Freightliner gave Roberson (P) notice that it was terminating its contract with Roberson (P), Roberson (P) began negotiations with Volvo (D) to take Freightliner's place. Their negotiations culminated in an email from Volvo (D), which indicated what the two companies agreed to, and that many details needed to be worked out. The email was captioned "Confirmation of our conversation," and recaps the status of the negotiations. It also identifies items that the parties agreed to and others that needed to be finalized, and that the contract would be complete only when these other subjects had been resolved. Roberson (P) and Freightliner then renewed their contract, and Roberson (P) sued Volvo (D) for breach of contract and fraud. Roberson (P) claimed the email constituted a contract. The district judge found that a jury could find that the email constituted Volvo's (D) assent to the items it mentioned, even if a full agreement had not been signed. The court of appeals granted review.

ISSUE: Does the agreement between parties on any particular term of a contract under negotiation give rise to a jury question as to whether there is a contract on that term alone?

HOLDING AND DECISION: (Easterbrook, J.) No. The agreement between parties on any particular term of a contract under negotiation does not give rise to a jury question as to whether there is a contract on that term alone. The email lists many documents that contain more of the required details for the contract, and which were necessary for the parties to review and finalize. The termination clause, truck purchases, maintenance cost per mile, trade-in value all referred to other documents that were necessary to fill in details. Volvo (D) protected itself by stating in the email that many required details "needed to be finalized." Because the details were required, there was no agreement without them. Reversed.

▶ ANALYSIS

This case stands for the not-so-bright line between preliminary negotiations and an offer. The description of terms agreed upon, in a letter of intent, does not necessarily amount to an offer.

■══■

Quicknotes

OFFER A proposed promise to undertake performance of an action, or to refrain from acting, that is to become binding upon acceptance by the offeree.

■══■

Lefkowitz v. Greater Minneapolis Surplus Store, Inc.

Responder to ad (P) v. Surplus store (D)

Minn. Sup. Ct., 251 Minn. 188, 86 N.W.2d 689 (1957).

NATURE OF CASE: Appeal from judgment for plaintiff in action to recover damages for breach of contract.

FACT SUMMARY: Greater Minneapolis Surplus Store (D) advertised one fur stole on a "first-come-first-served" basis but would not sell the stole to Lefkowitz (P) who accepted the alleged offer.

🏛 RULE OF LAW
A newspaper advertisement for the sale of an article which is clear, definite, and explicit, and leaves nothing to negotiation is an offer, acceptance of which will create a binding contract.

FACTS: Greater Minneapolis Surplus Store (Surplus Store) (D) published the following advertisement in a Minneapolis newspaper: "SATURDAY 9 A.M. 2 BRAND NEW PASTEL MINK 3-SKIN SCARFS Selling for $89.50 Out they go Saturday. Each . . . $1.00 1 BLACK LAPIN STOLE Beautiful, worth $139.50 . . . $1.00. FIRST COME FIRST SERVED." Lefkowitz (P) was the first to present himself on Saturday and demanded the Lapin Stole for one dollar. The Surplus Store (D) refused to sell to him because of a "house rule" that the offer was intended for women only. Lefkowitz (P) sued the Surplus Store (D) and was awarded $138.50 as damages. Surplus Store (D) appealed, and the state's highest court granted review.

ISSUE: Is a newspaper advertisement for the sale of an article which is clear, definite, and explicit, and leaves nothing to negotiation an offer, acceptance of which will create a binding contract?

HOLDING AND DECISION: (Murphy, J.) Yes. A newspaper advertisement for the sale of an article which is clear, definite, and explicit, and leaves nothing to negotiation is an offer, acceptance of which will create a binding contract. The test of whether a binding obligation may originate in advertisements addressed to the public is "whether the facts show that some performance was promised in positive terms in return for something requested." Whether an advertisement is an offer or merely an invitation for offers depends on the legal intention of the parties and the surrounding circumstances. Where an offer is clear, definite and explicit, and leaves nothing open for negotiation, it constitutes an offer such that acceptance of it will create a contract. With respect to the Lapin fur, Surplus Store's (D) advertisement was such an offer. As to Surplus Store's (D) alleged "house rule," while an advertiser has the right at any time before acceptance to modify his offer, he does not have the right, after acceptance to impose new or arbitrary conditions not contained in the published offer. Affirmed.

▶ ANALYSIS

Although most advertisements for goods at a certain price are held not to be offers, the present case presents an interesting exception to that rule. Restatement (Second) § 25 (illustration No. 1) indicates that the basis of the court's decision is that the words "First come first served" create language of promise which is ordinarily lacking in advertisement for the sale of goods. Probably it was this factor in conjunction with the statement of a quantity (to wit, one), which motivated the court. Caveat: The Uniform Commercial Code has dealt a blow to the present court's insistence that nothing be left open for negotiation [See UCC § 2-204(3)].

■■■

Quicknotes

MUTUALITY Reciprocal actions of two parties; in a contract context, refers to mutual promises between two parties to perform an action in exchange for performance on the part of the other party.

UNILATERAL CONTRACT An agreement pursuant to which a party agrees to act, or to forbear from acting, in exchange for performance on the part of the other party.

■■■

Continental Laboratories v. Scott Paper Co.

Hotel products supplier (P) v. Distributor (D)

759 F. Supp. 538 (S.D. Iowa 1990), *aff'd*, 938 F.2d 184 (8th Cir. 1991).

NATURE OF CASE: Defense motion for summary judgment in breach of contract action.

FACT SUMMARY: Scott Paper Co. (D) contended that summary judgment should be granted in its favor on the ground that there was no binding contract with Continental Laboratories (P).

🏛 RULE OF LAW
If either party intends not to be bound in the absence of a fully executed document, no binding contract will be formed.

FACTS: During early 1987, representatives of Continental Laboratories (Continental) (P) and Scott Paper Co. (Scott) (D) entered into negotiations concerning a potential supply and distribution agreement. Throughout the negotiations period, Scott (D) representatives prepared and submitted to Continental (P) at least five drafts of a written supply and distribution agreement, with each new draft incorporating changes from the negotiations. On July 19, 1987, Scott (D), through one Smith, announced internally that it had reached an agreement with Continental (P). Continental (P) representatives believed that a binding oral contract was reached by the parties during a telephone conference call on August 25, 1987. Smith's affidavit, on the other hand, demonstrated that Scott (D) through Smith never intended to be bound by an oral agreement but only by a written contract executed by both parties. Scott (D) representatives then sent a written agreement to Continental (P), but that document was never signed. Further negotiations continued until Scott (D) terminated any further discussions regarding the proposed venture. Continental (P) filed suit against Scott (D), alleging breach of a binding oral agreement. Scott (D) moved for summary judgment on the ground that there was no binding contract.

ISSUE: Will a binding contract be formed if either party does not intend to be bound in the absence of a fully executed document?

HOLDING AND DECISION: (Vietor, C.J.) No. If either party intends not to be bound in the absence of a fully executed document, a binding contract will not be formed. In ascertaining whether the parties intended to be bound prior to execution of a written document, the court should consider the following factors: (1) whether the contract is of a class usually found to be in writing; (2) whether it is of a type needing a formal writing for its full expression; (3) whether it has few or many details; (4) whether the amount is large or small; (5) whether the contract is common or unusual; (6) whether all details have been agreed upon or some remain unresolved; and (7) whether the negotiations show a writing was discussed or contemplated. Factors 1 and 2 support Scott's (D) position. The matter was a large and complex commercial undertaking, which is usually put into written form. Similarly, factors 3, 4, and 5 support Scott's (D) position. First, the 12-page contract contained many details and references to numerous exhibits. Second, the transaction at issue involved a commitment by Scott (D) to purchase a minimum of $2.25 million worth of products from Continental (P). Third, this particular contract was unusual for Scott (D) because of its entrance into a new market. Under factor 6, although Smith announced internally to Scott (D) officials that the parties had reached an agreement in principle in July 1987, many details were still unresolved. Finally, an analysis of the summary judgment record under factor 7 indicated that Scott (D) only intended to be bound by a written and executed contract. Continental (P) failed to generate a genuine issue of material fact regarding whether Scott (D) intended to be bound by an oral agreement or only by a written and executed agreement. Motion for summary judgment granted to Scott (D).

▶ ANALYSIS

Under Iowa law, a binding oral contract may exist even though the parties intend to memorialize their agreement in a fully executed document. On the other hand, the parties can make the execution of a written document a condition precedent to the birth of a binding contract. Therefore, it is imperative to look at the intent of the parties to see if a binding contract is what was contemplated by the contracting parties. If the true intent of the parties can be determined, then unjust decisions will be fewer and far between.

■=■

Quicknotes

AFFIDAVIT A declaration of facts written and affirmed before a witness.

ORAL CONTRACT A contract that is not reduced to written form.

SUMMARY JUDGMENT Judgment rendered by a court in response to a motion by one of the parties, claiming that the lack of a question of material fact in respect to an issue warrants disposition of the issue without consideration by the jury.

■=■

Kortum-Managhan v. Herbergers NBGL

Credit card user (P) v. Credit card issuer (D)

Mont. Sup. Ct., 349 Mont. 475, 204 P.3d 693 (2009).

NATURE OF CASE: Appeal from dismissal of action asserting multiple claims for violations of federal and state credit, consumer, and trade protection laws, and from order compelling arbitration.

FACT SUMMARY: Kortum-Managhan (P) contended, inter alia, that a credit card bill stuffer she received with numerous inserts in her monthly statement, which purported to give her notice that any claims she might have against the credit card issuer would have to be arbitrated, was insufficient notice to cause her to knowingly and intelligently waive her right to a jury trial on such claims.

🏛 RULE OF LAW
A credit card "bill stuffer" is insufficient notice to cause a consumer to knowingly and intelligently waive her fundamental constitutional right to a jury trial.

FACTS: Kortum-Managhan (P) filled out an in-store application for a Herbergers's (D) credit card. The application did not include the terms and conditions of the agreement. Subsequently, she received by mail her Herbergers (D) credit card, accompanied by a revolving credit card agreement, which did not include an arbitration clause. However, it did contain a provision purporting to allow Herbergers (D) to unilaterally change the agreement as it saw fit and specifying that a cardholder's continued use of their Herbergers (D) credit card or other services constituted agreement to Herbergers's (D) unilateral change in terms. Around a year later, Herbergers (D) mailed to Kortum-Managhan (P) a bill stuffer that, along with many ads, included a notice providing that resolution of any credit-card-related claims against Herbergers (D) could only be arbitrated. The notice purported to disallow jury trials, court litigation, and class actions of any kind. Around five years later, Kortum-Managhan (P) brought federal and state claims against Herbergers (D), asserting multiple violations of the Federal Fair Debt Collection Practices Act and her state's unfair trade practices and consumer protection act, alleging that Herbergers (D) reported to the various credit bureaus that she had several accounts with Herbergers (D) and its affiliates when, in reality, she had only one account. She maintained that this inaccurate reporting on Herbergers's (D) part negatively impacted her credit score and that her application for admittance to the state bar was impeded. Herbergers (D), relying on the notice it had previously sent, moved to dismiss her complaint and to compel arbitration. The trial granted Herbergers's (D) motion, notwithstanding that Kortum-Managhan (P) asserted that she either did not receive the change in terms or she did not notice the change in terms because her monthly billing statement came stuffed with copious piles of junk mail that she routinely threw away without reading, so that she did not agree to arbitrate all disputes with Herbergers (D) and that she did not knowingly and intelligently waive her fundamental constitutional rights to trial by jury and to access to the courts. The state's highest court granted review.

ISSUE: Is a credit card "bill stuffer" sufficient notice to cause a consumer to knowingly and intelligently waive her fundamental constitutional right to a jury trial?

HOLDING AND DECISION: (Nelson, J.) No. A credit card "bill stuffer" is insufficient notice to cause a consumer to knowingly and intelligently waive her fundamental constitutional right to a jury trial. While arbitration agreements between parties are valid and enforceable, the threshold issue is whether the parties agreed to arbitrate. Generally, a party cannot unilaterally change the terms of a contract, but must obtain the other party's consent before doing so. This is because a revised contract is merely an offer and does not bind the parties until it is accepted. Generally, an offeree cannot actually assent to an offer unless he knows of its existence. Some courts faced with a situation where, as here, a credit card issuer has attempted to add an arbitration clause to the parties' existing agreement by mailing out a change in terms with continued use of the credit account constituting acceptance, have held that as a matter of law, the cardholder has not accepted the issuer's offer to arbitrate their disputes. Other courts have found that a "bill stuffer" imposing a change in terms that takes away an individual's right to a jury trial is fundamentally different than imposing a change in the interest rate, late charges, or other terms, so that the issuer does not act in an "objectively reasonable" manner when it attempts to "recapture" a forgone opportunity by adding an entirely new term which has no bearing on any subject, issue, right, or obligation addressed in the original contract and which was not within the reasonable contemplation of the parties when the contract was entered into. Moreover, these courts have determined that the credit issuer's unilateral right to change the terms of the parties' agreement is constrained by the implied covenant of good faith and fair dealing. Here, Herbergers's (D) amendment did not relate to financial terms or rates, so it was not within the contemplation of the parties when the original card agreement was entered into. Because the agreement in this case is a contract of adhesion, and because such contracts will not be enforced against the weaker party where it is not within their reasonable expectations, the arbitration provision will not be enforced against Kortum-Managhan (P),

Continued on next page.

who clearly did not reasonably expect it. In addition, while a party is free to contract away the right to a jury trial, the waiver must be made knowingly, voluntarily, and intelligently—especially when it is a waiver of a fundamental constitutional right such as the right to trial by jury. Here, Kortum-Managhan's (P) waiver cannot be said to have been made knowingly, voluntarily and intelligently since the parties did not negotiate over the provision; the "bill stuffer" was a take-it-or-leave-it part of Herbergers's (D) form contract, so that Kortum-Managhan's (P) only options were to either waive her right to access to the courts and trial by jury or to discontinue use of the credit card; and the arbitration provision was not conspicuous— bold type, capital letters, and larger fonts were used to draw attention to other clauses. For these and other reasons, not only was Herbergers's (D) unilateral attempt to amend its original cardholder agreement to include an arbitration clause sneaky and unfair, it was also ineffective. Accordingly, the trial court erred in granting Herbergers's (D) motion to compel arbitration and to dismiss. Reversed and remanded.

DISSENT: (Rice, J.) Kortum-Managhan (P) should have read the mail she received from her credit issuers carefully, as it is commonplace for issuers to make changes to agreements with their customers through notices mailed with the customers' monthly bills. This is done pursuant to the specific authority granted to the companies to do so under the original agreement. When Kortum-Managhan (P) entered into an agreement under which Herbergers (D) could unilaterally make changes and send notice of those changes, that contractual authority was not qualified by a requirement that notices be sent in a separate envelope. Therefore, Kortum-Managhan (P) should not be able to escape her duty to read legal notices by way of her assertion that "she routinely throws away the junk mail without reading it."

▶ ANALYSIS

Other courts have upheld a company's unilateral change in contract terms, including the addition of an arbitration provision. Arbitration clauses in contracts are valid even in contracts of adhesion, if the clause is within the reasonable expectation of the weaker party and is not unduly oppressive, unconscionable, or against public policy. Thus, the court here arguably would have upheld the Herbergers's (D) arbitration provision if, for example, it had been included in a letter along with a copy of the revised agreement, rather than in the monthly statement.

■■■

Quicknotes

ARBITRATION CLAUSE Provision contained in a contract pursuant to which both parties agree that any disputes arising thereunder will be resolved through arbitration.

UNILATERAL One-sided; involving only one person.

■■■

ProCD, Inc. v. Zeidenberg

Software manufacturer (P) v. Purchaser (D)

86 F.3d 1477, 29 U.C.C. Rep. Serv. 2d 1109 (7th Cir. 1996).

NATURE OF CASE: Appeal from an order in favor of defendant in a case alleging breach of the terms of a shrinkwrap or end-user license.

FACT SUMMARY: When Zeidenberg (D), a customer, bought and then resold the data compiled on its CD-ROM software disk, ProCD (P) sued for breach of contract.

🏛 RULE OF LAW
A buyer accepts goods when, after an opportunity to inspect, he fails to make an effective rejection.

FACTS: ProCD, Inc. (P) compiled information from over 3,000 telephone directories into a computer database which it sold on CD-ROM disks. Every box containing the disks declared that the software came with restrictions stated in an enclosed license. This license, which was encoded on the CD-ROM disks as well as printed in the manual, and which appeared on a user's screen every time the software ran, limited use of the application program and listings to non-commercial purposes. Zeidenberg bought a ProCD (P) software package but decided to ignore the license and to resell the information in the database. Zeidenberg (D) also made the information from ProCD's (P) database available over the Internet for a price, through his corporation. ProCD (P) sued for breach of contract. The district court found that placing the package of software on the shelf was an "offer," which the customer "accepted" by paying the asking price and leaving the store with the goods. A contract includes only those terms which the parties have agreed to and one cannot agree to secret terms. Thus, the district court held that buyers of computer software need not obey the terms of shrinkwrap licenses. Such licenses were found to be ineffectual because their terms did not appear on the outsides of the packages. ProCD (P) appealed.

ISSUE: Does a buyer accept goods when, after an opportunity to inspect, he fails to make an effective rejection?

HOLDING AND DECISION: (Easterbrook, J.) Yes. A buyer accepts goods when, after an opportunity to inspect, he fails to make an effective rejection under § 2-602 of the Uniform Commercial Code. A vendor, as master of the offer, may invite acceptance by conduct, and may propose limitations on the kind of conduct that constitutes acceptance. ProCD (P) proposed a contract that a buyer would accept by using the software after having an opportunity to read the license at leisure. Zeidenberg (D) did this, since he had no choice when the software splashed the license across his computer screen and would not let

him proceed without indicating acceptance. The license was an ordinary contract accompanying the sale of products and was therefore governed by the common law of contracts and the Uniform Commercial Code. Transactions in which the exchange of money precedes the communication of detailed terms are common. Buying insurance or buying a plane ticket being two common examples. ProCD (P) extended an opportunity to reject if a buyer should find the license terms unsatisfactory. Zeidenberg (D) inspected the package, tried out the software, learned of the license, and did not reject the goods. Reversed and remanded.

▶ ANALYSIS

The sale of information contained in computer databases presented new challenges to courts. Some courts found that the sale of software was the sale of services, rather than of goods. This case treated the sale of software as a sale of goods governed by Article 2 of the Uniform Commercial Code.

■=■

Quicknotes

CD-ROM Compact disc read only memory.

INSPECTION OF GOODS The examination of goods, which are the subject matter of a contract for sale, for the purpose of determining whether they are satisfactory.

REJECTION The refusal to accept the terms of an offer.

SHRINKWRAP LICENSE Terms of restriction packaged inside a product.

■=■

Beard Implement Co. v. Krusa

Farm tool seller (P) v. Farmer (D)

Ill. App. Ct., 208 Ill. App. 3d 953, 567 N.E.2d 345 (1991).

NATURE OF CASE: Appeal from award of damages for breach of contract.

FACT SUMMARY: Krusa (D) contended that Beard Implement Co. (P) never accepted his offer to purchase a combine and that the trial court erred in finding a contract existed between the parties.

🏛 RULE OF LAW
Under UCC § 2-206, if an offer contained in a purchase order is unambiguous in inviting acceptance only by the signature of the offeree, no contract exists until the purchase order is signed accordingly.

FACTS: On December 23, 1985, Krusa (D) met with representatives of Beard Implement Co. (Beard) (P) at Beard's (P) office. Beard (P) filled out a purchase order for a new combine for the price of $52,800 cash and the trade-in of Krusa's (D) old combine. Krusa (D) signed the purchase order, but none of Beard's (P) representatives ever signed the purchase order. The bottom part of the purchase order specifically stated that the order was subject to acceptance by the dealer, with an area placed on the order for the dealer (Beard (P)) to sign. At that time, Krusa (D) signed a counter check as down payment for the combine. Three days later, after speaking with his wife, Krusa (D) decided that the combine was too expensive. Therefore, Krusa (D) purchased a cheaper combine from another company and sent a letter to Beard (P) stating that he did not want to go through with purchase. Beard (P) sued Krusa (D) for breach of contract, arguing that a contract existed between the parties even before their agreement was reduced to writing and that the verbal agreement was evidenced by a counter check which was signed by Krusa (D). The trial court found for Beard (P), holding that there was a breach of contract. Krusa (D) appealed, contending that there was no acceptance on behalf of Beard (P) because Beard (P) did not sign the purchase order. The state's intermediate appellate court granted review.

ISSUE: Under UCC § 2-206, if an offeror's offer contained on a purchase order is unambiguous in inviting acceptance only by the signature of the offeree, does a contract exist if the purchase order has not been signed?

HOLDING AND DECISION: (Steigmann, J.) No. Under UCC § 2-206, if an offeror's offer contained on a purchase order is unambiguous in inviting acceptance only by the signature of the offeree, no contract exists until the purchase order is signed accordingly. In the present case, the purchase order form signed by Krusa (D) constitutes an offer made by Krusa (D) to Beard (P). Beard's (P) purchase order form is subject to the acceptance by the dealer (Beard) (P), which acceptance shall be signified by the signature of the dealer. It was obvious from the purchase order that the parties intended the agreement to be bilateral and that the offer by Krusa (D) to purchase the combine be deemed accepted by Beard (P) only when he or his authorized representative signed the order. Based on the foregoing, the purchase order in this case unambiguously required the signature by Beard's (P) dealer in order to be a proper acceptance of Krusa's (D) offer. Because Beard's (P) dealer never signed the purchase order, no contract ever existed. Beard's (P) argument that it offered the combine to Krusa (D) and Krusa (D) accepted by signing a counter check as a down payment is unpersuasive. Reversed.

▶ ANALYSIS

The court relied on a number of cases that supported Krusa's (D) position. In *Brophy v. City of Joilet*, 14 Ill. App. 2d 443 (1957), the court held that where an offer requires an acceptance to be made in writing, no other form of acceptance can be made. In *Antonucci v. Stevens Dodge, Inc.*, 73 Misc. 2d 173, 340 N.Y.S.2d 979 (N.Y. Civ. Ct. 1973), the case which the court deemed most analogous to the case at bar, it was held that where the agreement takes the form of a written instrument, the acceptance is effective only when the document has been signed and delivered, unless it was clearly the intention of the parties that the earlier, verbal agreement be binding, and that the writing act merely as a memorandum or better evidence of an oral contract.

Quicknotes

ACCEPTANCE Assent to the specified terms of an offer, resulting in the formation of a binding agreement.

BILATERAL An agreement pursuant to which each party promises to undertake an obligation, or to forbear from acting, at some time in the future.

Fujimoto v. Rio Grande Pickle Co.

Employees (P) v. Pickle company (D)

414 F.2d 648 (5th Cir. 1969).

NATURE OF CASE: Appeal of award of damages for breach of contract.

FACT SUMMARY: After signing contracts of employment, Fujimoto (P) and Bravo (P) did not return the executed documents to the employer, Rio Grande Pickle Co. (D).

RULE OF LAW
Return of an executed contract to the offeror is not necessary to make the contract binding upon the offeror.

FACTS: Fujimoto (P) and Bravo (P) were important employees of Rio Grande Pickle Co. (Rio Grande) (D). They demanded greater compensation, and Rio Grande (D) responded by offering them employment contracts calling for each to receive 10 percent of Rio Grande's (D) net profits for the period covered by the contract. Both men signed the documents and kept the originals in their possession. Rio Grande (D) had made no request that the executed documents be returned. The pair continued to work for 14 months, until Rio Grande (D) ceased operations in the area where they worked. When Rio Grande (D) refused to pay the 10 percent bonus, Fujimoto (P) and Bravo (P) sued for breach. Rio Grande (D) contended that the employment contracts had never been formed because they had not returned the executed originals. The district court awarded each $8,964.25. Rio Grande (D) appealed. The court of appeals granted review.

ISSUE: Is return of an executed contract to the offeror necessary to make the contract binding upon the offeror?

HOLDING AND DECISION: (Goldberg, J.) No. Return of an executed contract to the offeror is not necessary to make the contract binding upon the offeror. An offeror can require notice of acceptance in any manner he chooses. However, absent any such requirement communicated to the offeree, acceptance may be communicated by any commercially reasonable means. Physical delivery of the documents is not required. Here, both Fujimoto (P) and Bravo (P) continued to work, and this was sufficient to put Rio Grande (D) on notice that they had accepted Rio Grande's (D) offer of an employment contract. The district court erred in its computation of damages. Affirmed in part; reversed and remanded in part.

▶ ANALYSIS

Three categories of notice of acceptance exist. The first is that an offeror may designate an exclusive manner of notice of acceptance. Secondly, he may specify a mode but not make it exclusive. The third category, that illustrated here, involves no specific manner of notification. As the court said, in this instance commercial reasonableness governs.

■=■

Quicknotes

EXECUTED An agreement whose obligations have been fully performed.

NOTICE Communication of information to a person by an authorized person or an otherwise proper source.

■=■

Day v. Caton

Wall builder (P) v. Neighbor (D)

Mass. Sup. Jud. Ct., 119 Mass. 513 (1876).

NATURE OF CASE: Action on a contract to recover the value of one-half of a party wall built upon and between adjoining estates.

FACT SUMMARY: Day (P) erected a valuable party wall between his and his neighbor Caton's (D) land, but Caton (D), who knew of the construction and that Day (P) expected payment in return, said nothing and refused to pay for one-half of the wall's construction.

🏛 RULE OF LAW

If a party voluntarily accepts and avails himself of valuable services rendered for his benefit, when he has the option to accept or reject them and knows that the party rendering the services expects payment in return, even if there is no distinct proof that they were rendered by his authority or request, a promise to pay for them may be inferred.

FACTS: Day (P) claimed he had an express agreement with the adjacent landowner, Caton (D), that in return for Day's (P) construction of a brick party wall upon and between their adjoining properties, Caton (D) would pay him one-half the value for the wall. When Caton (D) denied that any express agreement had ever been reached concerning payment for the party wall, Day (P) sued to enforce the alleged agreement.

ISSUE: If a party voluntarily accepts and avails himself of valuable services rendered for his benefit, when he has the option to accept or reject them and knows that the party rendering the services expects payment in return, even if there is no distinct proof that they were rendered by his authority or request, may a promise to pay for them be inferred?

HOLDING AND DECISION: (Devens, J.) Yes. If a party voluntarily accepts and avails himself of valuable services rendered for his benefit, when he has the option to accept or reject them and knows that the party rendering the services expects payment in return, even if there is no distinct proof that they were rendered by his authority or request, a promise to pay for them may be inferred. Where one person knows that another is conferring a valuable benefit on him with expectation of payment and allows him to do so without objection, then a jury may infer a promise of payment. Silence may be interpreted as assent in the face of facts that fairly call upon one to speak. The question is one for the jury. Exceptions overruled.

▶ ANALYSIS

Section 72(1)(a) of the Restatement (Second) of Contracts is in accord with the present decision. However, where one family member renders services to another family member, the presumption is that the services were made without expectation of payment. This is a rebuttable presumption.

■═■

Quicknotes

REBUTTABLE PRESUMPTION A rule of law, inferred from the existence of a particular set of facts, which is conclusive in the absence of contrary evidence.

■═■

Davis v. Jacoby

Business owners (P) v. Distant cousins (D)

Cal. Sup. Ct., 1 Cal. 2d 370, 34 P.2d 1026 (1934).

NATURE OF CASE: Denial of action for specific performance of an alleged contract to make a will.

FACT SUMMARY: Whitehead invited the Davises (P) to help him with his business affairs and to look after his sick wife; the Davises (P) accepted by letter, but before they could move down, Whitehead killed himself.

🏛 RULE OF LAW
In case of doubt it is presumed that an offer invites the formation of a bilateral rather than a unilateral contract.

FACTS: Mr. Whitehead, whose health, as well as his business, was ailing, invited by means of a series of letters his wife's niece, Mrs. Davis (P), and her husband (P), to settle their affairs in Canada and to come and stay with him and his wife. The two families were very close and the Whiteheads regarded Mrs. Davis (P) as their daughter. In one letter, Mr. Whitehead stated that if Mr. Davis (P) could help him with his failing business, and if Mrs. Davis (P) would look after his sick wife, Mrs. Davis (P) "will inherit everything." This letter further asked, "Will you let me hear from you as soon as possible." The Davises (P) immediately dispatched a letter in which they accepted Mr. Whitehead's offer, and started to pack their belongings. Mr. Whitehead again wrote a letter in which he acknowledged receipt of the Davises (P) acceptance. Before the Davises (P) could leave, Mr. Whitehead committed suicide. The Davises (P) nonetheless came down and tended after Mrs. Whitehead until her death. It was not until that point that the Davises (P) realized that Mr. Whitehead had failed to make a will in their favor and had instead left all his property to some distant nephews (D). In an action brought by the Davises (P) for specific enforcement of the alleged contract to make a will, the trial court ruled that Mr. Whitehead's offer was one to enter into a unilateral contract and, since they had not performed prior to his death, the Davises' (P) acceptance by letter was ineffective.

ISSUE: In case of doubt is it presumed that an offer invites the formation of a bilateral rather than a unilateral contract?

HOLDING AND DECISION: (Per curiam) Yes. In case of doubt it is presumed that an offer invites the formation of a bilateral rather than a unilateral contract. Where there is ambiguity, it is presumed that an offer invites the formation of a bilateral contract by an acceptance amounting in effect to a promise by the offeree to perform what the offer requests, rather than the formation of one or more unilateral contracts by actual performance on the part of the offeree. A bilateral contract is favored since it immediately and fully protects the expectations of both parties. Mr. Whitehead's offer was one to enter into a bilateral contract since the facts suggest that he wanted only a promise to perform and not performance. The parties, being very close, were not dealing at arm's length. Mr. Whitehead was looking to the Davises (P) for assurance and peace of mind. He had asked for a reply. When an offer has indicated the mode and means of acceptance, an acceptance in accordance with that mode or means is binding on the offeror. Finally, since the offer contemplated a service that could not be fully performed until after his death (caring for Mrs. Whitehead), he had to rely on the Davises' (P) promise. Consequently, specific performance should be granted. Reversed.

▶ ANALYSIS

UCC § 2-206(1) provides: "Unless otherwise unambiguously indicated by the language or circumstances, (a) an offer to make a contract shall be construed as inviting acceptance in any manner . . . reasonable in the circumstances; (b) an order or other offer to buy goods for prompt or current shipment shall be construed as inviting acceptance either by a prompt promise to ship or by the prompt or current shipment of . . . goods."

■══■

Quicknotes

BILATERAL CONTRACT An agreement pursuant to which each party promises to undertake an obligation, or to forbear from acting, at some time in the future.

DEALING AT ARM'S LENGTH A course of dealing between parties who are unrelated and are motivated by purely independent interests.

SPECIFIC PERFORMANCE An equitable remedy whereby the court requires the parties to perform their obligations pursuant to a contract.

UNILATERAL CONTRACT An agreement pursuant to which a party agrees to act, or to forbear from acting, in exchange for performance on the part of the other party.

■══■

Dickinson v. Dodds

Land buyer (P) v. Land seller (D)

Ct. App., Ch. Div., 2 Ch. D. 463 (1876).

NATURE OF CASE: Appeal from decree of specific performance of a land sale contract.

FACT SUMMARY: Dodds (D) offered to sell land to Dickinson (P), giving Dickinson (P) a couple of days to think it over, but before Dickinson (P) could accept, Dodds (D) sold the land to Allan, and this sale was communicated to Dickinson (P) by his agent, Berry, after which Dickinson (P) attempted to formally accept Dodds's (D) offer.

> 🏛 **RULE OF LAW**
> An open offer to sell terminates when the offeree learns that the offeror has already agreed to sell to someone else.

FACTS: On Wednesday, Dodds (D) offered in writing to sell certain real estate to Dickinson (P) and purported to leave the offer open until Friday morning. On Thursday, however, Dodds (D) sold the land to Allan, and Berry, Dickinson's (P) agent, informed Dickinson (P) of the sale on Thursday afternoon. After learning of the sale, Dickinson (P) attempted, on Thursday evening, to formally accept Dodds's (P) offer by leaving an acceptance at the place Dodds (D) was residing, but Dodds (D) never received that acceptance, and then both Berry and Dickinson (P) attempted to formally accept in person, but Dodds (D) told both of them that it was too late, as the property had been sold. Dickinson (P) sued for specific performance. The vice-chancellor issued a decree of specific performance, and Dodds (D) appealed.

ISSUE: Does an open offer to sell terminate when the offeree learns that the offeror has already agreed to sell to someone else?

HOLDING AND DECISION: (Lord James, J.) Yes. An open offer to sell terminates when the offeree learns that the offeror has already agreed to sell to someone else. An offeree may not bind an offeror by accepting the offer after learning that the subject of the offer has been sold. A binding contract requires a "meeting of the minds." When an offeror withdraws his offer and the offeree accepts, no meeting has occurred. Even if the offer is still open to the knowledge of the offeree, the fact is that the offeror is no longer of a mind to form the contract, so acceptance does not bind him. Here, the document Dodd (D) gave to Dickinson (P) was merely an offer, notwithstanding that, most likely, both Dodd (D) and Dickinson (P) were under the belief that Dickinson (P) had until Friday morning to accept. Being unsupported by consideration, the promise to keep the offer open was not binding. Accordingly,

Dodds (D) was not required to communicate his retraction to Dickinson (P), and, when Dickinson (P) found out that Dodds (D) had sold the property, Dickinson (P) was on notice that there was no meeting of the minds, just as if Dodds (D) had expressly told him he had withdrawn the offer. Here, even though the revocation was not communicated to Dickinson (P), Dodds's (D) revocation was effective against Dickinson (P), so no contract was formed. Reversed.

CONCURRENCE: (Lord Mellish, J.) Dodds's (D) promise to keep the offer open was not binding, so the agreement between Dodds (D) and Allan was binding, as nothing in law or equity prevented Allan from making a more favorable bid on the property. Then Berry found out about the agreement and communicated that knowledge to Dickinson (P), who was then on notice of the sale. Once Dickinson (P) had such notice, he could not create a binding contract with Dodd (D), as there could be no meeting of their minds. Moreover, at that point it is clear that the performance of the offer is impossible. Therefore, there was no binding contract between Dodd (D) and Dickinson (P).

CONCURRENCE: (Baggallay, J.A.) The judgments that have been announced are correct.

▌ *ANALYSIS*

A traditional requirement for a contract was a "meeting of the minds," as described by the court here. The term used today is "mutual assent," as stated in § 17 of the Restatement (Second) of Contracts. The concept is the same.

▬═■

Quicknotes

MEETING OF THE MINDS A requirement of a valid contract that the parties possess a mutuality of assent as manifested by the terms of the agreement and not by a hidden intent; enforceability of the contract is limited to those terms to which the parties assented.

SPECIFIC PERFORMANCE An equitable remedy, whereby the court requires the parties to perform their obligations pursuant to a contract.

▬═■

Petterson v. Pattberg

Estate executor (P) v. Mortgage holder (D)

N.Y. Ct. of App., 248 N.Y. 86, 161 N.E. 428 (1928).

NATURE OF CASE: Appeal from affirmance of judgment for plaintiff in action for breach of contract.

FACT SUMMARY: Pattberg (D) offered to discount the mortgage on J. Petterson's (P) estate on the condition that it is paid on a certain date. Pattberg (D) then sold the mortgage before Petterson (P), as executor of the estate, had paid him.

🏛 RULE OF LAW
An offer to enter into a unilateral contract may be withdrawn at any time prior to performance of the act requested to be done.

FACTS: Pattberg (D) held a mortgage on property belonging to J. Petterson's estate. Petterson (P) was executor of that estate. Pattberg (D) offered to discount the amount of the mortgage on the condition it be paid on a certain date. Before that date, Petterson (P) went to Pattberg's (D) home and offered to pay him the amount of the mortgage. Pattberg (D) told Petterson (P) that he had already sold the mortgage to a third person. Petterson (P) sued for the amount of the offered discount, the trial court rendered judgment in his favor, and the state's intermediate appellate court affirmed. The state's highest court granted review.

ISSUE: Can an offer to enter into a unilateral contract be withdrawn prior to performance of the act requested to be done?

HOLDING AND DECISION: (Kellogg, J.) Yes. An offer to enter into a unilateral contract may be withdrawn at any time prior to performance of the act requested to be done. Here, Pattberg's (D) offer proposed to Petterson (P) the making of a unilateral contract, the gift of a promise (to discount the mortgage) in exchange for the performance of an act (payment by a certain date). Pattberg (D) was free to revoke his offer any time before Petterson (P) accepted by performing the act. He revoked the offer by informing Petterson (P) that he had sold the mortgage. An offer to sell property may be withdrawn before acceptance without any formal notice to the person to whom the offer is made. It is sufficient if that person has actual knowledge that the person who made the offer has done some act inconsistent with the continuance of the offer, such as selling the property to a third person. Reversed.

DISSENT: (Lehman, J.) Pattberg (D) made payment of the mortgage by Petterson (P), before the stipulated time, a condition precedent to performance by Pattberg (D) of his promise to accept payment at a discount. If the condition precedent was not performed, it is because Pattberg (D)

made performance impossible by refusing to accept payment, when Petterson (P) came with an offer of immediate performance. "It is a principle of fundamental justice that if a promisor is himself the cause of the failure of performance either of an obligation due him or of a condition upon which his own liability depends, he cannot take advantage of the failure." Until the act requested was performed, Pattberg (D) had the right to revoke his offer. However, he could not revoke it after Petterson (P) had offered to make the payment, since the language of Pattberg's (D) offer should not be construed to mean that Pattberg (D) could defeat his own offer after it had been accepted by Petterson (P) in the very way which Pattberg (D) must have intended it should be accepted.

▶ ANALYSIS

Other facts in *Petterson* which do not appear in the opinion may have influenced the court. The trial record shows that Pattberg (D) was prevented from testifying as to a letter sent to J. Petterson (P), in which the offer was revoked. The record also suggests that Petterson (P) knew of the sale of the mortgage. Note, 1928, 14 *Cornell L.Q.* 81. The Restatement (Second) of Contracts provides, "Where an offer invites an offeree to accept by rendering performance, an option contract is created when the offeree begins performance." Actual performance is necessary. Preparations to perform, though they may be essential to performance, are not enough. However, they may constitute justifiable reliance sufficient to make the offerer's promise binding under § 90.

■═■

Quicknotes

EXECUTOR OF ESTATE A person designated by a deceased individual to effectuate the disposition of his property pursuant to a testamentary instrument.

UNILATERAL CONTRACT An agreement pursuant to which a party agrees to act, or to forbear from acting, in exchange for performance on the part of the other party.

■═■

Marchiondo v. Scheck

Real estate broker (P) v. Seller of real estate (D)

N.M. Sup. Ct., 78 N.M. 440, 432 P.2d 405 (1967).

NATURE OF CASE: Appeal from dismissal of action to recover real estate commission.

FACT SUMMARY: Scheck (D) offered to sell realty to a specified prospective buyer and agreed to pay Marchiondo (P) a broker's commission. Later Scheck (D) revoked the offer. Shortly after the revocation and within the time limit set by the offer, Marchiondo (P) obtained the offeree's acceptance.

RULE OF LAW
Partial performance by the offeree of an offer of a unilateral contract results in a binding contract that is conditional upon the offeree's full performance.

FACTS: Scheck (D) offered to sell real estate to a specified prospective buyer and agreed to pay Marchiondo (P) a percentage of the sales price as a commission. The offer set a six-day time limit for acceptance, and Marchiondo (P) received Scheck's (D) revocation of the offer on the sixth day. Later that day Marchiondo (P) obtained the offeree's acceptance. Marchiondo (P) brought suit for the commission, but the trial court dismissed the complaint. The state's highest court granted review.

ISSUE: Does partial performance by the offeree of an offer of a unilateral contract result in a binding contract that is conditional upon the offeree's full performance?

HOLDING AND DECISION: (Wood, J.) Yes. Partial performance by the offeree of an offer of a unilateral contract results in a binding contract that is conditional upon the offeree's full performance. Where an offer invites an offeree to accept by rendering a performance, an option contract is created when the offeree begins to partially perform. The offeror's duty of performance under an option contract so created is conditional on the offeree's completion of performance in accordance with the terms of the offer. In such a case, the offeree's part performance furnishes the acceptance and consideration for a binding contract conditional upon the offeree's full performance. Hence, here, Scheck's (D) right to revoke his offer depended upon whether Marchiondo (P) had partially performed before he received Scheck's (D) revocation. What constitutes partial performance will vary from case to case since what can be done toward performance is determined by what is authorized to be done. Hence it is a question of fact to be determined at the trial. This case is remanded to the trial court so that it can make a finding on the issue of Marchiondo's (P) partial performance prior to the revocation. Reversed and remanded.

▶ ANALYSIS

In many cases involving real estate brokers, it has been held that the owner is no longer privileged to revoke after the broker has taken substantial steps toward rendering performance by advertising the property, soliciting prospective sellers, showing the property, or otherwise. Where notice of revocation is given when the broker's services have proceeded to the point where success is probable, the court may be convinced that it was given for the purpose of avoiding payment of the commission while at the same time enjoying the benefit of the services. Such a revocation is in bad faith and the broker may be held entitled to the commission on the ground that the owner has wrongfully prevented fulfillment of the condition precedent to the right to payment.

Quicknotes

CONDITION PRECEDENT The happening of an uncertain occurrence, which is necessary before a particular right or interest may be obtained or an action performed.

OPTION CONTRACT A contract pursuant to which a seller agrees that property will be available for the buyer to purchase at a specified price and within a certain time period.

QUESTION OF FACT An issue relating to a factual assertion that is disputed at trial and left to the jury to resolve.

Loring v. City of Boston

Reward collector (P) v. City (D)

Mass. Sup. Jud. Ct., 7 Metc. 409, 48 Mass. 409 (1844).

NATURE OF CASE: Action for damages for breach of contract.

FACT SUMMARY: Loring (P) attempted to collect on a reward offered years earlier, during a period of civic crisis.

🏛 RULE OF LAW
An offer which is otherwise not revoked and not limited in duration by its express terms remains open only for a reasonable time, as determined under the particular circumstances of the offer.

FACTS: In 1837, the City of Boston (City) (D) was encountering an epidemic of arson. The mayor offered a $1,000 reward for information leading to the conviction of the arsonist. The offer's duration was not limited, and the offer was not revoked. In 1841, Loring (P) obtained the arrest and conviction of one Marriott for the arson. Marriott had moved to New York, and the epidemic of arson had been over for some time. City (D) refused to pay the reward, and Loring (P) sued. The trial court certified to the state supreme judicial court the issue of whether the offer had lapsed with time.

ISSUE: Does an offer that is otherwise not revoked and not limited in duration by its express terms remain open only for a reasonable time, as determined under the particular circumstances of the offer?

HOLDING AND DECISION: (Shaw, C.J.) Yes. An offer which is otherwise not revoked and not limited in duration by its express terms remains open only for a reasonable time, as determined under the particular circumstances of the offer. Thus, a party cannot collect on a reward offered years earlier, during a civic crisis, if the crisis has passed. When an offer is made which contains no textual time limit, the limit of the offer's duration will be that which is considered reasonable. What is reasonable depends upon the circumstances of each case. This in turn demands an examination of the offeror's objectives. When a reward is offered as a result of a specific set of conditions, reasonableness demands that, once the conditions no longer exist, the offeror's motivations no longer are present, so the offer would be considered withdrawn. Here, the rash of arsons which prompted the offer had ceased, so the offer would be considered to have been withdrawn, and this is how the trial court must rule.

▶ ANALYSIS

The type of contract involved here is what is called unilateral. A unilateral contract starts with a promise conditioned on performance of some act. The contract is sealed not by another promise, as with a bilateral contract, but by performance itself.

■━■

Quicknotes

BILATERAL CONTRACT An agreement pursuant to which each party promises to undertake an obligation, or to forbear from acting, at some time in the future.

UNILATERAL CONTRACT An agreement pursuant to which a party agrees to act, or to forbear from acting, in exchange for performance on the part of the other party.

■━■

Phillips v. Moor

Hay seller (P) v. Hay buyer (D)

Me. Sup. Jud. Ct., 71 Me. 78 (1880).

NATURE OF CASE: Appeal of action seeking damages for breach of contract.

FACT SUMMARY: All terms of a sale of hay by Phillips (P) to Moor (D) had been agreed upon, including pick-up by Moor (D), when fire destroyed the hay.

🏛 RULE OF LAW
When all terms of a sale have been agreed upon, including receipt by the vendee, risk of loss passes to the vendee.

FACTS: Phillips (P) and Moor (D) agreed that the latter would pick up from the former certain hay for processing and possible purchase. Moor (D) then offered to pay $9.50 per ton to purchase, and Phillips (P) agreed. Prior to Moor (D) picking up the hay, as they agreed he would do, the hay was destroyed by fire. When Moor (D) refused to pay, Phillips sued (P) for damages. [The casebook excerpt did not state the result in the trial court.]

ISSUE: When all terms of a sale have been agreed upon, including receipt by the vendee, does risk of loss pass to the vendee?

HOLDING AND DECISION: (Barrows, J.) Yes. When all terms of sale have been agreed upon, including receipt by the vendee, risk of loss passes to the vendee. Where the contract calls for delivery by the vendor, risk of loss does not pass until time of delivery because the goods sold cannot be precisely identified by the vendee until then. However, when the goods have been identified and all terms agreed upon and all that remains is for the vendee to take possession, risk of loss has passed. This was the case here, and judgment should be entered in favor of Phillips (P).

▶ ANALYSIS

Phillips (P) had agreed to part with the hay for $9.50 per ton, although his acceptance did contain language to the effect that he "wished" Moor (D) would pay $10.00. Moor (D) argued that this was not a valid acceptance. The court disagreed, noting that precatory language like this did not constitute a rejection and counter offer.

Quicknotes

PRECATORY LANGUAGE Words of desire as opposed to words that command action to be taken.

RISK OF LOSS Liability for damage to or loss of property that is the subject matter of a contract for sale.

Morrison v. Thoelke

Prospective buyer of land (P) v. Seller of land (D)

Fla. Dist. Ct. App., 155 So. 2d 889 (1963).

NATURE OF CASE: Appeal from summary judgment for plaintiff in an action to quiet title.

FACT SUMMARY: After mailing an acceptance, Morrison (P) informed Thoelke (D) that the offer was being rejected, the rejection being received before the acceptance.

🏛 RULE OF LAW
An acceptance is effective when it is posted even though a subsequent rejection is actually received before the acceptance.

FACTS: Thoelke (D) offered to purchase land from Morrison (P). Morrison (P) agreed, had a deed made out, and mailed it to Thoelke (D). Prior to receipt of the deed by Thoelke (D) Morrison (P) used a faster means to reject the offer, the rejection having reached Thoelke (D) before the acceptance. Thoelke (D) had the deed recorded and tendered the purchase price alleging that a valid contract had been entered into by them. Morrison (P) sued to quiet title alleging that an acceptance was not valid until received and could be withdrawn by the prior receipt of a rejection. Thoelke (D) alleged that the acceptance was binding upon posting. The trial court entered summary judgment for Morrison (P). The state's intermediate appellate court granted review.

ISSUE: Is an acceptance effective when it is posted even though a subsequent rejection is actually received before the acceptance?

HOLDING AND DECISION: (Allen, C.J.) Yes. An acceptance is effective when it is posted even though a subsequent rejection is actually received before the acceptance. While courts are split over this issue, and while there are persuasive arguments on both sides, an acceptance is valid upon posting, not upon receipt, and may not thereafter be recalled. The act of posting effectively places the acceptance beyond the control of the party and is an effective point at which to find a contract has been formed. This rule, also known as the "deposited acceptance" rule, is consistent with modern business practices and serves the best interest of both parties to the contract and the community in general. Once Morrison (P) posted the acceptance, a valid contract was formed. Reversed and remanded.

▶ ANALYSIS

Jurisdictions are split over this issue. Those holding that an acceptance is valid only when received focus on several different factors: (1) the acceptance could be retrieved prior to delivery, (2) there is no reason to bind the acceptor prior to the offeror learning of the contract, (3) the risk of any loss should be on the person choosing the method of communication. If an acceptance is received prior to an earlier mailed rejection, Restatement (Second) § 39 would give effect to the acceptance though this rule is also in dispute among the various jurisdictions. The court in this case qualifies its holding by stating that its decision is limited to circumstances involving the mails and does not purport to determine the rule possibly applicable to cases involving other modern methods of communication—such as those involving instantaneous communication—thus anticipating, before the advent of the Internet and email, the possibility of a different rule for situations involving electronic communications.

■■■

Quicknotes

ACTION TO QUIET TITLE Equitable action to resolve conflicting claims to an interest in real property.

MAILBOX RULE Common law rule that acceptance of an offer is binding upon dispatch at which time an enforceable contract is formed so long as it complies with the requirements for acceptance.

■■■

Livingstone v. Evans

Buyer of land (P) v. Seller of land (D)

Alberta Sup. Ct., 4 D.L.R. 769 (1925).

NATURE OF CASE: Action for specific performance for the sale of real estate.

FACT SUMMARY: Livingstone (P) submitted a counter-offer to Evans's (D) original offer, which counter-offer Evans (D) rejected. Livingstone (P) then unsuccessfully attempted to accept the original offer, based on Evans (D) saying "cannot reduce price," which Livingstone (P) took to mean that Evans (D) was reiterating his initial offer.

> 🏛 **RULE OF LAW**
> After an offer is rejected by a counter-offer, the original offer may be accepted where the offeror reestablishes it.

FACTS: Evans (D) offered to sell land to Livingstone (P) for $1,800. Livingstone (P) telegraphed that he would offer $1,600 or to send lowest price. Evans (D) telegraphed back "cannot reduce price." Livingstone (P) immediately wired an acceptance. Evans (D) refused to enter into a written contract or to convey the land alleging that his original offer was rejected by Livingstone's (P) counter-offer and could not be revived without an acceptance of the offer in Livingstone's (P) second telegram.

ISSUE: After an offer is rejected by a counter-offer, may the original offer be accepted where the offeror reestablishes it?

HOLDING AND DECISION: (Walsh, J.) Yes. After an offer is rejected by a counter-offer, the original offer may be accepted where the offeror reestablishes it. A counter-offer is a rejection of the original offer. It states a new contract which the original offeror is now free to accept or reject. If he rejects it, the other party cannot then unilaterally accept the original offer. He, in effect, makes a new offer at the original terms, which the original offeror is then free to accept or reject. Here, Evans (D) rejected Livingstone's (P) counter-offer. However, this does not end the inquiry herein. Evans's (D) telegram "cannot reduce price" is a reaffirmation of the original offer and demonstrates intent to be bound by it. It reestablishes the original offer and Livingstone's (P) acceptance forms a binding contract. Specific performance is therefore granted. Judgment for Livingstone (P).

▌ *ANALYSIS*

Courts, to ameliorate the harshness of the "mirror image" rule, that the acceptance must exactly match the terms of the offer, found that some acceptances were binding where there was a mere inquiry whether the offeror would accept some other terms. *Stevenson v. McLean*,

5 Q.B.D. 346 (1880). For example, "I accept but would like payment to be due 30 days after delivery." Courts would generally find that this was an unequivocal acceptance of the offer with a request for the addition of another term.

■=■

Quicknotes

REJECTION OF OFFER The refusal to accept the terms of an offer.

SPECIFIC PERFORMANCE An equitable remedy whereby the court requires the parties to perform their obligations pursuant to a contract.

■=■

Commerce & Industry Ins. Co. v. Bayer Corp.

Property insurers (P) v. Seller of nylon tow (D)

Mass. Sup. Jud. Ct., 433 Mass. 388, 742 N.E.2d 567 (2001).

NATURE OF CASE: Appeal from an order denying defendant's motion to compel arbitration and to stay further litigation.

FACT SUMMARY: An explosion and fire destroyed several Malden Mills' (P) buildings at its manufacturing facility. Subsequently, Malden Mills (P) and its property insurers commenced suit against numerous defendants, including Bayer Corp. (D). Bayer (D) brought a motion to compel arbitration in accordance with an arbitration provision in Malden Mills' (P) purchase orders.

🏛 **RULE OF LAW**
Where a contract is formed by the parties' conduct, only terms that are common to both parties' forms become terms of the resulting contract.

FACTS: Malden Mills (P) purchased nylon tow from Bayer Corp. (D). On the reverse side of Malden Mills' (P) purchase orders was an arbitration provision. In response, Bayer (D) remitted to Malden Mills (P) its own standard form invoice, which did not state a preference for arbitration or litigation, but did include a conditional acceptance provision. On December 11, 1995, an explosion and fire destroyed several Malden Mills' (P) buildings at its manufacturing facility. Subsequently, Malden Mills (P) and its property insurers commenced suit against numerous defendants, including Bayer (D), alleging the cause of the fire was ignition of nylon tow sold by Bayer (D). Based on the arbitration provision in Malden Mills' (P) purchase orders, Bayer (D) moved to compel arbitration. The trial court denied Bayer's (D) motion, and the state's highest court granted review.

ISSUE: Where a contract is formed by the parties' conduct, do only terms that are common to both parties' forms become terms of the resulting contract?

HOLDING AND DECISION: (Greaney, J.) Yes. Where a contract is formed by the parties' conduct, only terms that are common to both parties' forms become terms of the resulting contract. When the seller's invoice states that its acceptance is made expressly conditional on the buyer's assent to additional or different terms in the invoice and the buyer does not express its affirmative acceptance of seller's counteroffer, the provision is not enforceable. Bayer's (D) invoice expressly conditioned acceptance on Malden Mills' (P) assent to additional terms. Because Malden Mills (P) did not express assent to these additional terms, but merely remitted payment and accepted the goods, this contract was formed by the parties' conduct (as opposed to writings). Where a contract is

formed by the parties' conduct, the terms of the contract are determined exclusively by subsection (3) of UCC § 2-207. Under subsection (3) of UCC § 2-207, only terms that are common to both parties' forms become terms of the resulting contract. The arbitration provision was not common to both Malden Mills' (P) purchase orders and Bayer's (D) invoices. In fact, Bayer's (D) invoice did not state a preference either way for arbitration. Thus, the resulting contract did not include an arbitration provision, so that the order denying the motion to compel arbitration and to stay litigation is affirmed. Affirmed.

▶ **ANALYSIS**

The proviso clause shunts the parties into either subsection (2) or subsection (3) of UCC § 2-207, but never both.

■═■

Quicknotes

ARBITRATION An agreement to have a dispute heard and decided by a neutral third party, rather than through legal proceedings.

■═■

Klocek v. Gateway, Inc.

User (P) v. Computer manufacturer (D)

104 F. Supp. 2d 1332 (D. Kan. 2000).

NATURE OF CASE: Defense motion to dismiss fraud suit.

FACT SUMMARY: Klocek (P) sued Gateway (D) alleging that Gateway (D) induced him to purchase a computer and support package by making false promises of technical support and also breached certain warranties that its computer would be compatible with standard peripherals and standard internet services. Gateway (D) moved to dismiss the suit, asserting that an arbitration provision in its Standard Terms and Conditions Agreement, included with the computer, was binding.

🏛 RULE OF LAW
Terms received with a product purchased by a consumer do not become part of the contract for the sale of that product where there is no evidence that the consumer expressly agreed to those terms, that the seller informed the consumer of any conditions to the sale, or that the parties agreed to or contemplated additional terms to the sale agreement.

FACTS: Klocek (P), the purchaser of a computer brought individual and class action claims against Gateway, Inc. (D), alleging that Gateway (D) induced him to purchase the computer and support package by making false promises of technical support and also breached certain warranties that its computer would be compatible with standard peripherals and standard internet services. Gateway (D) asserted that Klocek (P) had to arbitrate his claims under Gateway's Standard Terms and Conditions Agreement ("Standard Terms"), which was included in the box that contained the computer battery power cables and instruction manuals. At the top of the first of four pages, the Standard Terms indicated that the consumer accepted the terms by retaining the computer five days past delivery. The 10th of 16 paragraphs included a provision for binding arbitration of disputes. Based on this provision, Gateway (D) moved to dismiss Klocek's (P) claims under the Federal Arbitration Act (FAA), which ensures that written arbitration agreements in maritime transactions and transactions involving interstate commerce are "valid, irrevocable, and enforceable," and which embodies federal policy that favors arbitration agreements and requires that they be rigorously enforced.

ISSUE: Do terms received with a product purchased by a consumer become part of the contract for the sale of that product where there is no evidence that the consumer expressly agreed to those terms, that the seller informed the consumer of any conditions to the sale, or that the

parties agreed to or contemplated additional terms to the sale agreement?

HOLDING AND DECISION: (Vratil, J.) No. Terms received with a product purchased by a consumer do not become part of the contract for the sale of that product where there is no evidence that the consumer expressly agreed to those terms, that the seller informed the consumer of any conditions to the sale, or that the parties agreed to or contemplated additional terms to the sale agreement. Gateway (D) bears the burden of proving that the parties had a written agreement to arbitrate, which is a question of state law. Here, Gateway (D) has not met this burden and has not even presented enough evidence for the court to determine which state's law should apply. It is, however, clear that the parties had a contract for the sale of a computer, which is governed by the Uniform Commercial Code (UCC). Under UCC § 2-207, which applies to additional terms in acceptance or written confirmation, the Standard Terms constitute either an expression of acceptance or written confirmation. As an expression of acceptance, the Standard Terms would constitute a counteroffer only if Gateway (D), as the offeree, expressly made its acceptance conditional on Klocek's (P) assent to the additional or different terms. Here, there was no evidence that at the time of the sales transaction, Gateway (D) informed Klocek (P) that the transaction was conditioned on his acceptance of the Standard Terms. Moreover, the mere fact that Gateway (D) shipped the goods with the terms attached did not communicate to Klocek (P) any unwillingness to proceed without his agreement to the Standard Terms. Because Klocek (P) is not a merchant, additional or different terms contained in the Standard Terms did not become part of the parties' agreement unless plaintiff expressly agreed to them. Although the Standard Terms indicated that Klocek's (P) retention of the computer amounted to the acceptance of its terms, there is no evidence that Klocek (P) expressly accepted those conditions, or that Gateway (D) informed him of a five-day review-and-return period as a condition of the sales transaction, or that the parties contemplated additional terms to the sales agreement. Motion to dismiss denied.

▶ ANALYSIS

The courts have been split over this issue. Some courts, for example, have held that under § 2-204, the seller, as the master of the offer, may propose limitations on the kind of conduct that constitutes acceptance and that § 2-207 does

Continued on next page.

not apply in cases with only one form—such as here. Other courts view the issue as one of contract formation under § 2-204, rather than as contract alteration under § 2-207. Here, the court distinguished those cases, concluding that § 2-207 is not limited to situations involving more than one form (i.e., "battle of the forms"), and that there is no support for the proposition that the seller is the master of the offer; instead, the court here concluded that Klocek (P) was the offeror—he offered to buy the computer—and Gateway (D) accepted by providing the computer.

■══■

Quicknotes

ARBITRATION AGREEMENT A mutual understanding entered into by parties wishing to submit to the decision making authority of a neutral third party, selected by the parties and charged with rendering a binding decision amenable to those affected.

BATTLE OF FORMS Refers to the exchange of forms, pursuant to a contract for the sale of goods, between a buyer and a seller.

MUTUAL ASSENT A requirement of a valid contract that the parties possess a mutuality of assent as manifested by the terms of the agreement and not by a hidden intent.

■══■

Walker v. Keith

Property renter (P) v. Owner of property (D)

Ky. Ct. App., 382 S.W.2d 198 (1964).

NATURE OF CASE: Action alleging breach of an option to renew clause.

FACT SUMMARY: Walker (P) rented property from Keith (D) for ten years with an additional ten year option, rent to be fixed mutually by the parties, said rental values to reflect the comparative business conditions between the periods.

> ## 🏛 RULE OF LAW
> Where essential terms such as price are not contained in an option contract and no standards are included whereby those terms may be judicially determined, no binding contract exists.

FACTS: Walker (P) entered into a ten-year lease with Keith (D). The contract gave Walker (P) an option to renew the lease for ten additional years. The parties were to agree on a fair rental at that time to be fixed based on the "comparative basis of rental values at the date of renewal with rental values at this time reflected by the comparative business conditions of the two periods." Walker (P) attempted to renew his lease, but Keith (D) refused. Walker (P) brought suit for damages or specific performance. The trial court fixed the reasonable rental value at $125 per month. Keith (D) appealed, arguing that there was no way to fix the price and, therefore, no binding contract existed. The state's intermediate appellate court granted review.

ISSUE: Where essential terms such as price are not contained in an option contract and no standards are included whereby those terms may be judicially determined, does a binding contract exist?

HOLDING AND DECISION: (Clay, Comm.) No. Where essential terms such as price are not contained in an option contract and no standards are included whereby those terms may be judicially determined, no binding contract exists. The failure of the parties to include essential contract terms renders the offer and acceptance ineffective and no contract is formed. The price term (rent) is essential in a lease contract. The option clause here failed to fix the rent or to provide any standard whereby the court could fix it. Equity cannot re-write a contract supplying essential terms which the parties failed to provide. Reasonable rent to one party may be unreasonable to the other, so that the language in the option regarding the comparative basis of rental values and comparative business conditions does not help to fix the rent. These terms are too broad, and the record shows the parties were in conflict—rather than in accord—as to their meaning; there has been no meeting of the minds. The parties herein have merely agreed to agree. Their failure to agree renders the option/offer incapable of being accepted. No contract was ever formed, and it was erroneous for the trial court to attempt to supply the rental term when the parties failed to do so with any degree of certainty. Reversed.

▶ ANALYSIS

A number of courts have tried to supply missing terms, even essential ones, by making reasonable judgments as to value, rental, etc. *Hall v. Weatherford*, 32 Ariz. 370 (1927). Courts feel that "reasonable" rental can be determined by comparison with the rental of similar property, for a similar period of time and a similar use. *Edwards v. Tobin*, 132 Or. 38 (1930). In *Walker*, the court focuses on whether a contract exists. Only once it is found to exist may the court supply terms.

■═■

Quicknotes

ESSENTIAL TERMS Terms without which a contract may not be entered.

OPTION CONTRACT A contract pursuant to which a seller agrees that property will be available for the buyer to purchase at a specified price and within a certain time period.

SPECIFIC PERFORMANCE An equitable remedy whereby the court requires the parties to perform their obligations pursuant to a contract.

■═■

Rego v. Decker

Service station owner (D) v. Lessee (P)

Alaska Sup. Ct., 482 P.2d 834 (1971).

NATURE OF CASE: Appeal of order mandating specific performance of a land sale contract.

FACT SUMMARY: A court granted specific performance of an option contract for the purchase of land by Decker (P) notwithstanding that it did not provide Rego (D), the seller, with any security interest.

🏛 RULE OF LAW
A court may grant specific performance as to those terms in a contract that are uncertain where it can fashion a remedy that is fair to the parties.

FACTS: Decker (P) leased a service station from Rego (D) with an option to buy. The option specified a price as well as a schedule of amounts already paid as rent that would be deducted from the purchase price, depending on when the option was exercised. Rego (D) was required, in exchange, to furnish Decker (P) with a warranty deed and title insurance in the amount of the purchase price. The option, however, did not address whether Decker (P) would have to provide any security in the transaction. Decker (P) sought to exercise the option, but Rego (D) refused, and instead sold the property to a third party. Decker (P) sued for specific performance. The trial court granted specific performance as to the purchase option, and Rego (D) appealed, arguing that the terms of the option provisions of the lease were uncertain and too harsh, or in the alternative, that if granted, the specific performance provisions of the decree should have been conditioned upon various provisions protecting Rego's (D) interests. The state's highest court granted review.

ISSUE: May a court grant specific performance as to those terms in a contract that are uncertain where it can fashion a remedy that is fair to the parties?

HOLDING AND DECISION: (Rabinowitz, J.) Yes. A court may grant specific performance as to those terms in a contract that are uncertain where it can fashion a remedy that is fair to the parties. To be specifically enforceable, a contract must be reasonably definite and certain as to its terms. Here, Rego (D) contended that some of the terms were uncertain, and Decker (P) countered with explanations for why those terms were not uncertain. While a court may fill gaps in a contract where the expectations of the parties are reasonably clear, a court should not impose on a party any performance to which he did not and probably would not have agreed. Where the character of a gap in an agreement manifests failure to reach an agreement rather than a sketchy agreement, or where gaps cannot be filled with confidence that the reasonable

expectations of the parties are being fulfilled, then specific enforcement should be denied for lack of reasonable certainty. However, where one or more terms are left open and uncertain, an entire contract should not be invalidated for indefiniteness where the parties intended to make a contract and there is a reasonably certain basis for giving an appropriate remedy. Here, the key uncertainty was whether the parties intended to include a security provision, and the trial court failed to make findings on this issue. If the parties did not intend security, then the agreement is not uncertain. If, however, they did contemplate security, but failed to include it in the purchase option, that would amount to uncertainty. Such uncertainty, however, should not result in the unconditional denial of specific performance where a remedy can be crafted that is fair to the parties. In this instance, such a remedy can be fashioned by requiring Decker (P) to furnish adequate security for his performance. Thus, while the trial court's order of specific performance of the purchase option agreement was not erroneous, the court's decree should have been made conditional upon Decker's (P) either paying the purchase price in full or furnishing adequate security embodying such terms as the court considered appropriate. Therefore, the case must be remanded so the trial court can make its order conditional on the giving by Decker (P) of appropriate security. Affirmed and remanded.

▶ ANALYSIS

The Restatement (Second) of Contracts, § 33(2) provides that the terms of a contract are definite enough to be enforced if they allow the determination of whether a breach exists and whether an appropriate remedy may be fashioned. In practice, under today's more liberal approach to the degree of definiteness required for a contract, four essential elements must still be present, wither expressly or impliedly for a contract to be specifically enforced, i.e., the contract's parties, subject matter, time for performance, and price. Nonetheless, even when one of the elements is missing, it will be supplied by the court, if the parties intended to leave it to reasonable implication, agreed to determine it later in a further agreement, or "filled in the term" through performance under the contract.

■■■

Continued on next page.

Quicknotes

LAND SALE CONTRACT Contract for the sale of real property pursuant to which title to the property is transferred from the seller to buyer.

MUTUALITY OF PERFORMANCE The requirement for a valid contract that the parties be required to perform.

SPECIFIC PERFORMANCE An equitable remedy whereby the court requires the parties to perform their obligations pursuant to a contract.

■══■

Consideration

Quick Reference Rules of Law

Hamer v. Sidway

Nephew's estate (P) v. Uncle's estate (D)

N.Y. Ct. App., 124 N.Y. 538, 27 N.E. 256 (1891).

NATURE OF CASE: Action on appeal to recover upon a contract which is supported by forbearance of a right as consideration.

FACT SUMMARY: William Story (D) promised to pay $5,000 to William Story, 2d (P) if he would forbear in the use of liquor, tobacco, swearing or playing cards or billiards for money until he became twenty-one years of age.

RULE OF LAW

Forbearance on the part of a promisee is sufficient consideration to support a contract.

FACTS: William Story (D) agreed with his nephew William Story, 2d (P), that if W. Story 2d (P) would refrain from drinking liquor, using tobacco, swearing and playing cards or billiards for money until he became twenty-one years of age, W. Story (D) would pay him $5,000. Upon becoming twenty-one years of age, W. Story, 2d (P) received a letter from W. Story (D) stating he had earned the $5,000 and it would be kept at interest for him. Twelve years later, W. Story (D) died and this action was brought by the assignees of W. Story, 2d (P) against the executor (D) of the estate of W. Story (D). Judgment was entered in favor of W. Story, 2d (P) at the trial at special term and was reversed at general term of the supreme court. The assignee of W. Story, 2d (P) appealed. The state's highest court granted review.

ISSUE: Is forbearance on the part of a promisee sufficient consideration to support a contract?

HOLDING AND DECISION: (Parker, J.) Yes. Forbearance on the part of a promisee is sufficient consideration to support a contract. Valuable consideration may consist either of some right, interest, profit, or benefit accruing to the one party, or some forbearance, detriment, loss, or responsibility given, suffered or undertaken by the other. Courts "will not ask whether the thing which forms the consideration does in fact benefit the promisee or a third party, or is of any substantial value to any. It is enough that something is promised, done, forborne, or suffered by the party to whom the promise is made as consideration for the promise made to him." Thus, the court here rejects the argument that there was no consideration because W. Story 2d's (P) forbearance benefited him. Reversed.

▶ ANALYSIS

The surrendering or forgoing of a legal right constitutes a sufficient consideration for a contract if the minds of the parties meet on the relinquishment of the right as a consideration. Consideration may be forbearance to sue on a claim, extension of time, or any other giving up of a legal right in consideration of a promise.

■══■

Quicknotes

CONSIDERATION Value given by one party in exchange for performance, or a promise to perform, by another party.

FORBEARANCE Refraining from the assertion of a lawful right or other action.

■══■

Batsakis v. Demotsis

Lender (P) v. Borrower (D)

Tex. Ct. Civ. App., 226 S.W.2d 673 (1949).

NATURE OF CASE: Appeal from judgment in action to recover on a promissory note.

FACT SUMMARY: Batsakis (P) loaned Demotsis (D) 500,000 drachmae (which, at the time, had a total value of $25 in American money) in return for Demotsis's (D) promise to repay $2,000 in American money.

🏛 RULE OF LAW
Mere inadequacy of consideration will not void a contract.

FACTS: During World War II, Batsakis (P), a Greek resident, loaned Demotsis (D), also a Greek resident, the sum of 500,000 drachmae which at the time had a distressed value of only $25 in American money. In return, Demotsis (D), eager to return to the United States, signed an instrument in which she promised to repay Batsakis (P) $2,000 of American money. When Demotsis (D) refused to repay, claiming that the instrument was void at the outset for lack of adequate consideration, Batsakis (P) brought an action to collect on the note and recovered a judgment for $750 (which, at the time, after the war, reflected the rising value of drachmae), plus interest. Batsakis (P) appealed on the ground that he was entitled to recover the stated sum of the note—$2,000—plus interest.

ISSUE: Will mere inadequacy of consideration void a contract?

HOLDING AND DECISION: (McGill, J.) No. Mere inadequacy of consideration will not void a contract. Only where the consideration for a contract has no value whatsoever will the contract be voided. A plea of want of consideration amounts to a contention that the instrument never became a valid obligation in the first instance. As a result, mere inadequacy of consideration is not enough. Here, the trial court obviously placed a value on the consideration—the drachmae—by deeming them to be worth $750. Thus, the trial court felt that there was consideration of value for the original transaction. Furthermore, the 500,000 drachmae was exactly what Demotsis (D) bargained for. It may not have been a good bargain, but she nonetheless agreed to repay Batsakis (P) $2,000. Accordingly, Batsakis (P) is entitled to recover $2,000, and not just $750, plus interest. Affirmed as reformed.

▌ ANALYSIS

Official comment (e) to the Restatement (Second) of Contracts § 81, states, "gross inadequacy of consideration may be relevant in the application of other rules, (such as) . . . lack of capacity, fraud, duress, undue influence or mistake."

Section 234 provides for the avoidance of a contract which, at the time it is made, contains an unconscionable term. The official comment to this section states that "gross disparity in the values exchanged . . . may be sufficient ground, without more, for denying specific performance."

■■■

Quicknotes

CONSIDERATION Value given by one party in exchange for performance, or a promise to perform, by another party.

PROMISSORY NOTE A written promise to tender a stated amount of money at a designated time and to a designated person.

UNCONSCIONABILITY Rule of law whereby a court may excuse performance of a contract, or of a particular contract term, if it determines that such term(s) are unduly oppressive or unfair to one party to the contract.

■■■

Schnell v. Nell

Husband of testator (D) v. Beneficiary of will (P)

Ind. Sup. Ct., 17 Ind. 29 (1861).

NATURE OF CASE: Appeal from overruled demurrer to the complaint in an action for breach of contract.

FACT SUMMARY: Out of consideration for his deceased wife, Schnell (D) agreed to pay Nell (P) $200 in return for Nell's (P) payment of one cent, and agreed to forbear all claims against the wife's estate.

> 🏛 **RULE OF LAW**
> A contract will be vitiated for lack of consideration where the consideration given by one party is only nominal and intended to be so.

FACTS: Theresa Schnell's will left $200 to Nell (P). The will was declared a nullity because Theresa, at the time of her death, held no property in her own name. Nonetheless, Theresa's husband, Zacharias Schnell (D), agreed to give Nell (P) $200 out of the love and respect he had for his wife. In return, Nell (P) agreed to pay Schnell the sum of one cent, and also agreed to forbear any claim he might have against Theresa's estate. When Schnell (D) refused to honor his promise, Nell (P) sued for breach. The trial court overruled Schnell's (D) demurrer to the complaint, and the state's highest court granted review.

ISSUE: Will a contract be vitiated for lack of consideration where the consideration given by one party is only nominal and intended to be so?

HOLDING AND DECISION: (Perkins, J.) Yes. A contract will be vitiated for lack of consideration where the consideration given by one party is only nominal and intended to be so. The general proposition that inadequacy of consideration will not vitiate a contract does not apply where consideration offered by one party is plainly intended to be nominal. Since Schnell (D) was not bound to honor his promise on a tender of one cent, it is necessary to determine if there was any other sufficient consideration. A moral consideration will not support a promise; nor will forbearance of a legally groundless claim. Honor of a deceased wife for her past services is inadequate since the consideration is past, and also because veneration in memory of a deceased person is not a legal consideration for a promise to pay any third party money. Schnell's promise (D) is therefore unenforceable. Reversed, with costs, and remanded.

▶ **ANALYSIS**

The holding here represents an exception to general rule that where an action is at law for breach of contract, a court will not examine the fairness of the bargained-for exchanges. However, where the action is in equity for specific performance of the contract, the general rule is reversed: before relief will be granted, there must be a showing that the agreed exchanges were substantially equal in value.

■■■

Quicknotes

FORBEARANCE Refraining from the assertion of a lawful right or other action.

MORAL CONSIDERATION An inducement to enter a contract which is not enforceable at law, but is made based on a moral obligation and may be enforceable in order to prevent unjust enrichment on the part of the promisor.

NOMINAL CONSIDERATION Consideration that is so insignificant that it does not represent the actual value received from the agreement.

■■■

Fiege v. Boehm

Suspected father (D) v. Unmarried woman (P)

Md. Ct. App., 210 Md. 352, 123 A.2d 316 (1956).

NATURE OF CASE: Appeal from a jury verdict judgment for plaintiff, and from the denials of a motion for a directed verdict and of a motion for a new trial or judgment n.o.v. in an action to recover damages for breach of contract.

FACT SUMMARY: Fiege (D) promised to pay money if Boehm (P) would refrain from instituting bastardy proceedings; but Fiege (D), after blood tests, determined that Boehm's (P) bastardy claim was invalid and refused to pay.

RULE OF LAW
Forbearance to assert a claim that turns out to be invalid may serve as consideration for a return promise if the parties at the time of the settlement reasonably believed in good faith that the claim was valid.

FACTS: Boehm (P), an unmarried woman, became pregnant and believed in good faith that Fiege (D) was the father. Fiege (D) promised to pay expenses incident to the birth and make regular payments for the raising of the child on condition that Boehm (P) would not institute bastardy proceedings against him. Subsequent to the child's birth, Fiege (D) had blood tests made which demonstrated that he could not have been the father. Fiege (D) then stopped making payments, whereupon Boehm (P) unsuccessfully instituted bastardy proceedings against him. Boehm (P) brought suit to recover the balance of the expenses as promised, and a jury returned a verdict in her favor. The trial court denied Fiege's (D) motion for a directed verdict and for a new trial or judgment n.o.v., and the state's highest court granted review.

ISSUE: May forbearance to assert a claim that turns out to be invalid serve as consideration for a return promise if the parties at the time of the settlement reasonably believed in good faith that the claim was valid?

HOLDING AND DECISION: (Delaplaine, J.) Yes. Forbearance to assert a claim that turns out to be invalid may serve as consideration for a return promise if the parties at the time of the settlement reasonably believed in good faith that the claim was valid. Although forbearance to assert a claim known to be invalid will not support a return promise, if the parties to a settlement agreement reasonably believe in good faith that the claim forgone is valid (or if there is at least a bona fide dispute) the forbearance is consideration for a return promise. Thus, a promise not to prosecute a claim which is not founded in good faith does not of itself give a right of action on an agreement to pay for refraining from so acting, because a release from mere annoyance and unfounded litigation does not furnish valuable consideration. On the other hand, forbearance to sue for a lawful claim or demand is sufficient consideration for a promise to pay for the forbearance if the party forbearing had an honest intention to prosecute litigation which is not frivolous, vexatious, or unlawful, and which she believed to be well founded. To determine if the forbearance is sufficient consideration, the subjective requisite that the claim be bona fide is combined with the objective requisite that the claim has a reasonable basis of support. Here, because Boehm (P) subjectively believed her claim was valid, and because that claim had a reasonable basis of support, her agreement to forbear from bringing bastardy proceedings constituted consideration to support the agreement entered with Fiege (D). Affirmed.

ANALYSIS

Basic public policy underlies this decision. The law seeks to encourage out-of-court settlements which are not coerced. Such settlements (1) tend to promote good will, (2) are much less expensive for the parties to pursue than a full-blown court battle, and (3) help relieve unnecessary (and expensive) congestion on court dockets. However, a settlement based on forbearance to assert a claim known to be invalid is likely to be coercive and in bad faith, and courts will not enforce it.

Quicknotes

CONSIDERATION Value given by one party in exchange for performance, or a promise to perform, by another party.

FORBEARANCE TO ASSERT CLAIM Refraining from the assertion of a legal claim upon the date at which it becomes due.

INVALID CLAIM An interest or right that is not legally enforceable.

Wood v. Lucy, Lady Duff-Gordon

Marketer (P) v. Fashion designer (D)

N.Y. Ct. App., 222 N.Y. 88, 118 N.E. 214 (1917).

NATURE OF CASE: Action for damages for breach of a contract for an exclusive right.

FACT SUMMARY: Wood (P), in a complicated agreement, styled as an employment agreement, received the exclusive right for one year, renewable on a year-to-year basis if not terminated by 90 days' notice, to endorse designs with Lucy's (D) name and to market all her fashion designs for which she would receive one half of the profits derived. Lucy (D) broke the contract by placing her endorsement on designs without Wood's (P) knowledge and without paying him any of the profits.

🏛 RULE OF LAW
If a promise in exchange may be implied from the writing even though such a promise is imperfectly expressed or not expressed at all, such promise will support a valid contract.

FACTS: Lucy, Lady Duff-Gordon (Lucy) (D), a famous-name fashion designer, hired Wood (P) and granted to him an exclusive right to endorse designs of others with her name and to market and license all of her own designs, with the agreement that they were to split the profits derived by Wood (P) in half. The exclusive right was for a period of one year, renewable on a year-to-year basis, and terminable upon 90 days' notice. Lucy (D) placed her endorsement on fabrics, dresses, and millinery without Wood's (P) knowledge in violation of the contract and without paying him any profits. Wood (P) sued for damages. Lucy (D) claimed that the agreement lacked the elements of a contract as Wood (P) was not expressly bound to do anything. The trial court held for Wood (P), but the state's intermediate appellate court reversed. The state's highest court granted review.

ISSUE: If a promise in exchange may be implied from the writing even though such a promise is imperfectly expressed or not expressed at all, will such promise support a valid contract?

HOLDING AND DECISION: (Cardozo, J.) Yes. If a promise in exchange may be implied from the writing even though such a promise is imperfectly expressed or not expressed at all, such promise will support a valid contract. While the contract did not precisely state that Wood (P) had promised to use reasonable efforts to place Lucy's (D) endorsement and market her designs, such a promise can be implied. The implication arises from the circumstances. Lucy (D) gave an exclusive privilege and the acceptance of the exclusive agency was an acceptance of its duties. Lucy's (D) sole compensation was to be one-half the profits resulting from Wood's (P) efforts. Unless he gave his

efforts, she could never receive anything. Without an implied promise, the transaction could not have had such business efficacy as they must have intended it to have. Wood's (P) promise to make monthly accounts and to acquire patents and copyrights as necessary showed the intention of the parties that the promise has value by showing that Wood (P) had some duties. The promise to pay Lucy (D) half the profits and make monthly accounts was a promise to use reasonable efforts to bring profits and revenues into existence. Reversed.

▶ ANALYSIS

A bilateral contract can be express, implied in fact, or a little of each. The finding of an implied promise for the purpose of finding sufficient consideration to support an express promise is an important technique of the courts in order to uphold agreements which seem to be illusory and to avoid problems of mutuality of obligation. This case is the leading case on the subject. It is codified in UCC § 2-306(2) where an agreement for exclusive dealing in goods imposes, unless otherwise agreed, an obligation to use best efforts by both parties.

■══■

Quicknotes

BILATERAL CONTRACT An agreement pursuant to which each party promises to undertake an obligation, or to forbear from acting, at some time in the future.

IMPLIED PROMISE A promise inferred by law from a document as a whole and the circumstances surrounding its implementation.

■══■

Sylvan Crest Sand & Gravel Co. v. United States

Bidder on government contracts (P) v. Federal government (D)

150 F.2d 642 (2d Cir. 1945).

NATURE OF CASE: Appeal from summary judgment for defendant in action for damages for breach of four contracts for the sale of goods.

FACT SUMMARY: Sylvan Crest Sand & Gravel Co. (Sylvan) (P) successfully bid on four contracts to supply the United States (D) trap rock for an airport. The contract had printed on it that cancellation by the United States (D) could be made at any time. When the United States (D) refused to request or accept any rock in a timely way, thus depriving Sylvan (P) of its expected profits, Sylvan (P) filed suit claiming breach.

RULE OF LAW
In agreements that purport to reserve to one party the right to cancel at any time, it is reasonable to construe the agreement to require notice of cancellation, so that even though such notice may be given at any time, it constitutes a detriment, hence, valid consideration that supports the contract.

FACTS: Sylvan Crest Sand & Gravel Co. (Sylvan) (P) bid successfully on four government contracts of similar nature to supply trap rock for construction of an airport. The alleged breach by United States (D) was the Government's (D) refusal to request or accept delivery within a reasonable time after the date of the contract, depriving Sylvan (P) of $10,000 in profits. The contracts, basically the same, were government forms stating "Invitation," "Bid," and "Acceptance by the Government." Under "Bid," Sylvan (P) signed, stating all items would be furnished subject to all conditions of the invitation. The rock was to be delivered "as required," and "cancellation by the procurement office may be effected at any time." The back of the form stated conditions as to liabilities in case of default and that this form meets the requirements of a formal contract . . . After Sylvan (P) sued for damages, the United States (D) claimed that its promise was illusory and that there could be no binding obligation. The district court granted summary judgment to the United States (D). The court of appeals granted review.

ISSUE: In agreements that purport to reserve to one party the right to cancel at any time, is it reasonable to construe the agreement to require notice of cancellation, so that even though such notice may be given at any time, it constitutes a detriment, hence, valid consideration that supports the contract?

HOLDING AND DECISION: (Swan, J.) Yes. In agreements that purport to reserve to one party the right to cancel at any time, it is reasonable to construe

the agreement to require notice of cancellation, so that even though such notice may be given at any time, it constitutes a detriment, hence, valid consideration that supports the contract. Through a process of interpretation, consideration to uphold the contract can be found. The statements on the reverse of the contract form clearly presuppose the making of a valid contract. Those terms stated liabilities of the contractor in case of default. In construing the form, the court follows a presumption that both parties were acting in good faith. While the acceptance contained no promissory words, it is conceded that a promise by the United States (D) to pay the stated price for the rock which was delivered was to be implied. Since exact delivery times were not specified, it was implied that delivery within a reasonable time was intended. The express provision of "delivery to start immediately" implied a promise to give delivery instructions. Sylvan (P) made a promise to deliver rock at a stated price and if the Government (D) were suing for breach, the question would be whether the Government's (D) acceptance was sufficient consideration. Since the United States (D) is being sued, the question is whether it made any promise that has been broken, and its acceptance must be interpreted as a reasonable businessman would have understood it. It is reasonable to interpret the form as saying the Government (D) accepted Sylvan's (P) offer to deliver within a reasonable time and promised to take rock and pay the price unless the United States (D) gave Sylvan (P) notice of cancellation within a reasonable time. This is because the United States (D) intended to bind the bidder to the contract and the bidder thought that acceptance of his bid made a contract. Good faith requires no less and gives the effect of the parties' mutual intentions. Accordingly, United States (D) could not have an unrestricted power of cancellation. Even the words "Cancellation may be effected at any time" imply affirmative action, the giving of reasonable notice of intent to cancel. The words should be interpreted in favor of finding a contract and not to render illusory the promises of the parties. The Government's (D) obligation to give delivery instructions or notice of cancellation within a reasonable time constituted consideration for Sylvan's (P) promise to deliver in accordance with instructions and made the contract valid. Reversed and remanded.

⯈ ANALYSIS

This case has attracted great comment. Notice that the court was very careful to show the intent of the parties to

Continued on next page.

create a contract. In order to carry out that intention, the Government (D) would have to have promised to purchase or, instead, give reasonable notice of cancellation. This case removes the illusory promise problem by interpreting the cancellation clause to call for notice of cancellation within a reasonable time. Many critics find it difficult, if not impossible, to say Sylvan (P) bargained for notice of cancellation in exchange for the promise to supply rock. This premise seems to be a fiction designed to uphold the agreement. Without the fiction, the case supports the view that a promise is not rendered insufficient as consideration by reason of a power of cancellation reserved by the promisor. This view finds support in UCC § 2-309 (3) which requires notice of cancellation which is reasonable and an agreement dispensing with it is invalid if its operation would be unconscionable. This case, considered to be on the "frontier" of contract law, rests on solid precepts of good faith and reasonableness which are found codified in federal law requiring auto dealers to be treated in good faith by auto manufacturers who must give reasonable notice of cancellation or termination of the dealership. The court appears to have read into the agreement principles similar to those here. For Sylvan (P) to collect expectation damages, it must show clear-cut damages, reliance by one party, and a clear breach by the other party. If the above cannot be shown, reliance damages can still be had but will be considerably less. Reliance damages will restore plaintiff to where the plaintiff was before the contract; expectation damages will put the plaintiff where the plaintiff would have been had the contract been carried out.

■══■

Quicknotes

DETRIMENT A loss or injury sustained by an individual personally or to his interest in property.

EXPECTATION DAMAGES The measure of damages necessary to place the nonbreaching party in the same position as he would have enjoyed had the contract been fully performed.

ILLUSORY PROMISE A promise that is not legally enforceable because performance of the obligation by the promisor is completely within his discretion.

■══■

McMichael v. Price

Sand supplier (D) v. Sand salesman (P)

Okla. Sup. Ct., 177 Okla. 186, 58 P.2d 549 (1936).

NATURE OF CASE: Appeal of award of damages for breach of contract.

FACT SUMMARY: Price (P) contended that McMichael (D) breached a requirements contract.

RULE OF LAW
A requirements contract is valid if the buyer realistically anticipates the requirements set forth in the contract.

FACTS: Price (P), an experienced salesman of sand and sand-related products, contracted with McMichael (D), a supplier of sand, for the latter to supply him with all the sand he required in a retail sand business he wished to open. After a period of time, McMichael (D) refused to honor the contract, claiming that Price (P) had failed to timely pay as agreed, and Price (P) had to procure sand elsewhere. Price (P) sued for breach. A jury awarded Price (P) $7,512.51, and the trial court ordered a remittitur of $2,500, for a total judgment of $5,012.51. McMichael (D) appealed, and the state's highest court granted review.

ISSUE: Is a requirements contract valid if the buyer realistically anticipates the requirements set forth in the contract?

HOLDING AND DECISION: (Osborn, V.C.J.) Yes. A requirements contract is valid if the buyer realistically anticipates the requirements set forth in the contract. The argument is made that a requirements contract is illusory for want of valid consideration and mutuality because the buyer is under no obligation to require any amount of the goods at issue. However, where the buyer realistically will have a need for the product in question, this proposition fails, for, as a practical matter, the buyer will be required to buy from the seller. Here, Price (P) was an experienced sand salesman, and his anticipated future requirement for sand, which formed the premise of the contract, was realistic. Price (P) was obligated by the contract to purchase from McMichael (D) all the sand Price (P) could sell; correspondingly, McMichael (D) was required to supply that sand, and a valid, mutual contract was formed. Affirmed.

▶ ANALYSIS

Contracts, to be enforceable, must be concrete, which is to say, sufficiently definite that a party can know what is expected of him. Requirements contracts of necessity cannot specify the amount of goods sold. For this reason they have been challenged as lacking concreteness. Such challenges are usually unsuccessful as long as the parties

intended to be bound by this agreement, there is a mutuality of obligation under the agreement, and they agree to do something that will be a detriment sufficient to support this promise.

■═■

Quicknotes

ILLUSORY CONTRACT A contract that is unenforceable for lack of consideration because a promise by one of the parties to perform is completely within his discretion.

MUTUALITY OF OBLIGATION Requires that both parties to a contract are bound or else neither is bound.

REQUIREMENTS CONTRACT An agreement pursuant to which one party agrees to purchase all his required goods or services from the other party exclusively for a specified time period.

■═■

Hayes v. Plantations Steel Co.

Employee (P) v. Steel company (D)

R.I. Sup. Ct., 438 A.2d 1091 (1982).

NATURE OF CASE: Appeal of award of damages for breach of contract.

FACT SUMMARY: Hayes (P) tried to enforce a promise made to him upon announcing his retirement that he would receive a pension.

🏛 RULE OF LAW
A promise made to an employee upon the announcement of his retirement is not enforceable.

FACTS: Hayes (P) had been an employee of Plantations Steel Co. (Plantations) (D) for many years. No pension plan had ever been agreed to between them. After Hayes (P) announced his retirement, an officer of Plantations (D) promised him that he would be paid a $5,000 annual pension, and Hayes (P) received this annual amount for four years. Subsequent to this, a change of management occurred, and Plantations (D) refused to honor the commitment. Hayes (P) sued for breach. The trial court found Plantations (D) liable for the $5,000 annual pension, and Plantations (D) appealed. The state's highest court granted review.

ISSUE: Is a promise made to an employee upon the announcement of his retirement enforceable?

HOLDING AND DECISION: (Shea, J.) No. A promise made to an employee upon the announcement of his retirement is not enforceable. To be binding, a contract must involve the exchange of present or future performance obligations. A promise made based on past performance does not fall within this situation, for the promisee has not been placed under a legal obligation to perform any future act. Here, Plantations's (D) promise was meant to induce Hayes (P) to refrain from retiring when he could have chosen to do so in return for further service, nor was the promise made to encourage long service from the start of his employment. Instead, it was intended merely "as a token of appreciation for [Hayes's] many years of service." As such it was in the nature of a gratuity paid to Hayes (P) for as long as the company chose. While promissory estoppel may provide the requisite consideration if the promisee detrimentally relies upon the promise, in this instance, however, no evidence exists that Hayes (P) took the promise to pay $5,000 annually into account in formulating his retirement plans, so no detrimental reliance has been shown. Reversed and remanded.

▶ ANALYSIS

It is an elementary principle of contract law that a binding contract must involve an exchange of obligations. A contract based on past performance does not meet this criterion. Such a so-called contract is often termed an "illusory contract."

■■▬■

Quicknotes

ILLUSORY CONTRACT A contract that is unenforceable for lack of consideration because a promise by one of the parties to perform is completely within his discretion.

PROMISSORY ESTOPPEL A promise that is enforceable if the promisor should reasonably expect that it will induce action or forbearance on the part of the promisee, and does in fact cause such action or forbearance, and it is the only means of avoiding injustice.

■■▬■

Mills v. Wyman

Caretaker (P) v. Father (D)

Mass. Sup. Jud. Ct., 3 Pick. 207 (1825).

NATURE OF CASE: Appeal from nonsuit of action to recover upon a promise.

FACT SUMMARY: Mills (P) took care of Wyman's (D) son without being requested to do so and for so doing was promised compensation for expenses arising out of the rendered care by Wyman (D). Wyman (D) later refused to compensate Mills (P).

 RULE OF LAW
A moral obligation is insufficient consideration for a promise.

FACTS: Mills (P) nursed and cared for Levi Wyman, the son of Wyman (D). Upon learning of Mills's (P) acts of kindness toward his son, Wyman (D) promised to repay Mills (P) his expenses incurred in caring for Levi Wyman. Later, Wyman (D) refused to compensate Mills (P) for his expenses. Mills (P) filed an action in the Court of Common Pleas where Wyman (D) was successful in obtaining a nonsuit against Mills (P). Mills (P) appealed.

ISSUE: Is a moral obligation sufficient consideration for a promise?

HOLDING AND DECISION: (Parker, C.J.) No. A moral obligation is insufficient consideration for a promise. It is said a moral obligation is sufficient consideration to support an express promise. However, the universality of the rule cannot be supported. Therefore, notwithstanding that Wyman (D) acted disgracefully, there must be some other preexisting legal (rather than merely moral) obligation which will suffice as consideration. Affirmed.

▶ ANALYSIS

In cases such as this one, the nearly universal holding is that the existing moral obligation is not a sufficient basis for the enforcement of an express promise to render the performance that it requires. The general statement is that it is not sufficient consideration for the express promise. The difficulties and differences of opinion involved in the determination of what is a moral obligation are probably much greater than those involved in determining the existence of a legal obligation. This tends to explain the attitude of the majority of courts on the subject and justifies the generally stated rule.

Quicknotes

MORAL OBLIGATION A duty that is not enforceable at law, but is consistent with ethical notions of justice.

PREEXISTING DUTY A common law doctrine that renders unenforceable a promise to perform a duty, which the promisor is already legally obligated to perform, for lack of consideration.

Webb v. McGowin

Lumber employee (P) v. Estate of passerby (D)

Ala. Ct. App., 27 Ala. App. 82, 168 So. 196 (1935), *cert. denied*, 232 Ala. 374, 168 So. 199 (1936).

NATURE OF CASE: Action on appeal to collect on a promise.

FACT SUMMARY: Webb (P) saved the now deceased J. McGowin from grave bodily injury or death by placing himself in grave danger and subsequently suffering grave bodily harm. J. McGowin, in return, promised Webb (P) compensation. McGowin's executors (D) then refused to pay the promised compensation.

RULE OF LAW
A moral obligation is a sufficient consideration to support a subsequent promise to pay where the promisor has received a material benefit.

FACTS: Webb (P), while in the scope of his duties for the W. T. Smith Lumber Co., was clearing the floor, which required him to drop a 75-lb. pine block from the upper floor of the mill to the ground. Just as Webb (P) was releasing the block, he noticed J. McGowin below and directly under where the block would have fallen. In order to divert the fall of the block, Webb (P) fell with it, breaking an arm and leg and ripping his heel off. The fall left Webb (P) a cripple and incapable of either mental or physical labor. In return for Webb's (P) act, J. McGowin promised to pay Webb (P) $15 every two weeks for the rest of Webb's (P) life. J. McGowin paid the promised payments until his death eight years later. Shortly after J. McGowin's death, the payments were stopped and Webb (P) brought an action against N. McGowin (D) and J. F. McGowin (D) as executors of J. McGowin's estate for payments due him. The executors (D) of the estate were successful in obtaining a nonsuit against Webb (P) in the lower court. Webb (P) appealed.

ISSUE: Is a moral obligation a sufficient consideration to support a subsequent promise to pay where the promisor has received a material benefit?

HOLDING AND DECISION: (Bricken, J.) Yes. A moral obligation is a sufficient consideration to support a subsequent promise to pay where the promisor has received a material benefit. It is well settled that a moral obligation is a sufficient consideration to support a subsequent promise to pay where the promisor has received a material benefit, although there was no original duty or liability resting on the promisor. Reversed and remanded.

CONCURRENCE: (Samford, J.) Remand is appropriate to serve the ends of justice, but the majority's certainty that the plaintiff may recover is in doubt, given these facts.

ANALYSIS

In most cases where the moral obligation is asserted, the court feels that the promise ought not to be enforced; instead of going into the uncertain field of morality the court chooses to rely upon the rule that moral obligation is not a sufficient consideration. On the other hand, in cases where the promise is one which would have been kept by most citizens and the court feels that enforcement is just, a few courts will enforce the promise using the *Webb v. McGowin* rule. In general the *Webb v. McGowin* rule is the minority rule and the *Mills v. Wyman* rule, 3 Pick. 207 (Mass. 1825), is the majority rule.

Quicknotes

MORAL OBLIGATION A duty that is not enforceable at law, but is consistent with ethical notions of justice.

PROMISOR Party who promises to render an obligation to another in the future.

Harris v. Watson

Seaman (P) v. Master and Commander (D)

K.B., Peake 72, 170 Eng. Rep. 94 (1791).

NATURE OF CASE: Suit to recover extra wages promised by the Master and Commander of a ship.

FACT SUMMARY: Watson (D) promised extra wages to Harris (P) for labor performed while the ship was in danger. Harris (P) sued to recover these wages.

> **🏛 RULE OF LAW**
> Performing a legal duty that is already owed under a contract does not constitute consideration.

FACTS: The ship "Alexander" encountered difficulty at sea. Watson (D), the Master and Commander of the ship, agreed to pay five guineas above and beyond Harris's (P) common wages for Harris (P), a seaman, to navigate the ship out of danger. Harris (P) sued to recover these additional wages.

ISSUE: Does performing a legal duty that is already owed under a contract constitute consideration?

HOLDING AND DECISION: (Lord Kenyon, J.) No. Performing a legal duty that is already owed under a contract does not constitute consideration. There is no consideration for Harris's (P) request for additional wages, because he was already obligated to perform the work he did so perform. As a matter of policy, sailors should not get additional pay for work in times of danger, lest they threaten to sink the ship unless the captain pays them any extravagant demand they make. Thus, Harris's (P) action is nonsuited.

▶ ANALYSIS

Harris v. Watson states the basic principle behind the pre-existing duty rule.

■==■

Stilk v. Myrick

Ship's crew (P) v. Captain (D)

C.P., 6 Esp. 129, 170 Eng. Rep. 1168 (1809).

NATURE OF CASE: Action to enforce an oral modification of a contract.

FACT SUMMARY: Due to the desertion of other sailors, Captain Myrick (D) offered Stilk (P) and the other crewmen additional wages to complete a sea voyage shorthanded.

🏛 RULE OF LAW
Modifications of employment contracts which are occasioned by emergency or duress are unenforceable.

FACTS: Two crew members of a ship deserted. The Captain, Myrick (D), was unable to hire any replacements. He therefore agreed to divide the pay of the two deserters among Stilk (P) and the rest of the crew. Myrick (D) later refused to pay the additional wages, and Stilk (P) sued.

ISSUE: Are modifications of employment contracts which are occasioned by emergency or duress enforceable?

HOLDING AND DECISION: (Lord Ellenborough, J.) No. Modifications of employment contracts which are occasioned by emergency or duress are unenforceable. Although the result reached in *Harris v. Watson* K.B., Peake 72, 170 Eng. Rep. 94 (1791), is correct in these circumstances, public policy is not the principle on which the decision is to be supported. Where crew members have signed on for a voyage and are obligated to complete it, there is no consideration for an oral agreement to pay additional wages for performing, under emergency conditions, the duties already required of them. This case might be different if the crewmen could have left the ship at any port, or members of the crew had been discharged. But neither of these situations was presented here. The loss of two crew members, through no fault of the captain, produced an emergency situation. There is no reason under these circumstances to award the crew additional compensation for merely performing the duties they already owed Myrick (D). Judgment for Myrick (D).

▶ ANALYSIS

One who has a legal duty to perform an obligation cannot recover additional funds for performing on a day on which his employment contract does not require him to work. For example, a public health inspector cannot require a restaurant owner to pay him for an inspection made outside his normal working orders. However, the application of the present case to less artificial situations than a ship might cause greater problems. For example, suppose one's employer asked him to work an extra day for an additional $50. This would probably be enforceable unless the employee, like the seamen, already owed his employer the duty to work as many hours as were necessary to complete a given task.

■══■

Quicknotes

CONSIDERATION Value given by one party in exchange for performance, or a promise to perform, by another party.

PRE-EXISTING DUTY A common law doctrine that renders unenforceable a promise to perform a duty, which the promisor is already legally obligated to perform, for lack of consideration.

■══■

Lingenfelder v. Wainwright Brewery Co.

Architect (P) v. Brewery (D)

Mo. Sup. Ct., 103 Mo. 578, 15 S.W. 844 (1891).

NATURE OF CASE: Appeal of order denying damages for breach of contract.

FACT SUMMARY: Wainwright Brewery Co. (D) reneged on a promise to pay certain monies to Jungenfeld for the latter to perform a contract under which he was already obligated to perform, the promise being made after Jungenfeld threatened non-performance.

▥ RULE OF LAW
A promise made to induce compliance with a valid contract is not enforceable.

FACTS: Jungenfeld, an architect, contracted with Wainwright Brewery Co. (Wainwright) (D) to design a brewery. Subsequent to the agreement, but prior to performance, Jungenfeld threatened to quit. Wainwright (D) offered him extra compensation to honor the contract. Jungenfeld then provided the agreed-upon services. Jungenfeld subsequently died, and Lingenfelder (P), the executor of his estate, sued on the promise. The trial court held for Lingenfelder (P), and the state's highest court granted review.

ISSUE: Is a promise made to induce compliance with a valid contract enforceable?

HOLDING AND DECISION: (Gantt, J.) No. A promise made to induce compliance with a valid contract is not enforceable. A promise, to be enforceable, must involve consideration flowing from the promise to the promisor. When a promisee only agrees to do that which he is already obligated to do, he has in fact given nothing to the promisor. Here, Jungenfeld was already contractually obligated to perform the services induced by the offer of extra compensation, so Jungenfeld did not in fact supply consideration for the promise of extra compensation. The promise by Wainwright (D) was therefore unenforceable. If, however, there had been additional consideration flowing from Jungenfeld to Wainwright (D) for the additional compensation, nothing would have prevented the parties from modifying their original agreement or entering into a new agreement that was supported by the additional consideration. Reversed.

▎ ANALYSIS

The rule here is a variation of what can be termed the "pre-existing duty rule." As one can gather from the rule's title, it deals with the enforceability of a contract involving one already under a duty to do what is called for in the contract.

The rule applies both in situations involving contractual obligations and those involving statutory obligations.

■■■■

Quicknotes

CONSIDERATION Value given by one party in exchange for performance, or a promise to perform, by another party.

PRE-EXISTING DUTY A common law doctrine that renders unenforceable a promise to perform a duty, which the promisor is already legally obligated to perform.

■■■■

Clark v. Elza

Automobile driver (D) v. Injured party (P)

Md. Ct. App., 286 Md. 208, 406 A.2d 922 (1979).

NATURE OF CASE: Appeal of denial of motion to enforce a settlement agreement.

FACT SUMMARY: A trial court refused to enforce an executory settlement agreement made between the parties, denying Clark's (D) motion to stay and permitting the trial to proceed notwithstanding the settlement agreement.

🏛 RULE OF LAW
An executory oral agreement to settle a lawsuit that is in the nature of an executory accord may be raised as a defense to the prosecution of that suit.

FACTS: Elza (P) filed a personal injury suit against Clark (D) and Woodward (D). Prior to trial, the parties agreed to settle. It was orally stipulated that Elza (P) would sign a release and order of satisfaction in exchange for $9,500. The draft was tendered, but Elza (P) reneged on the settlement, returning the draft unexecuted. Clark (D) and Woodward (D) moved the court for an order to enforce the settlement. The trial court denied this motion, finding that the parties had entered an executory accord rather than a substitute contract, and permitting the trial to proceed notwithstanding the settlement agreement. The state's intermediate appellate court denied Clark (D) and Woodward's (D) appeal as premature. An interlocutory appeal was taken, and the state's highest court granted review.

ISSUE: May an executory oral agreement to settle a lawsuit that is in the nature of an executory accord be raised as a defense to the prosecution of that suit?

HOLDING AND DECISION: (Eldridge, J.) Yes. An executory oral agreement to settle a lawsuit that is in the nature of an executory accord may be raised as a defense to the prosecution of that suit. When a party compromises a claim in exchange for some form of consideration, he enters into what is known as an executory accord—unless there is evidence that the parties intended to enter into a substitute contract, which was lacking here. An executory accord does not in itself extinguish the compromised claim; actual execution of the accord accomplishes this. It was on this basis that the court below denied the motion to enforce the agreement and stay the proceedings; the accord had never been executed. However, as with any other executory contract, an executory accord is an enforceable agreement. Consequently, because in this instance Elza (P) was in effect breaching a contract when he reneged on the settlement, the court

should have stayed the suit while Clark (D) and Woodward (D) sought enforcement. Reversed and remanded.

▶ ANALYSIS

A reneged settlement is a possibility in any lawsuit. Jurisdictions vary greatly as to how to deal with such a situation. Some permit a judge in the underlying suit to enforce the settlement. Others require a separate action for specific performance, which makes enforcing a settlement a cumbersome process indeed.

■═■

Quicknotes

ACCORD An agreement between two parties, one of which has a valid claim against the other, to settle the controversy.

INTERLOCUTORY APPEAL The appeal of an issue that does not resolve the disposition of the case, but is essential to a determination of the parties' legal rights.

■═■

Allegheny College v. National Chautauqua County Bank

College endowment (P) v. Executor of estate (D)

N.Y. Ct. App., 246 N.Y. 369, 159 N.E. 173 (1927).

NATURE OF CASE: Appeal from affirmance of a dismissal of a complaint for breach of contract.

FACT SUMMARY: National Chautauqua County Bank (National) (D), Johnston's executor, refused to pay the balance of a charitable subscription which Johnston made to Allegheny College's (Allegheny's) (P) endowment fund but later repudiated after paying a portion of it to Allegheny (P).

🏛 RULE OF LAW
The acceptance of a charitable subscription by the trustees of the charity implies a promise on their part to execute the work contemplated and to carry out the purposes for which the subscription was made, thus supplying the requisite consideration to support a contract between the donor and the charity.

FACTS: In response to a campaign by Allegheny College (Allegheny) (P) to increase its endowment fund, Johnston pledged $5,000 to become due 30 days after her death and to be paid by her executor. The money was to be added to the endowment fund or used to educate students preparing for the ministry, and, if the latter, the fund was to be called the "Mary Yates Johnston Memorial Fund." Before her death, Johnston paid Allegheny (P) $1,000 of the pledge which Allegheny (P) set aside as a scholarship fund for students preparing for the ministry. Later, Johnston notified Allegheny (P) that she had repudiated the pledge. Thirty days after Johnston's death, when National Chautauqua County Bank (National) (D), Johnston's executor, failed to pay the balance, Allegheny (P) brought this action for breach. National (D) argued that no consideration was given for the promise. The trial court ruled for National (D), dismissing the action, and the state's intermediate appellate court affirmed. The state's highest court granted review.

ISSUE: Does the acceptance of a charitable subscription by the trustees of the charity imply a promise on their part to execute the work contemplated and to carry out the purposes for which the subscription was made, thus supplying the requisite consideration to support a contract between the donor and the charity?

HOLDING AND DECISION: (Cardozo, C.J.) Yes. The acceptance of a charitable subscription by the trustees of the charity implies a promise on their part to execute the work contemplated and to carry out this purposes for which the subscription was made, thus supplying the requisite consideration to support a contract between the donor and the charity. While charitable subscriptions are unenforceable if given without consideration, when subscriptions have been in question, courts have found consideration where general contract law would have said it was absent. Also, the doctrine of promissory estoppel has been adopted as the equivalent of consideration in connection with charitable subscriptions. In this case, traditional consideration could be found without resorting to promissory estoppel. Allegheny (P), by accepting part of the pledge, was required to apply the money as conditioned but it did not have to fulfill all conditions until all of the pledge was paid. The duty assumed by Allegheny (D) "to perpetuate the name of the founder of the memorial is sufficient in itself to give validity to the subscription within the rules that define consideration for a promise of that order." When Allegheny (P) as promisee subjected itself to such a duty at the implied request of Johnston as promisor, the result was creation of a bilateral contract. Reversed.

DISSENT: (Kellogg, J.) Johnston offered the sum as a gift. Even if one strains to find a contract, there was never an acceptance because not all acts were performed. Also, the donation was not to take effect until death, but by her death, the offer was withdrawn.

▶ ANALYSIS

Though the facts as recited in this case do not make it clear, apparently Johnston repudiated her pledge because Allegheny (P) did not immediately create a fund in her name upon payment of the $1,000. Allegheny (P) only established a nameless fund. To this, Judge Cardozo said that Johnston would have had grounds to repudiate the pledge had Allegheny (P) announced the fund as coming from an anonymous donor, but Allegheny (P) said nothing as to the source and was held not to be obligated to do so until the whole pledge was paid. As for this case, Corbin commented, "The implied promise of the trustees is said to be a sufficient consideration for the subscriber's promise. By such an implied promise, the trustees may sometimes be assuming duties that were not already incumbent upon them as trustees, but this does not necessarily show that the transaction was a bargaining transaction." Corbin, Contracts, 1 vol. ed., § 198.

■=■

Quicknotes

BILATERAL CONTRACT An agreement pursuant to which each party promises to undertake an obligation, or to forbear from acting, at some time in the future.

Continued on next page.

PROMISSORY ESTOPPEL A promise that is enforceable if the promisor should reasonably expect that it will induce action or forbearance on the part of the promisee, and does in fact cause such action or forbearance, and it is the only means of avoiding injustice.

REPUDIATION The actions or statements of a party to a contract that evidence his intent not to perform, or to continue performance, of his duties or obligations thereunder.

■══■

Universal Computer Systems v. Medical Services Association of Pennsylvania

Computer bidder (P) v. Medical services company (D)

628 F.2d 820 (3d Cir. 1980).

NATURE OF CASE: Appeal from grant of judgment n.o.v. denying damages for breach of contract.

FACT SUMMARY: Medical Services Association of Pennsylvania (Blue Shield) (D) contended it was not bound by its employee's promise to aid Universal Computer Systems (P) in its bid, and thus no breach of contract occurred.

🏛 RULE OF LAW
A promisee who reasonably relies upon the apparent authority of the employee of another, to his detriment, may recover for breach of contract based upon promissory estoppel.

FACTS: Medical Services Association of Pennsylvania (Blue Shield) (D) announced it was accepting bids for a limited time for a computer system. It held out its employee Gebert as a liaison. Universal Computer Systems (Universal) (P) contacted Gebert and arranged to have Gebert pick up its bid at the airport so that the bid could be timely submitted. On the appointed day, the bid was sent; yet Gebert refused to pick it up. The bid was not timely received and was rejected on that basis. Universal (P) sued, contending Gebert had apparent authority to bind Blue Shield (D) to pick up the bid. It reasonably relied upon his representations and did not make alternative arrangements. Thus, it argued Blue Shield (D) was estopped from rejecting the bid. The trial court granted Blue Shield's (D) motion for judgment n.o.v., and Universal (P) appealed.

ISSUE: May a promisee who reasonably relies upon the apparent authority of the employee of another, to his detriment, recover for breach of contract on the basis of promissory estoppel?

HOLDING AND DECISION: (Rosenn, J.) Yes. A promisee who reasonably relies upon the apparent authority of the employee of another, to his detriment, may recover for breach of contract on the basis of promissory estoppel. Gebert was designated as liaison to coordinate the bids. As such, he had the apparent authority to arrange for the receipt of the bids. His failure to fulfill his promise in this case resulted in Universal's (P) detriment. Accordingly, Blue Shield (D) is estopped from denying the authority existed. Furthermore, the jury could have reasonably determined that had Blue Shield (D) carried out its promise, Universal's (P) bid would have been accepted. If Universal's (P) bid had timely arrived, it would have been the lowest bid by a margin of approximately $450 per month. Blue Shield's (D) agent testified that he would have recommended that negotiations be conducted with the lowest bidder. Thus, the jury's determination was not based upon conjecture and speculation as Blue Shield (D) alleges, and the district court's judgment denying Blue Shield's (D) motions for judgment n.o.v. and for a new trial on the issue of damages is affirmed. The court's order entering judgment n.o.v. for Blue Shield (D) on the issue of liability is reversed and remanded with instructions to reinstate the jury's verdict.

▶ ANALYSIS

This case comports with § 90 of the Restatement (Second) of Contracts (1932). It is a traditional promissory estoppel analysis where the formal elements of contract, offer, acceptance, and consideration, are lacking, yet because of reasonable detrimental reliance justice commands enforcement.

Quicknotes

APPARENT AUTHORITY The authority granted to an agent to act on behalf of the principal in order to effectuate the principal's objective, which is not expressly granted but which is inferred from the principal's conduct.

DETRIMENTAL RELIANCE Action by one party, resulting in loss, that is based on the conduct or promises of another.

JUDGMENT N.O.V. A judgment entered by the trial judge reversing a jury verdict if the jury's determination has no basis in law or fact.

PROMISSORY ESTOPPEL A promise that is enforceable if the promisor should reasonably expect that it will induce action or forbearance on the part of the promisee, and does in fact cause such action or forbearance, and it is the only means of avoiding injustice.

James Baird Co. v. Gimbel Bros.

Contractor (P) v. Merchant (D)

64 F.2d 344 (2d Cir. 1933).

NATURE OF CASE: Appeal from judgment for defendant in action for breach of a contract for the sale of goods.

FACT SUMMARY: James Baird Co. (Baird) (P), relying on Gimbel Bros.'s (Gimbel's) (D) quoted prices for linoleum it offered to various contractors who were bidding on a public construction project, submitted a bid and later the same day received a telegraphed message from Gimbel (D) that its quoted prices were in error. Baird's (P) bid was accepted.

🏛 RULE OF LAW
The doctrine of promissory estoppel may not be applied in cases where there is an offer that is not intended to become a promise until a consideration is received.

FACTS: Gimbel Bros. (Gimbel) (D), having heard that bids were being taken for a public building, had an employee obtain the specifications for linoleum required for the building and submitted offers to various possible contractors, including James Baird Co. (Baird) (P), of two prices for linoleum, depending upon the quality used. The offer was made in ignorance of a mistake as to the actual amount of linoleum needed, causing Gimbel's (D) prices to be about half the actual cost. The offer concluded as follows: "If successful in being awarded this contract, it will be absolutely guaranteed . . . and . . . we are offering these prices for reasonable (sic) prompt acceptance after the general contract has been awarded." Baird (P) received this on the 28th, the same day on which Gimbel (D) discovered its mistake and telegraphed all contractors of the error, but the communication was received by Baird (P) just after Baird (P) submitted its lump-sum bid relying on Gimbel's (D) erroneous prices. Baird's (P) bid was accepted on the 30th. Baird (P), who received Gimbel's (D) written confirmation of the error on the 31st, sent an acceptance despite this, two days later. Gimbel (D) refused to recognize a contract, and Baird (P) sued for breach of contract. The district court ruled for Gimbel (D), and the court of appeals granted review

ISSUE: May the doctrine of promissory estoppel be applied in cases where there is an offer that is not intended to become a promise until a consideration is received?

HOLDING AND DECISION: (Hand, J.) No. The doctrine of promissory estoppel may not be applied in cases where there is an offer that is not intended to become a promise until a consideration is received. First, looking at the language of Gimbel's (D) offer, Gimbel's (D) use of the

phrase "if successful in being awarded this contract" clearly shows Gimbel's (D) intent of not being bound simply by a contractor relying or acting upon the quoted prices. This is reinforced by the phrase ". . . prompt acceptance after the general contract has been awarded." No award has been made at the time and reliance on the prices cannot be said to be an award of the contract. Had a relying contractor been awarded the contract and then repudiated it, Gimbel (D) would not have any right to sue for breach; nor had the relying contractor gone bankrupt could Gimbel (D) have gone against the estate. The contractors could have protected themselves by insisting on a contract guaranteeing the prices before relying upon them. The court will not strain to find a contract in aid of one who fails to protect himself. The theory of promissory estoppel is not available as it is more appropriate in donative or charitable cases where harsh results to the promisee arising from the promisor's breaking his relied-upon promise are to be protected against. However, an offer for an exchange, either being an act or another promise, is not meant to become a promise until a consideration is received. Here, the linoleum was to be delivered for the contractor's acceptance, not his bid. An option contract has not arisen as it is clear from the language of the offer that Gimbel (D) had no intention of assuming a one-sided obligation. Affirmed.

▌ ANALYSIS

Later cases have held the doctrine of promissory estoppel not to be as narrow. The majority of courts which have considered the issue hold that justifiable detrimental reliance on an offer renders it irrevocable. Naturally, the contractor must have something upon which to justifiably rely. The court in its decision notes that Restatement § 90 follows its view. However, Restatement (Second) § 90 has expanded the sections as to enlarge its scope according to the more modern viewpoint. It must be shown that the offerer foresaw that his promise would reasonably induce the forbearance or action. The first inkling of this doctrine probably arose in the well-known *Hamer v. Sidway*, 27 N.E. 256 (1891), where an uncle promised to pay his nephew $5,000 for refraining from the use of liquor, swearing, and other activities until his 21st birthday; it reached full maturity in J. Traynor's decision in *Drennan v. Star Paving Company*, 51 Cal. 2d 409, 333 P.2d 757 (1958). Generally, this case is a good example of the manner of the parties in order to determine their intent and hence, the existence of a contract. It appears that Gimbel (D) could have used the defense of unilateral mistake based upon a

Continued on next page.

clerical error as seen in *M.F. Kemper Construction Co. v. City of Los Angeles*, 235 P.2d (1951).

■══■

Quicknotes

IRREVOCABLE OFFER An offer that may not be retracted by the promisor without the assent of the offeree.

PROMISSORY ESTOPPEL A promise that is enforceable if the promisor should reasonably expect that it will induce action or forbearance on the part of the promisee, and does in fact cause such action or forbearance, and it is the only means of avoiding injustice.

REPUDIATION The actions or statements of a party to a contract that evidence his intent not to perform, or to continue performance, of his duties or obligations thereunder.

UNILATERAL MISTAKE When only one party to a contract is mistaken as to its terms, which does not render the agreement unenforceable.

■══■

Branco Enterprises, Inc. v. Delta Roofing, Inc.

General contractor (P) v. Subcontractor (D)

Mo. Ct. App., 886 S.W.2d 157 (1994).

NATURE OF CASE: Appeal from an order granting damages to plaintiff on the basis of detrimental reliance.

FACT SUMMARY: When Delta Roofing, Inc. (Delta) (D), a subcontractor, failed to do roofing work at the agreed-upon price, Branco Enterprises, Inc. (P), a general contractor, was forced to contract with another company to get the work done and then sued Delta (D) for the extra sum expended.

RULE OF LAW

A contract may be effected between a general contractor and a subcontractor based on the general contractor's reliance on the subcontractor's bid for a component of the project being bid upon.

FACTS: Branco Enterprises, Inc. (Branco) (P) bid on a renovation of a building and subcontracted part of the job. Delta Roofing, Inc. (Delta) (D) successfully submitted a bid to Branco (P) for installation and warranty of the roof. Branco (P) told Delta (D) that it was relying on Delta's (D) bid in placing its bid as general contractor for the project. A general contract was signed. When Delta (D) later refused to do the work because it was not certified by Owens-Corning to install the roof, Branco (P) contracted with a new company to do the job at a higher cost and sued Delta (D) for damages. The trial court determined that the parties had a contract on which Branco (P) had detrimentally relied and granted Branco's (P) request for damages. Delta (D) appealed, contending that there was no contract and there was insufficient evidence for the trial court to have found that Branco (P) was entitled to rely on Delta's (D) bid when computing the cost for installing the roof. The state's intermediate appellate court granted review.

ISSUE: May a contract be effected between a general contractor and a subcontractor based on the general contractor's reliance on the subcontractor's bid for a component of the project being bid upon?

HOLDING AND DECISION: (Parrish, J.) Yes. A contract may be effected between a general contractor and a subcontractor based on the general contractor's reliance on the subcontractor's bid for a component of the project being bid upon. Damages may be based on the doctrine of promissory estoppel. The necessary elements for promissory estoppel are a promise, foreseeable reliance, reliance, and injustice absent enforcement. The trial court's finding that an oral agreement, finalized when the general contract was signed, had been made was not erroneous. The fact that a written subcontract was not tendered to Delta (D) by Branco (P) until after the general contract was signed was of no significance since the written contract was just a confirmation of the earlier oral promises. The doctrine of promissory estoppel applied and an injustice would occur if Branco (P) did not obtain reimbursement from Delta (D) for the greater sum it had to expend to get the job done. Affirmed.

▶ ANALYSIS

Section 87(2) of the Restatement (Second) of Contracts concerns the irrevocability of certain subcontractors' bids. If the offeree reasonably relied on the offer to his detriment, the reliance doctrine enforces an otherwise unenforceable promise. Not all jurisdictions permit general contractors to use promissory estoppel to bind subcontractors to their bids, however.

■═■

Quicknotes

PROMISSORY ESTOPPEL A promise that is enforceable if the promisor should reasonably expect that it will induce action or forbearance on the part of the promisee, and does in fact cause such action or forbearance, and it is the only means of avoiding injustice.

■═■

Hoffman v. Red Owl Stores

Grocery store purchaser (P) v. Agent of grocery business (D)

Wis. Sup. Ct., 26 Wis. 2d 683, 133 N.W.2d 267 (1965).

NATURE OF CASE: Appeal from award of damages based on promissory estoppel.

FACT SUMMARY: Hoffman (P) was assured by an agent of the Red Owl Stores (Red Owl) (D) that if he took certain steps he would obtain a supermarket franchise, but, after taking these steps at great expense, Hoffman (P) did not receive the franchise.

🏛 RULE OF LAW
When a promisor makes a promise that he should reasonably expect to induce action on the part of the promisee and which does induce such action, he can be estopped from denying the enforceability of that promise.

FACTS: An agent of the Red Owl Stores (Red Owl) (D) promised Hoffman (P) that Red Owl (D) would establish him in a supermarket store for the sum of $18,000. In reliance upon this promise, and upon the recommendations of the agent, Hoffman (P) purchased a grocery store to gain experience. Thereafter, upon further recommendations of the agent, Hoffman (D) sold his grocery store fixtures and inventory to Red Owl (D), before the profitable summer months started, and paid $1,000 for an option on land for building a franchise outlet. After moving near this outlet, Hoffman (P) was told that he needed $24,100 for the promised franchise. After Hoffman (P) acquired this amount, most of it through a loan from his father-in-law, he was told that he needed an additional $2,000 for the deal to go through. Finally, after acquiring the additional $2,000, Hoffman (P) was told he would be established in his new store as soon as he sold a bakery store which he owned. After doing this, though, Red Owl (D) told Hoffman (P) that in order to enhance his credit rating he must procure from his father-in-law a statement that the funds acquired from him were an outright gift and not a loan. In response, Hoffman (P) sued for damages to recover income which he lost and expenses which he incurred in reliance upon the promises of Red Owl (D). After an award of damages for Hoffman (P), Red Owl (D) appealed. The state's highest court granted review.

ISSUE: When a promisor makes a promise that he should reasonably expect to induce action on the part of the promisee and which does induce such action, can he be estopped from denying the enforceability of that promise?

HOLDING AND DECISION: (Currie, C.J.) Yes. When a promisor makes a promise that he should reasonably expect to induce action on the part of the promisee and which does induce such action, he can be estopped from denying the enforceability of that promise. Under the doctrine of promissory estoppel, as stated in § 90 of Restatement (First) of Contracts, "a promise which the promisor should reasonably expect to induce action for forbearance of a definite and substantial character on the part of the promisee and which does induce such action or forbearance is binding if injustice can be avoided only by enforcement of the promise." Of course, such damages as are necessary to prevent injustice can be awarded under the doctrine of promissory estoppel instead of specific performance. Furthermore, an action based upon promissory estoppel is not equivalent to a breach of contract action, and therefore, the promise does not have to "embrace all essential details of a proposed transaction between promisor and promisee so as to be the equivalent of an offer that would result in a binding contract between the parties if the promisee were to accept the same." Here, it is not important that no final construction plans, etc. were ever completed. It is instead important that Hoffman (P) substantially relied to his detriment on Red Owl's (D) promise and that Red Owl (D) should have reasonably foreseen such reliance. Therefore, Hoffman (P) is entitled to those damages which are necessary to prevent injustice. He is entitled to losses resulting from selling his bakery, from purchasing the option on land for a franchise, from moving near the franchise outlet, and from selling his grocery store fixtures and inventory. Hoffman's (P) reasonable damages from selling his grocery store fixtures and inventory, though, do not include any future lost profits, since he only purchased the grocery store temporarily to gain experience (i.e., he is only entitled to any loss measured by the difference between the sales price and fair market value). Affirmed.

▶ ANALYSIS

This case illustrates the doctrine of promissory estoppel. At common law, such doctrine afforded protection to any party threatened with "substantial economic loss" after taking "reasonable steps in foreseeable reliance upon a gratuitous promise." The Restatement (Second), however, does not require that the promise be gratuitous or that the reliance be "substantial." It only requires reasonable, foreseeable reliance upon any promise. Note that an action under the doctrine of promissory estoppel is not equivalent to an action for breach of contract, and, therefore, no consideration is necessary to make the promise binding. Furthermore, the promise upon which a person reasonably relies will be enforced specifically or by

Continued on next page.

damages whenever the court decides that the interests of justice would be served by such enforcement.

■━━■

Quicknotes

PROMISSORY ESTOPPEL A promise that is enforceable if the promisor should reasonably expect that it will induce action or forbearance on the part of the promisee, and does in fact cause such action or forbearance, and it is the only means of avoiding injustice.

SPECIFIC PERFORMANCE An equitable remedy, whereby the court requires the parties to perform their obligations pursuant to a contract.

■━━■

Remedies

Quick Reference Rules of Law

Hawkins v. McGee

Patient (P) v. Surgeon (D)

N.H. Sup. Ct., 84 N.H. 114, 146 A. 641 (1929).

NATURE OF CASE: Action in assumpsit for breach of an alleged warranty.

FACT SUMMARY: McGee (D), a surgeon, performed an unsuccessful operation on Hawkins's (P) hand after having guaranteed to make the hand 100 percent perfect. Hawkins (P) was awarded damages for pain and suffering and for "what injury he has sustained over and above the injury he had before."

> ### 🏛 RULE OF LAW
> The measure of damages for breach of contract is that amount of damages that will put the plaintiff in as good a position as he would have been in had the defendant kept his contract.

FACTS: McGee (D), a surgeon, performed an operation on Hawkins's (P) hand. Before the operation, McGee (D) had repeatedly solicited an opportunity to perform the operation and had guaranteed to make the hand 100 percent perfect. The operation was not successful, and Hawkins (P) sought to recover on the basis of McGee's (D) warranty. The trial court instructed the jury that Hawkins (P) would be entitled to recover for his pain and suffering and for "what injury he has sustained over and above the injury he had before." The jury rendered a verdict for Hawkins (P). The state's highest court granted review.

ISSUE: Is the measure of damages for breach of contract that amount of damages that will put the plaintiff in as good a position as he would have been in had the defendant kept his contract?

HOLDING AND DECISION: (Branch, J.) Yes. The measure of damages for breach of contract is that amount of damages that will put the plaintiff in as good a position as he would have been in had the defendant kept his contract. McGee's (D) words, if taken at face value, indicate the giving of a warranty. Coupled with the evidence that McGee (D) repeatedly solicited the opportunity to perform the operation, there is a reasonable basis for a jury to conclude that McGee (D) spoke the words with the intention that they be taken at face value as an inducement for Hawkins's (P) submission to the operation. The jury instruction on damages was erroneous. The purpose of awarding damages is to put a plaintiff in as good a position as he would have been in had the defendant kept his contract. The measure of recovery is what the defendant should have given the plaintiff, not what the plaintiff has given the defendant or otherwise expended. Hence, the measure of Hawkins's (P) damages is the difference between the value of a perfect hand, as promised by McGee (D), and the value of his hand in its present condition. Hawkins's (P) pain is not relevant to this determination. Also, damages might be assessed for McGee's (D) failure to improve the hand, but it would be erroneous and misleading to submit to the jury as a separate element of damages any change for the worse in the condition of Hawkins's (P) hand resulting from the operation. New trial ordered.

▌ANALYSIS

The measure of damages is the actual loss sustained by reason of the breach, which is the loss of what the promisee would have made if the contract had been performed, less the proper deductions. The plaintiff may recover damages not only for the net gains which were prevented by the breach, but also for expenses incurred in reliance on the defendant's performance of his contract promise. In a proper case, prospective profits which were lost because of the breach are also recoverable.

■═■

Quicknotes

ACTION IN ASSUMPSIT Action to recover damages for breach of an oral or written promise to perform or pay pursuant to a contract.

EXPECTATION DAMAGES The measure of damages necessary to place the nonbreaching party in the same position as he would have enjoyed had the contract been fully performed.

■═■

Peevyhouse v. Garland Coal & Mining Co.

Lessor of farm (P) v. Lessee (D)

Okla. Sup. Ct., 382 P.2d 109 (1962).

NATURE OF CASE: Appeal from award of damages for breach of contract.

FACT SUMMARY: After Willie and Lucille Peevyhouse (P) leased their farm to Garland Coal & Mining Co. (Garland) (D) for coal strip-mining operations, Garland (D) violated the lease terms by failing to perform the work necessary to restore the farm.

🏛 RULE OF LAW
If the lessee's performance of remedial work at the end of the lease period is incidental to the main lease purpose, and the economic benefit which would result to the lessor by full performance of the work is grossly disproportionate to the cost of performance, the lessor's damages are limited to the diminution in value resulting to the premises because of the lessee's nonperformance.

FACTS: The Peevyhouses (P) leased their farm to Garland Coal & Mining Co. (Garland) (D) for coal strip-mining operations. At the end of the five-year lease period, Garland (D) was obligated to perform the work necessary to restore the farm to its original condition. After Garland (D) failed to perform the restoration provided for in the lease, the Peevyhouses (P) sued Garland (D) for damages for breach of contract. The jury found for Peevyhouses (P) in the amount of $5,000. The Peevyhouses (P) appealed, contending that the correct measure of damages was the cost of the restorative work, which was valued at around $29,000. Garland (D) cross-appealed.

ISSUE: If the lessee's performance of remedial work at the end of the lease period is incidental to the main lease purpose, and the lessee's economic benefit from full performance of the work is grossly disproportionate to the cost of performance, are the lessor's damages limited to the diminution in value to the premises because of the lessee's nonperformance?

HOLDING AND DECISION: (Jackson, J.) Yes. If the lessee's performance of remedial work at the end of the lease period is incidental to the main lease purpose, and the lessee's economic benefit from full performance of the work is grossly disproportionate to the cost of performance, lessor's damages are limited to the diminution in value to the premises because of the lessee's nonperformance. Here, the cost of restoring the farm to its original condition was estimated to be $29,000. Under the most liberal view of the evidence, the diminution in value to the premises because of the nonperformance of the remedial work was $300. Therefore, the $5,000 jury verdict was clearly excessive. Modified and affirmed.

DISSENT: (Irwin, J.) If the value of the performance of a contract is considered in determining the measure of damages for breach of contract, the value of the benefits received by the breaching party should also be considered. However, to consider either of these factors in a case such as this ignores the contract the parties entered into and writes a new contract. There is no reason Garland (D) should not be required to pay for the accomplishment of what it promised to do, since when it entered the contract, it could reasonably anticipate that the cost of performance might be disproportionate to the value or benefits received by the Peevyhouses (P) for the performance.

▶ ANALYSIS

The case might have a different outcome in today's present environment of public awareness of environmental concerns. In a more recent case, one court has predicted that it would no longer follow the *Peevyhouse* holding. See *Rock Island Improvement Co. v. Helmerick & Payne*, 698 F.2d 1075 (10th Cir. 1983).

■≡■

Quicknotes

BREACH OF CONTRACT Unlawful failure by a party to perform its obligations pursuant to contract.

■≡■

John Thurmond & Associates, Inc. v. Kennedy

Construction company (D) v. Homeowner (P)

Ga. Sup. Ct., 284. Ga. 469, 668 S.E.2d 666 (2008).

NATURE OF CASE: Appeal from reversal of directed verdict for defendant in action for defective construction.

FACT SUMMARY: Kennedy (P), whose house John Thurmond & Associates, Inc. (JTA) (D) repaired after it was severely damaged by fire, contended that he did not have to present evidence of the fair market value of his house as a prerequisite to prevailing on his defective construction claim against JTA (D).

🏛 RULE OF LAW
A plaintiff in a breach of contract and negligent construction case does not have to prove fair market value of the property as a prerequisite to any recovery.

FACTS: Kennedy (P) hired John Thurmond & Associates, Inc. (JTA) (D) to repair his house after it was severely damaged by fire, at a contract price of $311,156. Kennedy (P) subsequently discovered problems with the construction and sued JTA (D) for breach of contract, breach of warranty, negligent construction, and negligence. At trial, Kennedy (P) presented evidence of the cost of repairing the allegedly faulty construction estimated at $751,632. After the close of evidence, the trial court granted JTA's (D) motion for a directed verdict on the ground that Kennedy (P) had not presented evidence of the fair market value of his home after the allegedly faulty repairs. The state's intermediate appellate court reversed, concluding that evidence of the fair market value of the home after the repairs were made was not required. The state's highest court granted review.

ISSUE: Does a plaintiff in a breach of contract and negligent construction case have to prove fair market value of the property as a prerequisite to any recovery?

HOLDING AND DECISION: (Thompson, J.) No. A plaintiff in a breach of contract and negligent construction case does not have to prove fair market value of the property as a prerequisite to any recovery. Generally, damages for defective construction are measured by the cost of repairing or restoring the damage, unless the cost of repair is disproportionate to the property's probable loss of value. Where demanded by the facts of a case, courts also have determined damages in such cases by measuring the diminution in value of the property after the injury occurred. Often, both measures of damages are in evidence and are complementary to the other. Thus, cost of repair and diminution in value are alternative, although oftentimes interchangeable, measures of damages in defective construction cases, and an injured party may choose to present his case using either or both methods of measuring

damages. Where the plaintiff chooses cost of repair as the measure of damages, evidence of the fair market value of the improved property is not a necessary element of his claim for damages. Contrary to JTA's (D) contention, recovery for cost of repair damages is not always limited by the fair market value of the property. Instead, the amount of damages may vary with the facts of each case and the method of calculating damages must be flexible to best place the injured party, as nearly as possible, in the same position they would have been in had the injury not occurred. Here, because Kennedy (P) adequately presented proof of the cost of repair, the trial court erred in directing a verdict against him. Affirmed.

DISSENT: (Carley, J.) Because Kennedy (P) is seeking recovery for JTA's (D) failing to improve the property in accordance with their contract, not for damaging existing improvements to the realty, Kennedy (P) must show the fair market value of the property as it should have been improved, since that is what Kennedy (P) claims he lost as the result of JTA's (D) breach or negligence. Kennedy (P) must show the fair market value of property had it been improved properly according to the contract and the fair market value of the property as it was actually improved by JTA (D). The difference between those two fair market values is the measure of recoverable damages. The cost of repairs is not admissible as an alternative measure of damages, but as evidence showing the recoverable difference in the market values. Where the defective construction cannot be repaired, it is pointless to use cost of repair as the measure of the loss in property value between what it is and as it should have been. Nevertheless, evidence of those values must be demonstrated to quantify the damages. In either situation, evidence of fair market value must be presented. Here, Kennedy's (P) cost to repair far exceeds the contract price, and if he recovers his cost of repair, he will receive a windfall. Thus, he should be limited to recovering damages that represent the diminution in value of the house that resulted from JTA's (D) breach/ negligence. Because he failed to prove that diminution in value, the trial court correctly rendered judgment for JTA (D).

▶ ANALYSIS

Under the Restatement (Second) of Contracts, § 348, if a breach results in defective or unfinished construction and the loss in value to the injured party is not proved with sufficient certainty, he may recover damages based on

Continued on next page.

either (a) the diminution in the market price of the property caused by the breach, or (b) the reasonable cost of completing performance or of remedying the defects if that cost is not clearly disproportionate to the probable loss in value to him. Here, the dissent is arguing that the cost of repair is not "reasonable" and is likely disproportionate to the loss in value to the property, so that Kennedy (P) should be limited to damages based on the diminution in the fair market value of his house caused by JTA's (D) construction defects.

■━■

Quicknotes

COST OF REPAIR RULE A measure of computing damages pursuant to a breach of contract, representing the cost to the non-breaching party to place himself in the same position he would have been in had the contract not been breached.

DIMINUTION IN VALUE A measure of computing damages pursuant to a breach of contract representing the decrease in the value of the subject matter of the contract as a result of the breach.

DIRECTED VERDICT A verdict ordered by the court in a jury trial.

FAIR MARKET VALUE The price of particular property or goods that a buyer would offer and a seller would accept in the open market following full disclosure.

■━■

Sullivan v. O'Connor

Entertainer (P) v. Plastic surgeon (D)

Mass. Sup. Jud. Ct., 363 Mass. 579, 296 N.E.2d 183 (1973).

NATURE OF CASE: Appeal from jury verdict on damages in action for medical malpractice and breach of contract.

FACT SUMMARY: O'Connor (D), a doctor, promised to improve Sullivan's (P) appearance by cosmetic surgery. In fact, O'Connor's (D) efforts left Sullivan (P) with more of a disfigurement than previously.

🏛 RULE OF LAW
A physician who breaches his contractual obligation to effect a particular result is liable to his patient for the cost of any measures or treatment necessitated by the physician's breach and for any pain and suffering resulting therefrom.

FACTS: Dr. O'Connor (D) expressly promised to enhance and improve the appearance of Sullivan (P), an entertainer, by performing cosmetic surgery on her nose. However, after two operations, Sullivan's (P) nose looked worse than it had previously. As a result of the surgery, the nose was disfigured, apparently permanently. Sullivan (P) sued to recover damages from O'Connor (D), alleging both breach of contract and medical malpractice, the latter theory of recovery being based on negligence. A jury trial resulted in a verdict for Sullivan (P) on the contract count and for O'Connor (D) on the count alleging malpractice. On appeal, O'Connor (D) took exception to the trial judge's instruction that Sullivan (P) could recover all out-of-pocket expenses occasioned by O'Connor's (D) breach of his promise plus any pain and suffering caused by her condition or by a third operation, which Sullivan (P) endured in a vain attempt to restore her nose to its previous shape.

ISSUE: Is a physician who breaches his contractual obligation to effect a particular result liable to his patient for the cost of any measures or treatment necessitated by the physician's breach and for any pain and suffering resulting therefrom?

HOLDING AND DECISION: (Kaplan, J.) Yes. A physician who breaches his contractual obligation to effect a particular result is liable to his patient for the cost of any measures or treatment necessitated by the physician's breach and for any pain and suffering resulting therefrom. Because contracts involving promises by physicians are necessarily predicated on matters which can be no more certain than medical science itself, it does not seem fair to award a patient the difference in value between the actual condition of his bodily part after treatment and the condition which the physician promised to bring about (i.e., expectancy value). But the patient should be entitled to recover more than just the money he expended on the doctor's treatment (i.e., more than just restitution value). It is a reasonable compromise which permits the patient to recover all his out-of-pocket expenses, including additional costs incurred in trying to remedy the doctor's failure to perform his promise, plus an amount which compensates him for any pain and suffering, physical or mental, occasioned by the physician's breach. Plaintiff's exceptions waived, and defendant's exceptions overruled.

▶ ANALYSIS

Ordinarily, a nonbreaching party is entitled to recover such compensatory damages as will place him in the same situation as he would have enjoyed had the contract never been breached. Under some circumstances, the nonbreaching party will be awarded restitution only of whatever he has given in performance of the contract, i.e., he will be restored to the position he occupied prior to execution.

■═■

Quicknotes

COMPENSATORY DAMAGES Measure of damages necessary to compensate victim for actual injuries suffered.

NEGLIGENCE Conduct falling below the standard of care that a reasonable person would demonstrate under similar conditions.

■═■

Anglia Television Ltd. v. Reed

Television company (P) v. Performer (D)

Ct. App., Civ. Div., 3 All Eng. Rep. 690 (1971).

NATURE OF CASE: Appeal from award of damages for breach of contract.

FACT SUMMARY: Reed (D), an actor, contended that Anglia Television Ltd. (Anglia) (P) could not ask for damages for wasted expenditures incurred before the contract was concluded with Reed (D) because these expenditures were for Anglia's (P) benefit at a time when it was uncertain whether there would be any contract or not.

🏛 RULE OF LAW
In a breach of contract action, wasted expenditure can be recovered when it is wasted by reason of the defendant's breach of contract.

FACTS: Anglia Television Ltd. (Anglia) (P) entered into a contract with Reed (D) whereby Reed (D) would perform in a play for television. Because of a booking error, Reed (D) repudiated the contract. Anglia (P) tried to find a substitute for Reed (D), could not, and then accepted Reed's (D) repudiation. Anglia (P) abandoned the proposed project and sued Reed (D) for damages. Anglia (P) did not claim their loss of profits as damages, but instead claimed wasted expenditures. They had incurred director's, designer's and manager's fees and claimed that money had been wasted because Reed (D) did not perform his contract. Reed (D) did not dispute his liability, but contended that Anglia (P) could not ask for damages for wasted expenditures incurred before the contract was concluded with Reed (D) because the expenditures were for Anglia's (P) benefit at a time when it was uncertain whether there would be any contract or not. The trial court allowed Anglia (P) to recover for expenditures incurred both before and after the contract was concluded, if such expenditure was reasonably in contemplation of the parties as likely to be wasted if the contract was broken. Reed (D) appealed.

ISSUE: In a breach of contract action, can wasted expenditure be recovered when it is wasted by reason of the defendant's breach of contract?

HOLDING AND DECISION: (Lord Denning, J.) Yes. In a breach of contract action, wasted expenditure can be recovered when it is wasted by reason of the defendant's breach of contract. A plaintiff in a breach of contract case has an election as far as damages are concerned. He can claim for his loss of profits; or for his wasted expenditure. He must elect between them. He cannot claim both. He can also claim expenditures which happened both before and after the contract were concluded, provided that the expenditures were such as would reasonably be in the contemplation of the parties as likely to be wasted if the contract was broken. Applying that principle here, it is plain that, when Mr. Reed (D) entered into this contract, he must have known perfectly well that a large amount of expenditures had already been incurred and that if he broke the contract, all those expenditures would be wasted. He must pay damages for all the expenditure so wasted. Affirmed.

▶ ANALYSIS

In a contract situation, the promisee may have changed his position in reliance on the contract, either incurring expenses in preparing to perform or foregoing opportunities to make other contracts. In such a case, the court may recognize a claim based on reliance rather than on the promisee's expectation. It does this by attempting to put him back in the same position as he would have been in had the contract not been made.

■■■

Quicknotes

DETRIMENTAL RELIANCE Action by one party, resulting in loss, that is based on the conduct or promises of another.

ELECTION OF DAMAGES The choosing from alternative measures of damages that are inconsistent; after such choice the elector is bound to his selection.

REPUDIATION The actions or statements of a party to a contract that evidence his intent not to perform, or to continue performance, of his duties or obligations thereunder.

■■■

Freund v. Washington Square Press

Author (P) v. Publisher (D)

N.Y. Ct. App., 34 N.Y.2d 379, 314 N.E.2d 419 (1974).

NATURE OF CASE: Appeal from affirmance of damages award in action for damages for breach of contract.

FACT SUMMARY: When Washington Square Press (D) breached its contract by failing to publish Freund's (P) book, the trial court awarded Freund (P) $10,000 to cover the cost of publishing it himself.

🏛 RULE OF LAW
For a plaintiff to recover damages for breach of contract, the amount of damages claimed must be measurable with a reasonable degree of certainty.

FACTS: Freund (P), an author and a professor, signed an agreement whereby Washington Square Press (Washington Square) (D) was to pay him certain royalties on the sale of his book, which it was obligated to publish in hardbound and paperback editions subject to its right to terminate the agreement within 60 days after submission of the manuscript. Washington Square (D) did not exercise its termination right but nonetheless failed to publish the book. The court that denied Freund's (P) prayer for specific performance set the matter for trial on the issue of money damages. Although Freund (P) argued that his academic promotion had been delayed, that he had lost anticipated royalties, and that it would cost him $10,000 to publish the book himself in hardback, the court allowed recovery only of the $10,000 cost of publishing the book. It denied any recovery for the cost of publishing it in paperback because the proof was conjectural. The state's intermediate appellate court affirmed, and the state's highest court granted review.

ISSUE: For a plaintiff to recover damages for breach of contract, must the amount of damages claimed be measurable with a reasonable degree of certainty?

HOLDING AND DECISION: (Rabin, J.) Yes. For a plaintiff to recover damages for breach of contract, the amount of damages claimed must be measurable with a reasonable degree of certainty. In allowing recovery for breach of contract, the law attempts to secure to the injured party the benefit of his bargain, subject to the limitations that the injury was foreseeable and that the amount of damages claimed is measurable with a reasonable degree of certainty and adequately proven. It is fundamental that the injured party should not recover more from the breach than he would have gained had the contract been fully performed. Here, an award of the cost of publication would enrich Freund (P) at Washington Square's (D) expense. What Freund (P) bargained for and lost were the royalties he would have been paid, but the

amount of royalties he could have expected to receive was not ascertainable with adequate certainty. Thus, only nominal damages are recoverable in this case, and the decision must be so modified. Affirmed as modified.

▶ ANALYSIS

Restatement (Second) of Contracts § 352, Comment provides: "Courts have traditionally required greater certainty in the proof of damages for breach of contract than in the proof of damages for a tort. . . . The main impact of the requirement of certainty comes in connection with recovery for [lost] profits."

▬▬■

Quicknotes

BENEFIT OF THE BARGAIN Calculation of assessing damages in actions for breach of contract measured as the difference between the actual value and the purported value of the goods being bought.

NOMINAL DAMAGES A small sum awarded to a plaintiff in order to recognize that he sustained an injury that is either slight or incapable of being established.

▬▬■

Humetrix, Inc. v. Gemplus S.C.A.

Health care consulting company (P) v. Microprocessor manufacturer (D)

268 F.3d 910 (9th Cir. 2001).

NATURE OF CASE: Appeal from jury verdict for the plaintiff in a cause of action alleging breach of contract, breach of fiduciary duty and intentional interference with contractual relations.

FACT SUMMARY: Humetrix, Inc. (P) brought suit against Gemplus S.C.A. (Gemplus) (D), alleging breach of contract, breach of fiduciary duty and intentional interference with contractual relations. The jury awarded Humetrix (P) $15 million on its breach of contract and breach of fiduciary duty claims and declared that Humetrix (P) was entitled to use a particular trademark which was in dispute. Gemplus (D) appealed on the contract counts and Inovaction (D) appealed as to the trademark decision.

🏛 **RULE OF LAW**
Lost profits are not speculative if there is reliable proof that such would have been garnered had the contract been performed.

FACTS: Humetrix, Inc. (P) contracted with Gemplus S.C.A. (Gemplus) (D) to provide portable patient data storage solutions to the U.S. health care market, via a health care data "Smart Card." Humetrix (P) then invested significant resources in market research, client development, and product development, applied to register the trademark "Vaccicard" for the Smart Card and had closed contracts with two California counties. Gemplus (D) failed to honor their oral agreements with Humetrix (P) when it was learned that a Gemplus (D) senior manager, Guy Guistini, was a 45 percent shareholder in Inovaction, a company that held the French trademarks for Vaccicard (the health care data Smart Card) and after Gemplus (D) acquired a new U.S. subsidiary that could perform many of the functions that Humetrix (P) was to have performed as Gemplus's (D) American partner. After ignoring Humetrix's (P) entreaties to enforce the partnership for several months, Gemplus (D) explained that it viewed Humetrix (P) as a reseller, rather than a partner (as was the original intent of their agreement). Humetrix (P) sued Gemplus (D) for breach of contract and breach of its fiduciary duty as Humetrix's (P) partner. Humetrix (P) also sued Guistini (D) for intentional interference with contract relations and Inovaction (D), seeking a declaration that Humetrix (P) was entitled to use the "Vaccicard" trademark in the United States. The jury returned awards for Humetrix (P). Gemplus (D) appealed, alleging error with the admission of evidence of lost profits, and that the $15 million dollar award by the jury was the result of passion, confusion and wild speculation. Inovaction (D) appealed as to the trademark decision. The court of appeals granted review.

ISSUE: Are lost profits speculative if there is reliable proof that such would have been garnered had the contract been performed?

DECISION AND HOLDING: (Tallman, J.) No. Lost profits are not speculative if there is reliable proof that such would have been garnered had the contract been performed. Humetrix (P) provided expert testimony of lost profits. This testimony was based upon contracts Humetrix (P) had closed, pilot projects for which Humetrix (P) had received commitments and contracts in negotiation at the time of breach. Gemplus (D) countered this expert testimony with its own expert testimony. In a battle of expert witnesses, the jury is equipped to make a determination as to whose experts were more credible on a given issue. Further, the evidence of lost profits was not made speculative by the nature of this business as a new venture. Humetrix (P) had been in the business of health care consulting for ten years before it entered into its agreement with Gemplus (D). In fact, it was the experience, the contacts and dynamism of the company that led Gemplus (D) to seek a partnership with Humetrix (P). Furthermore, Humetrix (P) offered reliable evidence of anticipated profits. For these and other reasons, the verdict was not a result of passion, confusion or wild speculation. Affirmed.

▶ **ANALYSIS**

The *Humetrix* case demonstrates that one can recover future damages as long as reliable evidence that such losses would occur can be presented.

■══■

Quicknotes

BREACH OF CONTRACT Unlawful failure by a party to perform its obligations pursuant to contract.

BREACH OF FIDUCIARY DUTY The failure of a fiduciary to observe the standard of care exercised by professionals of similar education and experience.

INTENTIONAL INTERFERENCE WITH CONTRACTUAL RELATIONS An intentional tort whereby a defendant intentionally elicits the breach of a valid contract resulting in damages.

TRADEMARK Any word, name, symbol, device or combination thereof that is either currently utilized, or which a person has a bona fide intent to utilize, in commerce in order to distinguish his goods from those of another.

■══■

Hadley v. Baxendale

Mill operator (P) v. Shipping company (D)

Ct. of Exchequer, 9 Exch. 341, 156 Eng. Rep. 145 (1854).

NATURE OF CASE: Action for damages for breach of a carrier contract.

FACT SUMMARY: Hadley (P), a mill operator in Gloucester, arranged to have Baxendale's (D) company, a carrier, ship his broken mill shaft to the engineer in Greenwich for a copy to be made. Hadley (P) suffered a £300 loss when Baxendale (D) unreasonably delayed shipping the mill shaft, causing the mill to be shut down longer than anticipated.

🏛 RULE OF LAW
The injured party to a contract may recover those damages as may reasonably be considered arising naturally from the breach itself and, the injured party may recover those damages as may reasonably be supposed to have been in contemplation of the parties, at the time they made the contract, as the probable result of a breach of it.

FACTS: Hadley (P), a mill operator in Gloucester, arranged to have Baxendale's (D) shipping company return his broken mill shaft to the engineer in Greenwich, who was to make a duplicate. Hadley (P) delivered the broken shaft to Baxendale (D), who, in consideration for his fee, promised to deliver the shaft to Greenwich in a reasonable time. Baxendale (D) did not know that the mill was shut down while awaiting the new shaft. Baxendale (D) was negligent in delivering the shaft within a reasonable time. Reopening of the mill was delayed five days, costing Hadley (P) lost profits and paid-out wages of £300. Hadley (P) had paid Baxendale (D) £24 to ship the mill shaft. Baxendale (D) paid into court £25 in satisfaction of Hadley's (P) claim. The jury awarded an additional £25, for a total £50 award.

ISSUE: May the injured party to a contract recover those damages as may reasonably be considered arising naturally from the breach itself, and may the injured party recover those damages as may reasonably be supposed to have been in contemplation of the parties, at the time they made the contract, as the probable result of a breach of it?

HOLDING AND DECISION: (Alderson, B.) Yes. The injured party to a contract may recover those damages as may reasonably be considered arising naturally from the breach itself and, the injured party may recover those damages as may reasonably be supposed to have been in contemplation of the parties, at the time they made the contract, as the probable result of a breach of it. The jury requires a rule for its guidance in awarding damages justly.

When a party breaches his contract, the damages he pays ought to be those arising naturally from the breach itself and, in addition, those as may reasonably be supposed to have been in contemplation of the parties, at the time they made the contract, as the probable result of the breach of it. Therefore, if the special circumstances under which the contract was made were known to both parties, the resulting damages upon breach would be those reasonably contemplated as arising under those communicated and known circumstances. But if the special circumstances were unknown, then damages can only be those expected to arise generally from the breach. Hadley's (P) telling Baxendale (D) that he ran a mill and that his mill shaft which he wanted shipped was broken did not notify Baxendale (D) that the mill was shut down. Baxendale (D) could have believed reasonably that Hadley (P) had a spare shaft or that the shaft to be shipped was not the only defective machinery at the mill. Here, it does not follow that a loss of profits could fairly or reasonably have been contemplated by both parties in case of breach. Such a loss would not have flowed naturally from the breach without the special circumstances having been told to Baxendale (D). New trial ordered.

▶ *ANALYSIS*

This case lays down two rules guiding damages. First, only those damages as may fairly and reasonably be considered arising from the breach itself may be awarded. Second, those damages which may reasonably be supposed to have been in contemplation of the parties at the time they made the contract as the probable result of a breach of it may be awarded. The second is distinguished from the first because with the latter, both parties are aware of the special circumstances under which the contract is made. Usually, those special circumstances are communicated by the plaintiff to the defendant before the making of the contract. But that is not an absolute condition. If the consequences of the breach are foreseeable, the party which breaches will be liable for the lost profits or expectation damages. Foreseeability and assumption of the risk are ways of describing the bargain. If there is an assumption of the risk, the seller or carrier must necessarily be aware of the consequences. A later English case held that there would be a lesser foreseeability for a common carrier than a seller as a seller would tend to know the purpose and use of the item sold, while the common carrier probably would not know the use of all items it carried. If all loss went on to the seller, this would obviously be an incentive

Continued on next page.

not to enter into contracts. Courts balance what has become a "seller beware" attitude by placing limitations on full recovery. The loss must be foreseeable when the contract is entered into. It cannot be overly speculative. The seller's breach must be judged by willingness, negligence, bad faith, and availability of replacement items. Restatement (First) § 331(2) would allow recovery in the situation in this case under an alternative theory. If the breach were one preventing the use and operation of property from which profits would have been made, damages can be measured by the rental value of the property or by interest on the value of the property. Uniform Commercial Code (UCC) § 2-715(2) allows the buyer consequential damages for any loss which results from general or particular needs that the seller had reason to know.

■═■

Quicknotes

CONSEQUENTIAL DAMAGES Monetary compensation that may be recovered in order to compensate for injuries or losses sustained as a result of damages that are not the direct or foreseeable result of the act of a party, but that nevertheless are the consequence of such act and which must be specifically pled and demonstrated.

EXPECTATION DAMAGES The measure of damages necessary to place the nonbreaching party in the same position as he would have enjoyed had the contract been fully performed.

■═■

AM/PM Franchise Assn. v. Atlantic Richfield Co.

Franchise association (P) v. Oil company (D)

Pa. Sup. Ct., 526 Pa. 110, 584 A.2d 915 (1990).

NATURE OF CASE: Appeal from affirmance of dismissal of action for damages for breach of warranty.

FACT SUMMARY: Atlantic Richfield Co. (D) contended that the damages sought by AM/PM Franchise Assn. (P) stemmed from a loss of good will, which is speculative and not a recoverable basis as a matter of law.

🏛 RULE OF LAW
Loss of primary profits, loss of secondary profits, and loss of good will are three types of lost profits recoverable as consequential damages.

FACTS: AM/PM Franchise Assn. (AM/PM) (P), a class of over 150 franchises, claimed that the gasoline they were required to sell did not conform to Atlantic Richfield Co.'s (ARCO) (D) warranties for the product. Numerous purchasers of the oxinol blend gasoline supplied by ARCO (D) experienced poor engine performance and physical damage to their fuel system components. As the problems with the oxinol blend became known, AM/PM (P) claimed to have suffered a precipitous drop in the volume of their business and a loss of profits. AM/PM (P) pointed to a rise in sales from 1973 until 1982, when sales began to fall dramatically, allegedly due to defective oxinol blend gasoline. AM/PM (P) sued for lost profits, consequential damages, and incidental damages. ARCO (D) demurred, contending that the damages sought by AM/PM (P) stemmed from a loss of good will, which is speculative and not a recoverable basis as a matter of law. The trial court sustained ARCO's (D) demurrer and dismissed AM/PM's (P) complaint. The state's intermediate appellate court affirmed. AM/PM (P) appealed, and the state's highest court granted review

ISSUE: Are loss of primary profits, loss of secondary profits, and loss of good will recoverable as consequential damages?

HOLDING AND DECISION: (Cappy, J.) Yes. Loss of primary profits, loss of secondary profits, and loss of good will are recoverable as consequential damages. Pursuant to the provisions of the Uniform Commercial Code, AM/PM (P) is entitled to seek general damages and consequential damages. Lost profits are the difference between what AM/PM (P) actually earned and what it would have earned had ARCO (D) not committed the breach. Because the gasoline was allegedly not in conformance with the warranties, AM/PM (P) may be entitled to lost profits. The loss of gasoline sales is "primary profits" and is recoverable upon further proof. Second, the present case presents compelling reasons for permitting damages for loss of "secondary profits," meaning the sales of other

AM/PM (P) products not made as a result of the breach of warranty. AM/PM (P) alleged that mini-mart sales declined during the period of time that ARCO (D) supplied nonconforming gasoline. Therefore, in a breach of warranty case, when a primary product of the defendant is alleged to be nonconforming and the plaintiff is unable to cover by purchasing substitute goods, the plaintiff, upon proper proof, should be entitled to sue for loss of secondary profits. Third, the phrase "good will damages" is coextensive with prospective profits and loss of business reputation. The rationale for precluding prospective profits under the rubric of "too speculative" ignores the realities of the marketplace and the science of modern economics. The claims for prospective profits should not be barred ab initio. Rather, AM/PM (P) should be given an opportunity to set forth and attempt to prove its damages. As long as AM/PM (P) can provide a reasonable basis from which the jury can calculate damages, it will be permitted to pursue its case. Reversed.

▶ ANALYSIS

Good will damages had been previously disallowed as being too speculative to permit recovery. However, the cases in which that decision was reached were not recent. They were written in a time when business was conducted on a simpler level, where market studies and economic forecasting were unexplored sciences.

Quicknotes

AB INITIO From its inception or beginning.

CONSEQUENTIAL DAMAGES Monetary compensation that may be recovered in order to compensate for injuries or losses sustained as a result of damages that are not the direct or foreseeable result of the act of a party, but that nevertheless are the consequence of such act and which must be specifically pled and demonstrated.

DEMURRER The assertion that the opposing party's pleadings are insufficient and that the demurring party should not be made to answer.

LOSS OF GOODWILL The diminishment of an intangible asset reflecting a corporation's favorability with the public and expectation of continuing patronage.

Rockingham County v. Luten Bridge Co.

County board (D) v. Bridge builder (P)

35 F.2d 301 (4th Cir. 1929).

NATURE OF CASE: Appeal from award of damages for breach of contract.

FACT SUMMARY: Rockingham County (D) contracted with Luten Bridge Co. (P) for construction of a bridge.

RULE OF LAW
After repudiation by one contract party to perform, the other party may not continue to perform and recover damages based on full performance.

FACTS: After the Rockingham County (the County) (D) board of commissioners voted to award a contract to Luten Bridge Co. (Luten) (P) for the construction of a bridge, three of the five commissioners resigned. The new board composed of three new commissioners and the two remaining commissioners unanimously voted to repudiate its contract with Luten (P). After receiving notice of the County's (D) repudiation, Luten (P) proceeded to construct the bridge. The total cost of labor and materials prior to the repudiation was $1,900. In a suit against the County (D), Luten (P) was awarded $18,301.07 in contract damages based on its full performance of its contract with the County (D). The County (D) appealed contending that Luten (P) was only entitled to damages it incurred prior to the County's (D) repudiation of the contract. The court of appeals granted review.

ISSUE: After repudiation by one contract party to perform, may the other party continue to perform and recover damages based on full performance?

HOLDING AND DECISION: (Parker, J.) No. After repudiation by one contract party to perform, the other party may not continue to perform and recover damages based on full performance. Here, the County (D) gave notice, while the contract was still executory, that it did not desire the bridge built and would not pay for it. Luten (D) at that point had a duty to desist from continuing to work on the bridge and piling on damages. Therefore, Luten (P) could not proceed to build the bridge and recover the full contract price. Reversed and remanded.

▶ ANALYSIS

The issue presented here is analogous to the duty of a terminated employee to minimize loss by finding suitable replacement employment. Judge Cardozo observed, "The servant is free to accept employment or reject it according to his uncensored pleasure. What is meant by the supposed duty is this: That if he reasonably rejects, he will not be heard to say that the loss of wages from then on shall be deemed the jural consequence of the earlier discharge. He has broken the chain of causation, and loss resulting to him thereafter is suffered through his own act." *McClelland v. Climax Hosiery Mills*, 252 N.Y. 347, 169 N.E. 605 (1930).

Quicknotes

EXECUTORY Something that has not been fully completed or performed.

JURAL Concerning the law or the justice system.

REPUDIATION The actions or statements of a party to a contract that evidence his intent not to perform, or to continue performance, of his duties or obligations thereunder.

Parker v. Twentieth Century-Fox Film Corp.

Actress (P) v. Movie company (D)

Cal. Sup. Ct., 3 Cal. 3d 176, 474 P.2d 689 (1970).

NATURE OF CASE: Appeal from summary judgment for plaintiff in action for damages for breach of a contract for employment.

FACT SUMMARY: Parker (P), an actress, was to have the lead role in the motion picture, "Bloomer Girl," to be produced by Twentieth Century-Fox Film Corp. (Fox) (D) and she was to receive $750,000 in salary. Fox (D) decided not to make the movie and offered Parker (P) the leading role in a film, "Big Country, Big Man," instead, which Parker (P) refused.

> 🏛 **RULE OF LAW**
> An employer may not claim mitigation where a wrongfully discharged employee refuses the employer's offer of different or inferior employment.

FACTS: Parker (P), an actress whose professional name is Shirley MacLaine, was hired for the lead role in the film, "Bloomer Girl," to be produced by Twentieth Century-Fox Film Corp. (Fox) (D). She was to receive a salary of $750,000 for 14 weeks. Under the contract, Parker (P) was to have approval over the director or any substitute, the dance director, and the screenplay. Twentieth Century-Fox Film Corp. (Fox) (D) decided not to make the film and offered Parker (P) the lead in "Big Country, Big Man," which, unlike the other film, was not a musical, but a western. Also, Fox (D) did not offer Parker (P) approval of the director or screenplay (and there was no need for a dance director). "Bloomer Girl" was to have been filmed in Los Angeles; "Big Country, Big Man" was to be made in Australia. Parker (P) rejected the second film offer and sued for her salary and resulting damages. The trial court granted summary judgment for Parker (P), and ordered Fox (D) to pay her $750,000 plus interest. The state's highest court granted review.

ISSUE: May an employer claim mitigation where a wrongfully discharged employee refuses the employer's offer of different or inferior employment?

HOLDING AND DECISION: (Burke, J.) No. An employer may not claim mitigation where a wrongfully discharged employee refuses the employer's offer of different or inferior employment. The general rule is that the measure of recovery by a wrongfully discharged employee is the amount of salary agreed upon for the period of service, less the amount which the employer affirmatively proves the employee has earned or with reasonable effort might have earned from other employment. However, before projected earnings from other employment opportunities not sought or accepted by the discharged employee can be applied in mitigation, the employer must show that the other employment was comparable, or substantially similar, to that of which the employee has been deprived; the employee's rejection of or failure to seek other available employment of a different or inferior kind may not be resorted to in order to mitigate damages. Fox (D), in claiming that Parker (P) unreasonably refused the second film offer, must show that the other employment was comparable to the first, or, at least, substantially similar to that which their employee has been deprived. If the western film offer were found different or inferior to the musical film offer, it makes no difference whether Parker (P) reasonably or unreasonably refused the second offer. The western was a different and inferior film where Parker (P) could not use her singing and dancing talents as in the musical. The western required travel to Australia for extensive outdoor filming rather than the use of sound stages in Los Angeles. The "Big Country" offer impaired or eliminated several rights of approval. Accordingly, as the second offer was different and inferior to the first, Parker (P) was correctly awarded $750,000 plus interest. Affirmed.

DISSENT: (Sullivan, C.J.) The issue of whether the offer by Fox (D) of "Big Country, Big Man" was an offer of work that was substantially similar to "Bloomer Girl" is one of fact and should have been left to a fact finder, rather than being decided on summary judgment as a matter of law. Employment which is different in kind should not be required to be accepted by the employee, but the mere existence of differences between two jobs in the same field should not be sufficient to release the employee from the employee's duty to mitigate, and, a rule based on such mere differences would effectively eliminate any obligation to attempt to minimize damage arising from a wrongful discharge—the only job the discharged employee would be required to accept is the job from which the employee was wrongfully terminated. Here, the majority merely points out differences between the two films, but not in the kind of employment that Parker (P) would be required to engage in if she accepted a role in the second film. Instead, the inquiry should focus on whether the differences which are present are substantial enough to constitute differences in the kind of employment or, alternatively, whether they render the substitute work employment of an inferior kind. This inquiry, at least here, would involve the kind of factual determinations not permitted on summary judgment. Parker's (P) declarations did not address these issues, and the trial court based its decision on its judicial notice of practices in the film industry and of various terms in the

Continued on next page.

employment contract. Such use of judicial notice on summary judgment was erroneous, but the majority avoids this issue. Contrary to the majority's determination, an offer that eliminates any contract right, regardless of its significance, cannot be said, as a matter of law, to be an offer of employment of an inferior kind. Instead, the relevant question in such cases is whether or not a particular contract provision is so significant that its omission creates employment of an inferior kind—which, again, can usually only be answered upon a factual inquiry.

▶ *ANALYSIS*

The court points out that if the other offer of employment is of a different or inferior kind, it does not matter whether the employee acts reasonably or unreasonably in rejecting the offer. The person with the duty to mitigate need not expose himself to undue risk, expense, or humiliation. It may be possible, considering the fact that Parker (P) made no westerns in the past, that in the management of an actress' career, such a film may have been considered a risk or, even possibly, a humiliation. Also, many cases have held that the employee is not required to accept employment unreasonably distant from the original location. The court apparently thought that Australia was unreasonably distant when Parker (P) was regularly working in Los Angeles and had intended to work on "Bloomer Girl" there. Note that in mitigating, the employee also does not have to accept a position of lesser rank or at a lower salary. Also, Parker (P) asked for damages in addition to her salary but such special damages are rarely awarded in cases of wrongful discharge. Damages for injury to the reputation of the employee are considered to be too remote and not within the contemplation of the parties. There is authority for damages when the denied employment would have enhanced the employee's reputation such as a motion picture credit, but this has only been applied once in the United States, but is common in England. The dissent would apparently foist an unacceptable film role upon an actress. Due to the nature of the industry and its regularly accepted business practices, the majority probably kept in mind the actor's need "to feel right" about a role and script before accepting it.

■═■

Quicknotes

MITIGATION OF DAMAGES Doctrine requiring the non-breaching party to a contract to exercise ordinary care in attempting to minimize the damages incurred as a result of the breach.

■═■

Lake River Corp. v. Carborundum Co.

Distributor (P) v. Powder manufacturer (D)

769 F.2d 1284 (7th Cir. 1985).

NATURE OF CASE: Appeal from judgments in diversity suit for liquidated damages and counterclaim for conversion.

FACT SUMMARY: Lake River Corp. (P) sued Carborundum Co. (D) for liquidated damages resulting from breach of a distributorship agreement. Carborundum Co. (D) counterclaimed under the theory of conversion. The district judge entered judgment for both parties. Both parties appealed.

🏛 RULE OF LAW
A minimum-guarantee provision is an unenforceable penalty, rather than an enforceable liquidated damages clause, where it is designed always to assure the promisee more than its actual damages.

FACTS: Carborundum Co. (D) manufactures "Ferro Carbo," an abrasive powder used in making steel. Carborundum (D) entered into a distributorship contract with Lake River Co. (P) to better serve its Midwestern clients. Lake River Co. (P) had a warehouse in Illinois and agreed to receive Ferro Carbo in bulk from Carborundum (D), "bag" it, and ship the bagged product to Carborundum's (D) customers. To honor this agreement, Carborundum (D) insisted that Lake River (P) install a new bagging system. Lake River (P) sought to ensure that it would be able to recover the cost of this new system ($89,000) and make a profit of 20 percent. Thus, Lake River (P) insisted on a minimum-quantity guarantee that in consideration of the new bagging system, Carborundum (D) would ship to Lake River (P) for bagging, a minimum of 22,500 tons of Ferro Carbo. If this minimum was not met, Lake River (P) would invoice Carborundum at the then-prevailing rates for the difference between the quantity bagged and the minimum guaranteed. Shortly after the contract between Carborundum (D) and Lake River (P) was signed, the demand for domestic steel fell dramatically and Carborundum (D) failed to ship the guaranteed amount. Lake River (P) demanded payment for the difference and Carborundum (D) refused. At this time, Lake River (P) had 500 tons of bagged Ferro Carbo in its warehouse, having a market value of $269,000, which it refused to release unless Carborundum (D) paid the $241,000 difference due under the formula. Carborundum (D) trucked in bagged Ferro Carbo from the East to serve its customers in Illinois at an additional cost of $31,000. Lake River (P) brought suit for $241,000 and Carborundum (D) counterclaimed for the value of the bagged Ferro Carbo which Lake River (P) had impounded. The district judge entered judgment for both parties. Both parties

appealed, and the court of appeals granted review. [The court affirmed the district court's ruling that Lake River (P) did not have a valid lien on the bagged powder.]

ISSUE: Is a minimum-guarantee provision an unenforceable penalty, rather than an enforceable liquidated damages clause, where it is designed always to assure the promisee more than its actual damages?

HOLDING AND DECISION: (Posner, J.) Yes. A minimum-guarantee provision is an unenforceable penalty, rather than an enforceable liquidated damages clause, where it is designed always to assure the promisee more than its actual damages. Leaving aside the theoretical question of whether courts should (paternalistically) refuse to enforce a contract provision that acts as a penalty against a large, sophisticated company—given that it can be argued on the one hand that there are some benefits to having penalties in contracts, but on the other hand that penalties also may discourage efficient as well as inefficient breaches of contract—the court must apply state law. Here, applicable state law requires that a liquidated damages clause, in order to be enforceable, must be a reasonable estimation at the time of contracting of the probable damages from breach, and the need for estimation must be based on the likely difficulty of assessing the actual damages suffered in the event of breach; otherwise, such clause is void as a penalty. Here, the damage formula is a penalty because it is designed always to assure Lake River (P) more than its actual damages. The formula—full contract price minus the amount already invoiced to Carborundum (D)—is invariant to the gravity of the breach. It also indicates a failure to reasonably estimate actual damages. Regardless of when a breach occurs, Lake River (P) will recover more than its expected profit at that point. If the breach occurs early, Lake River (P) will receive a windfall; if it occurs late, Lake River (P) still would get more than the profits it could reasonably anticipate if there had not been a breach. Despite the fact that the damage formula is invalid, Lake River (P) is still entitled to its common-law damages (the unpaid contract price of $241,000 minus the costs that Lake River (P) saved by not having to complete the contract (the variable costs on the other 45 percent of the Ferro Carbo that it never had to bag). Remanded to the district court to fix these damages.

▶ ANALYSIS

Although the court here sustains the distinction between penalty clauses and liquidated damages provisions, Judge

Continued on next page.

Posner expressly states his disagreement with such a dis-tinction. While he admits that penalty clauses impute a sense of exigency into the contract's terms, this advantage is heavily outweighed by countervailing concerns. First, the presence of the penalty clause increases the costs of con-tracting. Second, penalty clauses may discourage efficient breaches of contract. Nevertheless, he concludes that such a distinction is to be determined by the state courts in accordance with the common law, and may not be dictated by federal judges.

■══■

Quicknotes

LIQUIDATED DAMAGES An amount of money specified in a contract representing the damages owed in the event of breach.

PENALTY CLAUSE A provision in a contract imposing pen-alties for failure to comply with its terms and which is usually unenforceable.

■══■

Schurtz v. BMW of North America

Car buyer (P) v. Auto manufacturer (D)

Utah Sup. Ct., 814 P.2d 1108 (1991).

NATURE OF CASE: Appeal of a denial of attorney fees.

FACT SUMMARY: Schurtz (P) and BMW of North America (D) disputed the validity of a warranty provision disclaiming incidental and consequential damages due to the breach of warranty on a car.

RULE OF LAW
Consequential and incidental damages may be disclaimed pursuant to Uniform Commercial Code § 2-719, even when the warranty fails of its essential purpose.

FACTS: Schurtz (P) bought a 1982 BMW from a car dealer. The car carried a warranty from BMW of North America (BMW) (D), which was limited to repair or replacements of parts within 38,000 miles or three years. The warranty purported to disclaim any incidental and consequential damages resulting from any breach of warranty. Schurtz (P) found many problems with the car, and BMW (D) was unable to make repairs. Schurtz (P) filed suit against BMW (D) for damages, including incidental and consequential damages. BMW (D) filed a summary judgment motion to have these claims barred due to the warranty provision. Schurtz (P) responded that Uniform Commercial Code (UCC) § 2-719 provided that the disclaimer was ineffective where the warranty failed of its essential purpose. The trial court ruled for BMW (D) on this issue. Subsequently, the parties settled the matter, and as part of the agreement Schurtz (P) was entitled to seek attorney fees pursuant to consumer protection legislation. The court discounted the full amount of these fees based on the fact that the court felt Schurtz (P) should have known that consequential and incidental damages were not available. Schurtz (P) appealed, and the state's highest court granted review.

ISSUE: May consequential and incidental damages be disclaimed pursuant to UCC § 2-719, even when the warranty fails of its essential purpose?

HOLDING AND DECISION: (Zimmerman, J.) Yes. Consequential and incidental damages may be disclaimed pursuant to UCC § 2-719, even when the warranty fails of its essential purpose. UCC § 2-719 (3) states that consequential or incidental damages may be excluded unless the limitation is unconscionable. Although subpart (2) of § 2-719 provides that disclaimers may become invalid if the warranty fails of its essential purpose, the plain words of subsection (3) state that unconscionability is the sole test for consequential damages. From the

statute's language, it appears that subparts (2) and (3) are to operate independently—but courts around the country are split on this issue. Typically, where the buyer is a consumer with limited bargaining power, courts have ruled that the subparts are dependent, whereas in commercial transactions, courts have ruled that the subparts are independent. However, both the consumer and the non-consumer situation can be dealt with in a manner that reconciles the apparent split of authority in the cases by giving an independent reading to subparts (2) and (3). When trial courts are addressing the subpart (3) issue of unconscionability in any specific case, they should take an approach that frankly recognizes the differences that inhere in consumer, as opposed to commercial, settings and affect the determination of unconscionability. Because subparts (2) and (3) are independent, the disclaimer contained in BMW's (D) warranty is valid, as long as it meets the unconscionability standard, taking into account that in consumer transactions such limitations are not often negotiable. Accordingly, the trial court erred in deciding as a matter of law on summary judgment that Schurtz (P) was not entitled to incidental and consequential damages, and the case must be remanded in order to determine whether the disclaimer was unconscionable. Similarly, the trial court must readdress its reduction of attorney fees because its decision was based on the erroneous assumption that Schurtz (P) could never recover incidental and consequential damages. Reversed and remanded.

CONCURRENCE AND DISSENT: (Stewart, J.) The issue is one of contract interpretation, rather than statutory interpretation as the majority suggests. Section 2-719(1) authorizes a limited or exclusive remedy, and § 2-719(2) provides that if "circumstances cause an exclusive or limited remedy to fail of its essential purpose, remedy may be had as provided in this act." The phrase "as provided in this act" does not invalidate an otherwise valid contractual provision. The true question is whether, based on an interpretation of the contract, the failure of an exclusive or limited remedy also causes the failure of a consequential damages limitation. If the contract is interpreted in such a way that the consequential damages limitation must fail with the limited remedy, then incidental and consequential damages may be recovered as provided in the UCC. On the other hand, if the failure of the limited remedy does not cause the failure of the consequential damages limitation, then that limitation must be evaluated under the unconscionability standard of § 2-719(3). Thus, so long as a consequential damages

Continued on next page.

limitation is not unconscionable, it should be upheld where the exclusion is not so integrally related to the limited remedy that the failure of the essential purpose of that remedy, or its repudiation by the seller, necessarily invalidates the damages limitation.

▶ *ANALYSIS*

A warranty fails of its essential purpose when the seller is unable or unwilling to repair or replace the goods in an efficient manner under the warranty. In this case, UCC § 2-719 allows for remedies under the UCC rather than the remedies provided for in the warranty. For the standards of unconscionability, see UCC § 2-302.

■■■■

Quicknotes

CONSEQUENTIAL DAMAGES Monetary compensation that may be recovered in order to compensate for injuries or losses sustained as a result of damages that are not the direct or foreseeable result of the act of a party, but that nevertheless are the consequence of such act and which must be specifically pled and demonstrated.

SUMMARY JUDGMENT Judgment rendered by a court in response to a motion by one of the parties, claiming that the lack of a question of material fact in respect to an issue warrants disposition of the issue without consideration by the jury.

■■■■

Hibschman Pontiac, Inc. v. Batchelor

Car dealer (D) v. Auto buyer (P)

Ind. Sup. Ct., 266 Ind. 310, 362 N.E.2d 845 (1977).

NATURE OF CASE: Appeal from award of punitive damages.

FACT SUMMARY: Batchelor (P) purchased a new automobile from Hibschman Pontiac, Inc. (D) that contained many problems.

> ## 🏛 RULE OF LAW
> (1) Punitive damages may be awarded in cases where the elements of fraud, malice, and gross negligence mingle in the controversy.
> (2) Damages will be considered excessive if at first blush they appear to be outrageous and excessive or it is apparent that some improper element was taken into account by the jury in determining the amount.

FACTS: After Batchelor (P) purchased a new Pontiac GTO from Hibschman Pontiac, Inc. (Hibschman) (D), he noticed it contained several defects. Batchelor (P) brought the automobile back to the Hibschman's (D) service department five times for repairs without adequate results. Initially, Jim Hibschman (D) told Batchelor (P) that the service department "would do everything to get you happy." Eventually, Jim Hibschman (D) told Batchelor (P) that he was a habitual complainer whom they could not satisfy, and "I would rather you would leave and not come back. We are going to have to write you off as a bad customer." Batchelor (P) sued Hibschman (D) for breach of contract and was awarded damages of $1500 plus punitive damages of $15,000. Hibschman (D) appealed on the punitive damages issue, contending that the evidence failed to show that Hibschman (D) acted with fraud, malice, or gross negligence; and the state's intermediate appellate court reversed as to the punitive damages. The state's highest court granted review.

ISSUE:
(1) May punitive damages be awarded in cases where the elements of fraud, malice, and gross negligence mingle in the controversy?
(2) Will damages be considered excessive if at first blush they appear to be outrageous and excessive or it is apparent that some improper element was taken into account by the jury in determining the amount?

HOLDING AND DECISION: (Givan, C.J.)
(1) Yes. Punitive damages may be awarded in cases where the elements of fraud, malice, and gross negligence mingle in the controversy. Here, the jury could reasonably have found elements of fraud, malice, gross negligence, or oppression mingled into the breach of

warranty, since Batchelor (P) took the car to Hibschman (D) numerous times and was told that the car was "all ready to go," even though the service manager knew the repairs were not performed. Hibschman (D) gave Batchelor (P) specific representations of the excellence of the Hibschman (D) service department. Batchelor (P) relied on these representations in buying the car. Therefore, it was within the jury's province to award punitive damages, and the trial court did not err in denying a directed verdict on that issue. Affirmed as to this issue.

(2) Yes. Damages will be considered excessive if at first blush they appear to be outrageous and excessive or it is apparent that some improper element was taken into account by the jury in determining the amount. While there is no set ratio of actual damages to punitive damages that automatically renders punitive damages excessive, the amount here is too high on "first blush." Accordingly, the case is remanded to the trial court to either order remittitur of $7500, or to order a new trial on the appropriate amount of punitive damages. Transferred and remanded as to this issue.

CONCURRENCE: (DeBruler, J.) A standard of review of punitive damages should impose objective limitations upon such damages. The "first blush" rule does not do so.

▶ ANALYSIS

Factors that may affect the amount of punitive damages include: the plaintiff's costs of litigation, the financial condition of the defendant, and the grossness of the defendant's conduct. One court has held that such damages are appropriate whenever the defendant engages in conduct that is "malicious, oppressive, or gross." See *Winn-Dixie Montgomery, Inc. v. Henderson*, 395 So. 2d 475 (Ala. 1981).

Quicknotes

PUNITIVE DAMAGES Damages exceeding the actual injury suffered for the purposes of punishment, deterrence, and comfort to plaintiff.

Teradyne, Inc. v. Teledyne Industries

Transistor seller (P) v. Buyer (D)

676 F.2d 865 (1st Cir. 1982).

NATURE OF CASE: Appeal from award of damages for breach of contract action.

FACT SUMMARY: After Teledyne Industries (Teledyne) (D) contracted to buy a transistor system from Teradyne, Inc. (P), Teledyne (D) canceled the contract.

🏛 RULE OF LAW
(1) Under Uniform Commercial Code (UCC) § 2-708(2) if a seller resells goods after a breach by a buyer, the proceeds of the resale should not be credited to the buyer if the seller (absent the breach) would have made both the original sale and the resale, so that the seller is entitled to its expected "profit (including reasonable overhead)."
(2) In calculating a lost volume seller's profit on a lost sale, labor costs, including fringe benefits, should be included as direct costs deducted from profit where those costs are associated with testing, shipping, installing, servicing, or fulfilling warranties for the product that is being sold.
(3) There is no right to mitigation of damages where the offer of a substitute contract is conditioned on surrender by the injured party of his claim for breach.
(4) The cost of a master may be apportioned between parties in a manner that reflects the extent to which one party prevailed over the other in its request for damages.

FACTS: Teledyne Industries (Teledyne) (D) entered into a sales contract with Teradyne (P) for the purchase at a discount of Teradyne's (P) transistor test system, the T-347-A. Teledyne (D) canceled its order for the system two days prior to the system's scheduled delivery date, but offered to buy a different transistor system for $65,000. Teradyne (P) refused that offer, and then resold the system to another purchaser for a higher, non-discounted price. Teradyne (P) sued Teledyne (D) for breach of the sales contract. Teradyne (P) contended it was entitled to damages even though it resold the system for a higher price than the price contained in the original sales contract. Teradyne (P) argued it would have made the second sale even if Teledyne (D) had not broken the contract, and would have collected two profits instead of just one. The court appointed a master, whose report the court approved and based its decision on. The court ordered the parties to share equally the cost of the master. Teradyne (P) was awarded damages calculated under UCC § 2-708(2), equal to the contract price less ascertainable costs saved as a

result of the breach. The master based these costs on Teradyne's (P) inventory catalog; Teledyne (D) contended that a more complete source of costs was Teradyne's (P) public 10-K filing. The total damages awarded was $75,392, which was arrived at by subtracting from the original contract price of $98,400 a $984 quantity discount and $22,638 savings resulting from the breach, and adding $614 for preparing the product for the next customer. Teradyne (P) and Teledyne (D) both appealed. Teradyne (P) wanted Teledyne (D) to pay in full the master's cost. Teledyne (D) contended that additional variable costs, based on Teradyne's (P) 10-K, should have been used, as well as that certain direct and fringe labor costs associated with testing, shipping, installing, servicing, or fulfilling warranties should have been included rather than being treated as overhead—which would have reduced the award. Teledyne (D) also contended that its offer to purchase a different system should have offset the award as partial mitigation. The court of appeals granted review.

ISSUE:
(1) Under UCC § 2-708(2) if a seller resells goods after a breach by a buyer, should the proceeds of the resale be credited to the buyer if the seller (absent the breach) would have made both the original sale and the resale, so that the seller is not entitled to its expected "profit (including reasonable overhead)"?
(2) In calculating a lost volume seller's profit on a lost sale, should labor costs, including fringe benefits, be included as direct costs deducted from profit where those costs are associated with testing, shipping, installing, servicing, or fulfilling warranties for the product that is being sold?
(3) Is there a right to mitigation of damages where the offer of a substitute contract is conditioned on surrender by the injured party of his claim for breach?
(4) May the cost of a master be apportioned between parties in a manner that reflects the extent to which one party prevailed over the other in its request for damages?

HOLDING AND DECISION: (Wyzanski, J.)
(1) No. Under UCC § 2-708(2) if a seller resells goods after a breach by a buyer, the proceeds of the resale should not be credited to the buyer if the seller (absent the breach) would have made both the original sale and the resale, so that the seller is entitled to its expected "profit (including reasonable overhead)". A literal reading of § 2-708(2) would indicate that Teradyne (P) should recover nothing because the proceeds of

Continued on next page.

the resale exceeded the price set in the Teradyne (P)/ Teledyne (D) sales contract. However, it is universally agreed that statutory history mandates that the proceeds of the resale are not to be credited to the buyer if the seller is a lost volume seller. A lost volume seller is defined as one, whom had there been no breach by the buyer could and would have had the benefit of both the original contract and the resale contract. In this instance, Teradyne (P) was a lost volume seller. Therefore, it is entitled to the profit it expected on the contract. Affirmed as to this issue.

(2) Yes. In calculating a lost volume seller's profit on a lost sale, labor costs, including fringe benefits, should be included as direct costs deducted from profit where those costs are associated with testing, shipping, installing, servicing, or fulfilling warranties for the product that is being sold. While the master's conclusion that the variable costs were sufficiently accounted for by the inventory catalog is entitled to deference, the master's conclusion that labor costs and associated fringe benefits associated with testing, shipping, installing, servicing, or fulfilling warranties is not. Teradyne (P) argued that those wages would not have been affected if each of the testers, etc. handled one product more or less. However, the work of those employees entered as directly into production and supplying the transistor system as did the work of a fabricator of that system. Surely no one would regard as "reasonable overhead" within § 2-708(2) the wages of a fabricator of a T-347A even if his wages were the same whether he made one product more or less. Therefore, the wages of the testers, etc. likewise are not part of overhead and as a "direct cost" should have been deducted from the contract price. By the same reasoning, fringe benefits amounting to 12 percent of wages should also have been deducted as direct costs. Vacated and remanded as to this issue.

(3) No. There is no right to mitigation of damages where the offer of a substitute contract is conditioned on surrender by the injured party of his claim for breach. One is not required to mitigate his losses by accepting an arrangement with the repudiator if that is made conditional on his surrender of his rights under the repudiated contract. Therefore, Teradyne (P) was not required to accept Teledyne's (D) offer to purchase a different system as partial mitigation, and Teradyne (P) may claim all damages to which it is entitled. Affirmed as to this issue.

(4) Yes. The cost of a master may be apportioned between parties in a manner that reflects the extent to which one party prevailed over the other in its request for damages. Given that the district court will have to further reduce Teradyne's (P) award, the court may exercise its discretion in allocating the cost of the master. It is not required to impose all the master's costs on Teledyne (D) on the theory that since Teradyne (P) recovered a substantial part of what it sought, it was the prevailing party. If it so chooses, the district court

may adopt some other approach—for example, an allocation of the master's costs by reference to the ratio of the amount which Teradyne (P) finally recovers to the amount it originally sought in the complaint or to the amount it sought when the case was submitted to the master. Accordingly, the district court's order as to this issue is vacated and remanded. Vacated and remanded.

▶ *ANALYSIS*

A footnote in the instant case further illustrates the "lost volume seller" concept. "Boeing is able to make and sell in one year 100 airplanes. TWA contracts to buy the third plane off the assembly line, but it breaks the contract and Boeing resells the plane to Pan Am which had already agreed to buy the fourth plane. Because of the breach, Boeing sells only 99 aircraft during the year." Boeing is entitled to recover from TWA the net profit of the TWA contract price, no credit being given for any part of the proceeds Boeing received from its resale to Pan Am.

■=■

Quicknotes

LOST-VOLUME SELLER A seller who can accommodate more than one buyer and for whom a buyer's breach does not release the goods for sale to another customer; in such a case, the appropriate measure of damages is the net profit the seller would have earned pursuant to the sale.

RESALE OF GOODS BY SELLER AFTER BREACH When a vendor resells the goods, which are the subject matter of the breached contract, to another purchaser following default in payment by the original purchaser.

■=■

Maglica v. Maglica

Business partner (P) v. Owner (D)

Cal. Ct. App., 66 Cal. App. 4th 442, 78 Cal. Rptr. 2d 101 (1998).

NATURE OF CASE: Appeal from jury award in an action alleging breach of fiduciary duty and seeking recovery in quantum meruit.

FACT SUMMARY: Anthony Maglica (D) appealed from a jury award of $84 million granted to Claire Maglica (P) on breach of fiduciary duty and quantum meruit causes of action.

🏛 RULE OF LAW
Recovery in quantum meruit is measured by the reasonable value of services rendered to the benefiting party.

FACTS: Anthony Maglica (D) began his own machine shop business in 1955. He divorced in 1971, and kept the business. That year he met Claire (P). The two lived together, holding themselves out as husband and wife, although they never married. Claire (P) worked with Anthony (D) in establishing his business. When it incorporated in 1974, all the shares were held in Anthony's (D) name. Anthony (D) was president of the company and Claire (P) was the secretary. They both received salaries from the business. In 1992, Claire (P) discovered Anthony (D) was attempting to transfer stock to his children. The couple separated and in 1993, Claire (P) commenced suit against Anthony (D) for breach of contract, breach of partnership agreement, fraud, breach of fiduciary duty, and quantum meruit. The jury awarded Claire (P) $84 million on the breach of fiduciary duty and quantum meruit causes of action, finding that $84 million was the reasonable value of her services. Anthony (D) appealed. The state's intermediate appellate court granted review.

ISSUE: Is recovery in quantum meruit measured by the reasonable value of services rendered to the benefiting party?

HOLDING AND DECISION: (Sills, J.) Yes. Recovery in quantum meruit is measured by the reasonable value of services rendered to the benefiting party. The jury awarded Claire (P) damages based on her claim that Anthony (D) breached his fiduciary duty. No fiduciary duty, however, existed in this case. There was no contract stating that Anthony (D) agreed to give Claire (P) part of the business. Moreover, the couple remained unmarried, and thus Anthony (D) did not owe Claire (P) the fiduciary duties imposed on one spouse toward the other under the Family Code. Furthermore, in the absence of clear and convincing evidence of entrustment or an agreement to purchase property together, sufficient to overcome the presumption of the title of stock in Anthony's (D) name,

there can be no finding that there was a fiduciary duty owed and that Anthony (D) was in breach of that duty. Such a finding does not preclude Claire (P) from recovering in quantum meruit. Quantum meruit recovery is based on the reasonable value of services rendered that are of direct benefit to the defendant. Quantum meruit is awarded in order to prevent unjust enrichment by one of the parties. When one party receives a benefit that he may not fairly retain, he must restore the aggrieved party to his former position by return of the thing or its monetary equivalent. The initial inquiry is whether the defendant has received a benefit and what the measure of the resulting benefit was to the defendant. Here the jury was instructed that the reasonable value of Claire's (P) services was either the value it would have cost Anthony (D) to obtain the services elsewhere or the value to which he benefited as a result. While the services rendered must have been of benefit to the defendant to allow for recovery in quantum meruit, that benefit does not necessarily reflect the reasonable value of services rendered. Thus, the jury instruction was erroneous because it allowed the value of services to depend on their impact on the defendant's business rather than their reasonable value, thus impermissibly imposing an exchange of equity for services. Recovery based on benefit must be expressly agreed to by the parties pursuant to contract. The court erred in giving that instruction to the jury. Furthermore, the court erred in giving three of five jury instructions leading the jury to conclude that Claire (P) and Anthony (D) did not have an implied-in-fact contract. On remand, the three instructions should not be given. The jury should be told, rather, that while the facts that a couple live together, hold themselves out as married, and act as companions and confidants toward each other do not, by themselves, show an implied agreement to share property, those facts, when taken together and in conjunction with other facts bearing more directly on the alleged arrangement to share property, can show an implied agreement to share property. Reversed and remanded.

▶ ANALYSIS

The court erred in giving the jury an instruction regarding the issue of whether an implied-in-fact contract existed between the parties to share the stock in the company. The jury was told that the fact the parties were living together, holding themselves out as husband and wife, and that Claire (P) was providing services as a companion and confidant to Anthony (D), do not alone require a finding

Continued on next page.

of an implied contract. An implied-in-fact contract is one in which the parties, by engaging in particular conduct rather than words, evidence their intent. Courts have held that these factors, while not dispositive of the issue, are to be considered in determining whether there was an implied contract to share property. The jury here was misled to believe that they could not consider those facts at all in ascertaining whether there was an implied contract between Anthony (D) and Claire (P) to share the stock of the company. The jury should have been instructed that while such facts do not alone reflect an implied agreement to share property, such facts may support such an agreement when taken together with other factors more directly related to the presence of the alleged agreement.

■■■■

Quicknotes

BREACH OF FIDUCIARY DUTY The failure of a fiduciary to observe the standard of care exercised by professionals of similar education and experience.

QUANTUM MERUIT Equitable doctrine allowing recovery for labor and materials provided by one party, even though no contract was entered into, in order to avoid unjust enrichment by the benefited party.

■■■■

Feingold v. Pucello

Attorney (P) v. Alleged client (D)

Pa. Super. Ct., 439 Pa. Super. 509, 654 A.2d 1093 (1995).

NATURE OF CASE: Appeal from court finding for defendant in an action for quantum meruit.

FACT SUMMARY: Feingold (P), an attorney, alleged that Pucello (D) had orally agreed to retain him and requested payment in quantum meruit for the legal services he had purportedly rendered.

🏛 RULE OF LAW
An attorney will not be entitled to any quantum meruit recovery for work done on behalf of a prospective client where the attorney has failed to enter into a written contingency fee agreement with the prospective client; seeks to charge an unethically high fee; and in any event has not conferred a benefit on the prospective client.

FACTS: Pucello (D) was involved in an automobile accident and a co-worker gave Pucello's (D) name to Feingold (P), an attorney, with Pucello's (D) permission to do so. Feingold (P) called Pucello (D), orally discussed the case, and set up a medical appointment for Pucello (D) with a doctor he knew. Feingold (P) did not discuss fee arrangements at that time. After doing some research and securing an admission of liability from the other party, Feingold (P) sent Pucello (D) a formal contingency fee agreement calling for a 50/50 split of the recovery, after costs. When Pucello (D) refused to sign and found other counsel, Feingold (P) sued for the value of his services. A board of arbitrators found for Pucello (D) and, following Feingold's (P) appeal, the trial court at a de novo bench trial found that the parties had never entered into an attorney-client relationship and affirmed. Feingold (P) appealed, arguing that the circumstances implied a contract to support quantum meruit recovery.

ISSUE: Will an attorney be entitled to any quantum meruit recovery for work done on behalf of a prospective client where the attorney has failed to enter into a written contingency fee agreement with the prospective client; seeks to charge an unethically high fee; and in any event has not conferred a benefit on the prospective client?

HOLDING AND DECISION: (Olszewski, J.) No. An attorney will not be entitled to any quantum meruit recovery for work done on behalf of a prospective client where the attorney has failed to enter into a written contingency fee agreement with the prospective client; seeks to charge an unethically high fee; and in any event has not conferred a benefit on the prospective client. First, attorneys are required by law to state their contingency fees in writing before, or within a reasonable time after commencing representation. Quantum meruit is an equitable remedy and Feingold (P) came to this court with hands smudged by the ink which should have been used to sign his fee agreement. His abject failure to comply with the ethical rule requiring him to state his contingency fee up front and in writing precludes any equitable recovery. Second, the fee he sought to charge—50 percent of any recovery—was unethical, so this equitable consideration also precludes equitable recovery in the form of quantum meruit. Finally, regardless of these equitable considerations, Feingold's (P) claim fails on the merits, since he conferred no benefit on Pucello (D). If his work conferred a benefit on anyone, arguably it would be Pucello's (D) attorney. Affirmed.

CONCURRENCE: (Beck, J.) Feingold has failed to make out a claim in quasi-contract that would entitle him to restitution. It is clear that acceptance and retention of the benefits of Feingold's (P) services, a necessary element of the claim of unjust enrichment, has not been established. Since Feingold (P) introduced no competent evidence to support his assertion that his work on the case had the effect he alleged, the record could not support his claim that his services conferred a benefit upon Pucello (D). Feingold's (P) claim for quantum meruit cannot be sustained in the absence of a finding of unjust enrichment which, in equity, requires restitution. Here, the facts simply cannot support a finding that Pucello (D) was unjustly enriched by Feingold's (P) services. By refusing to accept Feingold's (P) files containing his work product, Pucello (D) affirmatively rejected any direct benefit from Feingold's (P) services. Because there can be no finding of unjust enrichment, the claim for quantum meruit must fail.

▶ ANALYSIS

The concurrence based its holding on the narrow basis that Feingold (P) had failed to make out a claim in quasi-contract. Feingold (P) had conceded that a contract for legal services had not been reached in this case. His sole claim was under an equitable claim in quasi-contract for quantum meruit.

■=■

Quicknotes

CONTINGENCY FEE AGREEMENT A fee agreement between an attorney and client that is contingent upon the ultimate disposition of the case and comprises a percentage of the party's recovery.

Continued on next page.

DE NOVO The review of a lower court decision by an appellate court, which is hearing the case as if it had not been previously heard and as if no judgment had been rendered.

QUANTUM MERUIT Equitable doctrine allowing recovery for labor and materials provided by one party, even though no contract was entered into, in order to avoid unjust enrichment by the benefited party.

■━━■

United States v. Algernon Blair, Inc.

Federal government (P) v. Contractor (D)

479 F.2d 638 (4th Cir. 1973).

NATURE OF CASE: Action to recover in quantum meruit the value of labor and equipment furnished.

FACT SUMMARY: Coastal Steel Erectors, a sub-contractor, brought suit in the name of the United States (P) against Algernon Blair, Inc. (D), the prime contractor on a government project, to recover in quantum meruit the value of the labor and materials it had furnished up to the point at which it justifiably ceased work.

> 🏛 **RULE OF LAW**
> A promisee is allowed to recover in quantum meruit the value of services he gave to a defendant who breached their contract irrespective of whether he would have lost money had the contract been fully performed and would thus be precluded from recovering in a suit on the contract.

FACTS: Algernon Blair, Inc. (Algernon) (D) was the prime contractor on a government project. Coastal Steel Erectors (Coastal), a subcontractor on the project, furnished materials and labor up to the point that Algernon (D) breached its contract with Coastal. At that point, Coastal ceased work and brought an action under the Miller Act, in the name of the United States (P), to recover in quantum meruit the value of the equipment and labor it had theretofore supplied. The district court found Algernon (D) had breached the contract, but held that Coastal would have lost money on the contract had it been fully performed. For this reason, it denied recovery, and Coastal appealed. The court of appeals granted review.

ISSUE: Is a promisee allowed to recover in quantum meruit the value of services he gave to a defendant who breached their contract irrespective of whether he would have lost money had the contract been fully performed and would thus be precluded from recovering in a suit on the contract?

HOLDING AND DECISION: (Craven, J.) Yes. A promisee is allowed to recover in quantum meruit the value of services he gave to a defendant who breached their contract irrespective of whether he would have lost money had the contract been fully performed and would thus be precluded from recovering in a suit on the contract. Regardless of whether or not the promisee would have lost money had he completed the contract, he can recover in quantum meruit the value of the services he gave to a defendant who breached the contract. It is an accepted principle of contract law, often applied in the case of construction contracts, that the promisee upon breach has the option to forgo any suit on the contract and

claim only the reasonable value of his performance. Thus, Coastal can recover for the equipment and labor it supplied despite the fact that it would have lost money on the contract and would thus have been unable to recover in a suit on the contract. Recovery in quantum meruit is measured by the reasonable value of the performance and is undiminished by any loss which would have been incurred by complete performance. Reversed and remanded for findings as to the reasonable value of the equipment and labor supplied by Coastal.

▶ ANALYSIS

The applicable standard in determining the "reasonable value" of services rendered is the amount for which such services could have been purchased from one in the plaintiff's position at the time and place the services were rendered. Some courts have held that the contract price is not only evidence of the reasonable value but is a ceiling on recovery, but others disagree. The rationale is that one should not recover more for part performance than he would have upon full performance.

■≡■

Quicknotes

QUANTUM MERUIT Equitable doctrine allowing recovery for labor and materials provided by one party, even though no contract was entered into, in order to avoid unjust enrichment by the benefited party.

■≡■

Rosenberg v. Levin

Lawyer (P) v. Client (D)

Fla. Sup. Ct., 409 So. 2d 1016 (1982).

NATURE OF CASE: Appeal from award for services rendered in breach of contract action.

FACT SUMMARY: After Levin (D) hired Rosenberg (P) to perform legal services, Rosenberg (P) was discharged without cause.

🏛 RULE OF LAW
A lawyer discharged without cause is entitled to the reasonable value of his services on the basis of quantum meruit, but recovery is limited to the maximum fee set in the fee contract.

FACTS: Levin (D) hired Rosenberg (P) to perform legal services pursuant to a fee agreement which provided for a fixed fee of $10,000, plus a contingent fee equal to fifty percent of all amounts recovered in excess of $600,000. Levin (D) later discharged Rosenberg (P) without cause before the case was settled. Levin (D) eventually settled the case for a net recovery of $500,000. Rosenberg (P) sued Levin (D) for his fees based on a quantum meruit evaluation of his services. The trial court awarded Rosenberg (P) $55,000 based on the quantum meruit value of his services. The district court lowered the amount of recovery to $10,000, holding that Rosenberg's (P) recovery in quantum meruit was limited to the amount Rosenberg (P) would have received had the contract not been prematurely discharged. Rosenberg (P) appealed. The state's highest court granted review.

ISSUE: Is a lawyer discharged without cause entitled to the reasonable value of his services on the basis of quantum meruit, with recovery limited to the maximum fee set in the fee contract?

HOLDING AND DECISION: (Overton, J.) Yes. A lawyer discharged without cause is entitled to the reasonable value of his services on the basis of quantum meruit, but recovery is limited to the maximum fee set in the fee contract. There is an overriding need to allow clients freedom to substitute attorneys without economic penalty. This approach creates the best balance between the desirable right of the client to discharge his attorney and the right of the attorney to reasonable compensation of his services. Affirmed.

▶ ANALYSIS

A footnote in the instant case details a rule in New York which provides that discharge of an attorney cancels the fee agreement. Under this rule an attorney can recover the full value of his services, even if it exceeds the contract price. Had the *Rosenberg* case been a New York case, the result would most likely have been different.

■══■

Quicknotes

QUANTUM MERUIT Equitable doctrine allowing recovery for labor and materials provided by one party, even though no contract was entered into, in order to avoid unjust enrichment by the benefited party.

■══■

Britton v. Turner

Laborer (P) v. Employer (D)

N.H. Sup. Ct., 6 N.H. 481 (1834).

NATURE OF CASE: Appeal from judgment for plaintiff in action in quantum meruit.

FACT SUMMARY: Britton (P) unjustly terminated a one-year contract for labor at a specified price after nine-and-one-half months.

🏛 RULE OF LAW
A party who unilaterally breaches a partially performed contract may recover in quasi contract for the labor and materials retained by the other party less damages resulting from the breach.

FACTS: Britton (P) agreed to perform labor for Turner (D) for one year for $120. After nine-and-one-half months Britton (P) quit without cause. Turner (D) refused to pay Britton (P) anything on the contract. Britton (P) brought suit to recover the reasonable value of his services in quantum meruit. The court directed the jury to find for Britton (P) in the amount of $95 since Turner (D) had retained the benefits of Britton's (P) services. Turner (D) appealed alleging that the contract made completion of the contract term a condition precedent to his duty to pay. The state's highest court granted review.

ISSUE: May a party who unilaterally breaches a partially performed contract recover in quasi contract for the labor and materials retained by the other party less damages resulting from the breach?

HOLDING AND DECISION: (Parker, J.) Yes. A party who unilaterally breaches a partially performed contract may recover in quasi contract for the labor and materials retained by the other party less damages resulting from the breach. It is true that Britton (P) cannot recover on the contract since Turner's (D) duty to pay is conditioned on Britton's (P) completion of one year's labor. However, a court of equity may allow recovery in quasi contract. By accepting the benefits of Britton's (P) labor there is found to be an implied promise to pay the reasonable value of such services. This implied promise arises outside of and in addition to the original contract. An offset on the amount due under the quasi contract is allowed for any damages sustained as a result of the breach of the express contract. It is a matter of simple justice to require the party to pay for the benefits actually received and retained by him. It must be assumed that he realized that there was a possibility that the laborer might breach the contract. It is unfair to reward the nonbreaching party out of all proportion to the damages actually sustained. He is left in the same position as he would have been in if the other party had not breached the contract under the theory herein. Affirmed.

▶ ANALYSIS

The reasonable value of the services rendered may not exceed the contract price when an action in quantum meruit is brought by the breaching party. Most courts calculate the award as the reasonable value of the services rendered to the particular defendant. If the efforts produced no substantial value to him, no award will be granted regardless of the reasonable value of the services rendered, e.g., labor and material costs.

■══■

Quicknotes

BREACH OF CONTRACT Unlawful failure by a party to perform its obligations pursuant to contract.

IMPLIED PROMISE A promise inferred by law from a document as a whole and the circumstances surrounding its implementation.

QUANTUM MERUIT Equitable doctrine allowing recovery for labor and materials provided by one party, even though no contract was entered into, in order to avoid unjust enrichment by the benefited party.

■══■

PHH Mortgage Corp. v. Barker

Mortgage holder (P) v. Mortgagor (D)

Ohio App. Ct., 190 Ohio App.3d 71, 940 N.E.2d 662 (2010).

NATURE OF CASE: Appeal from reinstatement of a mortgage in a foreclosure action.

FACT SUMMARY: PHH Mortgage Corp. (P), which had instituted mortgage foreclosure proceedings against the Barkers (D) on a loan they originally had with First Financial Bank, N.A (First Financial), contended that the trial court had abused its equitable discretion by reinstating the mortgage to a date clearly in default, thereby impermissibly reforming the parties' contract, notwithstanding the court found that the equities favored the Barkers (D), who had believed and acted on communications from First Financial that seemed to indicate that their loan had been modified so as to avoid default.

> ### 🏛 RULE OF LAW
> A court does not abuse its discretion and commit improper making of a contract where it reinstates a mortgage pursuant to the court's equitable powers after finding that the parties agreed to modify the original mortgage.

FACTS: The Barkers (D) executed a note and mortgage with First Financial Bank, N.A. (First Financial), but after around a year and a half defaulted on their monthly payment due to Mrs. Barker's (D) illness. After Mrs. Barker (D) recovered a couple of months later, the Barkers (D) attempted to contact First Financial on multiple occasions, and were finally informed about the bank's loss mitigation program, an assistance program that helps the homeowner cure the default and bring the mortgage current. Despite filling out and sending in the paperwork for that program, the Barkers (D) soon after received notice that their mortgage was in default. Shortly after that, they received a "coupon book" in the mail that had a new due date and an increased monthly payment amount, and the Barkers (D) started making payments in accordance with the seemingly revised mortgage terms at the bank's local branch, and the payments were accepted by the teller there. However, First Financial allegedly returned the payments on the grounds that the mortgage continued to be in default. The Barkers (D) claimed that they never received the returned payments, and they made another payment in person at the local branch. Not long thereafter, PHH Mortgage Corp. (PHH) (P) (to which First Financial apparently had sold the loan) sent a notice to the Barkers (D) along with a refund of the moneys they had paid informing them that the account had "been referred to an attorney to handle the foreclosure process." This was the first time PHH (P) formally communicated with the Barkers (D). The letter

further directed the Barkers (D) to call the "loss mitigation department" to learn about assistance programs to help bring the mortgage current. However, the Barkers (D) did not receive this letter until nearly five months after it was sent, and they made two more monthly payments at the local branch, which were accepted unconditionally. Then, when they attempted to make another payment, a month later, the teller at the bank refused payment, pursuant to PHH's (P) instructions. PHH (P), which had already instituted foreclosure proceedings, moved for summary judgment. The Barkers (D) defended by attaching an affidavit of Mr. Barker (D) attesting to the sequence of events that had transpired, and arguing that there were genuine issues of material fact based on First Financial having issued them the coupon book. PHH (D) objected to the use of Mr. Barker's (D) affidavit as the only evidence to establish a dispute of fact. During the pendency of the court proceedings, the loss mitigation department continued to send the Barkers (D) paperwork, which they dutifully completed and returned. The trial court denied summary judgment, and, after a bench trial, the court ordered reinstatement of the note and mortgage to terms consistent with those in the coupon book. PHH (P) appealed, arguing, inter alia, that the trial court had erred in reinstating the mortgage to a date clearly in default, thereby impermissibly reforming the parties' contract. The state's intermediate appellate court granted review.

ISSUE: Does a court abuse its discretion and commit improper making of a contract where it reinstates a mortgage pursuant to the court's equitable powers after finding that the parties agreed to modify the original mortgage?

HOLDING AND DECISION: (Shaw, J.) No. A court does not abuse its discretion and commit improper making of a contract where it reinstates a mortgage pursuant to the court's equitable powers after finding that the parties agreed to modify the original mortgage. A foreclosure involves a two-step process. Once it has been determined as a matter of law that a default on the obligation secured by the mortgage has occurred, the court must then consider the equities to determine if foreclosure is the appropriate remedy. Being an equitable remedy, foreclosure is reviewed for abuse of discretion. Here, based on the trial court's review of the equities and its finding that the Barkers (D) believed they had been granted a modification of their loan, based on the coupon book, and that they attempted to fulfill their obligations under the loan as so modified, the trial court did not abuse its discretion in

Continued on next page.

finding that foreclosure would be unjust. The surrounding circumstances support such a finding, given that the evidence at trial revealed that the Barkers (D) were receiving conflicting communications from First Financial/PHH (P) concerning their mortgage which obfuscated the situation, and given that First Financial's loss mitigation department continued to send the Barkers (D) paperwork throughout the foreclosure proceedings with PHH (P). There was ample evidence to support the trial court's decision that the equitable principles implicated in the case warranted a reinstatement of the Barkers' (D) mortgage. Further, the trial court did not err in order reinstatement of the mortgage as per the terms of the coupon books, because that was the last communication from First Financial/PHH (P) containing the terms of the revised payment schedule on the mortgage. Affirmed.

▶ ANALYSIS

The kind of equitable relief granted by the court in this case is considered "extraordinary" and to be granted only in the most limited of circumstances to avoid injustice. Here the equities seemed to favor the Barkers (D) because First Financial/PHH (P) sent them mixed messages, failed to communicate promptly, and failed to ensure that the Barkers (D) received communications that were purportedly sent, thus effectively misleading the Barkers (D). Had First Financial/PHH (P) responsibly communicated with the Barkers (D), the equities likely would not have been against First Financial/PHH (P)—but by the same token, the Barkers (D), who seemed to take their mortgage obligation seriously, upon receiving timely communications would have, upon receipt of such straightforward communications, been able to avoid foreclosure proceedings altogether.

■═■

Quicknotes

EQUITABLE REMEDY A remedy that is based upon principles of fairness as opposed to rules of law; a remedy involving specific performance rather than money damages.

EQUITY Fairness; justice; the determination of a matter consistent with principles of fairness and not in strict compliance with rules of law.

FORECLOSURE An action to recover the amount due on a mortgage of real property where the owner has failed to meet the mortgage obligations, terminating the owner's interest in the property which must then be sold to satisfy the debt.

■═■

Centex Homes Corp. v. Boag

Condominium builders (P) v. Apartment purchasers (D)

N.J. Super. Ct., 128 N.J. Super. 385, 320 A.2d 194 (1974).

NATURE OF CASE: Motion for summary judgment in breach of contract action.

FACT SUMMARY: After Boag (D) contracted to purchase a condominium from Centex Homes Corp. (P), Boag (D) was notified by his employer that he was being transferred.

🏛 **RULE OF LAW**
Specific performance is unavailable to a seller of real estate where the seller will suffer economic damage for which his remedy at law is adequate.

FACTS: Mr. and Mrs. Boag (D) contracted to purchase an apartment in Centex Home Corp.'s (Centex) (P) condominium project. Shortly thereafter, Boag (D) learned his employer was transferring him to Chicago. Consequently, Boag (D) advised Centex (P) that he was canceling the sale. Centex (P) sued Boag (D) for specific performance of the sale and filed a motion for summary judgment.

ISSUE: Is specific performance unavailable to a seller of real estate where the seller will suffer economic damage for which his remedy at law is adequate?

HOLDING AND DECISION: (Gelman, J.) Yes. Specific performance is unavailable to a seller of real estate where the seller will suffer economic damage for which his remedy at law is adequate. Here, the subject matter of the real estate transaction has no unique quality but is one of hundreds of virtually identical units being offered. The sales prices for the units are fixed, and the only variance in apartments with the same floor plans is their location within the project. Therefore, damages sustained by Centex (P) from Boag's (D) breach of contract are readily measurable and the damage remedy in law is wholly adequate. Centex's (P) specific performance complaint is dismissed.

▶ *ANALYSIS*

Section 2-506 of the Uniform Land Transaction Act provides that the seller of land is not entitled to specific performance unless the property cannot be resold by him at a reasonable price with reasonable effort. In the instant case, the condominium units were sold by Centex (P) through the showing of sample apartments, and Centex (P) was guaranteed a reasonable price.

■■■

Quicknotes

INADEQUACY OF REMEDY AT LAW Requirement for a suit to be brought in equity that the available legal remedy be unsatisfactory for the desired relief.

SPECIFIC PERFORMANCE An equitable remedy whereby the court requires the parties to perform their obligations pursuant to a contract.

■■■

Laclede Gas Co. v. Amoco Oil Co.

Gas company (P) v. Oil company (D)

522 F.2d 33 (8th Cir. 1975).

NATURE OF CASE: Appeal of order denying specific performance of a contract.

FACT SUMMARY: In a propane delivery contract with Amoco Oil Co. (D), Laclede Gas Co. (P) had the right unilaterally to terminate the agreement.

🏛 RULE OF LAW
A provision in a bilateral contract giving one party the right to terminate unilaterally does not render the contract unenforceable.

FACTS: The predecessors of Laclede Gas Co. (Laclede) (P) and Amoco Oil Co. (Amoco) (D) contracted for the latter to supply the former with propane for distribution to retail customers. The contract provided that the buyer had a right to terminate unilaterally. At one point, Amoco (D) ceased delivery and abrogated the contract. Laclede (P) sued for specific performance. The district court held the contract unenforceable due to Laclede's (P) right of abrogation and dismissed. Laclede (P) appealed. The court of appeals granted review.

ISSUE: Does a provision in a bilateral contract giving one party the right unilaterally to terminate render the contract unenforceable?

HOLDING AND DECISION: (Ross, J.) No. A provision in a bilateral contract giving one party the right unilaterally to terminate does not render the contract unenforceable. As long as a contract contains mutuality of consideration, which is to say, an exchange of obligations, the ability to cancel a contract will not render it unenforceable. Here, the contract had set terms for each side, so mutuality of consideration existed. Moreover, given that a long-term contract is at issue, specific performance is appropriate, since the record shows that Laclede (P) would be unable to find other propane suppliers who would be willing to enter into similar long-term contracts, and, even if it could, it would face considerable expense and trouble that cannot be estimated in advance in making such propane available to its clients. Therefore, Laclede's (P) remedy at law is inadequate, and, on remand, the district court must order specific performance. Reversed and remanded.

▶ ANALYSIS

Amoco (D) argued that, even if the contract was binding, specific performance was not indicated. One proffered reason was that specific performance was not mutually available as a remedy. The court rejected this, noting that this common-law requirement for specific performance had long been abandoned.

■═■

Quicknotes

ABROGATION Annulment; destruction; cancellation.

MUTUALITY OF CONSIDERATION The requirement, which in order for a contract to be enforceable if one party is obligated to render performance pursuant to a contract, then the other party must be similarly obligated.

TERMINATION OF CONTRACT The ending of a contract by either one party upon default by the other or by both parties pursuant to an agreement.

■═■

Lumley v. Wagner

Theater owner (P) v. Singer (D)

Lord Chan. Ct., 1 De C.M.&G. 604, 42 Eng. Rep. 687 (1852).

NATURE OF CASE: Appeal from order enjoining performer from accepting other employment.

FACT SUMMARY: Lumley (P), who had contracted with Wagner (D) for the latter to perform at his theater, sought to enjoin her from performing at another location.

> 🏛 **RULE OF LAW**
> A court may enjoin a performer from engaging in employment when the performer is under contract with another employer.

FACTS: Lumley (P) hired Wagner (D), a singer, to perform at his theater. After signing the contract, Wagner (D) sought to perform elsewhere. Lumley (P) obtained an injunction against Wagner (D) performing elsewhere. Wagner (D) appealed.

ISSUE: May a court enjoin a performer from engaging in employment when the performer is under contract with another employer?

HOLDING AND DECISION: (Lord Leonards, C.) Yes. A court may enjoin a performer from engaging in employment when the performer is under contract with another employer. A court of equity may fashion an order in the nature of specific performance even if, in a literal sense, performance is not ordered. Where an order not to do something tends to encourage the specific performance of a contract, such an order may be made if specific performance is a proper remedy. Here, the court cannot force Wagner (D) to sing; however, by enjoining her from engaging in other performance, it properly invoked its jurisdiction to compel compliance with the contractual terms. Affirmed.

▌ *ANALYSIS*

The court here did not discuss whether specific performance was a proper remedy. It apparently assumed that it was. Generally speaking, contracts involving performers are appropriate for specific performance because of the uniqueness of each performer.

■═■

Quicknotes

INJUNCTION A remedy imposed by the court ordering a party to cease the conduct of a specific activity.

SPECIFIC PERFORMANCE An equitable remedy whereby the court requires the parties to perform their obligations pursuant to a contract.

■═■

CHAPTER 4

The Statute of Frauds

Quick Reference Rules of Law

Yarbro v. Neil B. McGinnis Equipment Co.

Purchaser (D) v. Farm equipment company (P)

Ariz. Sup. Ct., 101 Ariz. 378, 420 P.2d 163 (1966).

NATURE OF CASE: Appeal of damages awarded under a suretyship agreement.

FACT SUMMARY: Yarbro (D) contended that the statute of frauds barred enforcement of an oral suretyship agreement he had made.

🏛 RULE OF LAW
The statute of frauds does not bar enforcement of an oral suretyship agreement if the surety's principal reason for acting was his own benefit.

FACTS: Russell (D) purchased a piece of farm equipment from Neil B. McGinnis Equipment Co. (McGinnis) (P), payments to be made in installments. Russell (D) defaulted, and McGinnis (P) threatened repossession. Yarbro (D), a neighbor of Russell (D), agreed to make payments for Russell (D). Yarbro (D), who had used the tractor extensively, eventually stopped making payments. McGinnis (P) brought a collection action against Russell (D) and Yarbro (D). The trial court awarded $8,751 jointly and severally, and Yarbro (D) appealed, contending that the statute of frauds barred enforcement of his surety agreement. The state's highest court granted review.

ISSUE: Does the statute of frauds bar enforcement of an oral suretyship agreement, if the surety's principal reason for acting was his own benefit?

HOLDING AND DECISION: (Bernstein, V.C.J.) No. The statute of frauds does not bar enforcement of an oral suretyship agreement if the surety's principal reason for acting was his own benefit. The statute of frauds requires that suretyship agreements must be in writing to be enforceable. However, courts have recognized the "primary purpose" exception. Where the primary concern of the guarantor has been to protect his own interest, as opposed to that of the individual benefiting from the surety agreement, the agreement need not have been in writing. Here, Yarbro (D) appears to have guaranteed Russell's (D) payments so that he himself could use the tractor. This shows Yarbro's (D) primary purpose to have been his own benefit, so the agreement did not have to be in writing. However, Yarbro (D) only agreed to pay Russell's (D) delinquent payments, not the entire contract amount, so his liability is reduced accordingly. Affirmed as modified.

▶ ANALYSIS

All states have some version of the statute of frauds. The agreements covered therein vary. The most common agreement found therein is a land sale contract. Suretyship agreements are not universally found in these statutes.

■══■

Quicknotes

JOINT AND SEVERAL LIABILITY Liability amongst tortfeasors allowing the injured party to bring suit against any of the defendants, individually or collectively, and to recover from each up to the total amount of damages awarded.

STATUTE OF FRAUDS A statute that requires specified types of contracts to be in writing in order to be binding.

SURETYSHIP A situation in which one party guarantees payment of the debt of another party to a creditor.

■══■

Professional Bull Riders, Inc. v. AutoZone, Inc.

Company (P) v. Sponsor (D)

Colo. Sup. Co., 113 P.3d 757 (2005).

NATURE OF CASE: State court's answer of question certified to it by federal court in action for breach of contract on an oral contract.

FACT SUMMARY: The parties entered into an oral agreement that would last for two years, but which allowed one party to withdraw halfway through the term. A party withdrew, and the other filed a suit for breach of contract.

🏛 RULE OF LAW
An agreement does not violate the statute of frauds where its terms can fairly and reasonably be interpreted to define alternate obligations, one or more of which can be performed within one year.

FACTS: Professional Bull Riders, Inc. (PBR) (P) conducted events that were sponsored by AutoZone, Inc. (D). For years 2001 and 2002, PBR (P) drafted a written contract under which AutoZone (D) could terminate the agreement by giving PBR (P) written notice of termination no later than Aug. 15, 2001. AutoZone (D) never signed the agreement, and in January 2002, notified PBR (P) that AutoZone (D) would not be sponsoring PBR (P) events in 2002. PBR (P) sued for breach of the oral agreement in federal district court. The district court found that the oral contract could not be performed within one year and was therefore unenforceable under the Colorado statute of frauds, and granted summary judgment to AutoZone (D). The federal court of appeals certified to the state's highest court the following question: is an oral agreement void when: (1) the agreement contemplates performance for a definite period of more than one year but (2) allows the party to be charged an option to terminate the agreement by a certain date less than a year from the making of the agreement and when (3) the party to be charged has not exercised that option to terminate the agreement? The state court answered the question.

ISSUE: Does an agreement violate the statute of frauds where its terms can fairly and reasonably be interpreted to define alternate obligations, one or more of which can be performed within one year?

HOLDING AND DECISION: (Coats, J.) No. An agreement does not violate the statute of frauds where its terms can fairly and reasonably be interpreted to define alternate obligations, one or more of which can be performed within one year. The statute of fraud's one-year provision should be construed narrowly, to bring within the statute only agreements that cannot possibly be performed within one year. It is unnecessary to decide whether an option to terminate a contract must always be construed as an alternative and sufficient means of performance, because the terms of this agreement make it possible that it could be performed within one year, and the one-year provision does not bring the agreement within the statute of frauds. Here, the word "terminate" not only applies to the agreement itself, but expressly limits AutoZone's (D) performance obligation to a specific task—sponsorship for one season—and an interpretation of the election to terminate as defining an alternate obligation is fair, reasonable, and clear. Question answered in the negative.

▶ ANALYSIS

Note that the court expressly states that the issue of whether an agreement was actually performed within one year of its making is not to be a consideration when determining whether the statute of frauds applies. The application of the statute of frauds depends on the terms of the agreement, not on whether it was or was not performed.

■≡■

Quicknotes

STATUTE OF FRAUDS A statute that requires specified types of contracts to be in writing in order to be binding.

■≡■

Eastern Dental Corp. v. Isaac Masel Co.

Retailer of dental products (P) v. Manufacturer (D)

502 F. Supp. 1354 (E.D. Pa. 1980).

NATURE OF CASE: Defense motion for summary judgment in action for breach of contract.

FACT SUMMARY: Eastern Dental Corp. (P) entered into an alleged oral requirements contract with Isaac Masel Co. (Masel) (D), a manufacturer of dental products, and contended that Masel (D) breached that contract when Masel (D) unilaterally terminated the purported agreement.

🏛 RULE OF LAW
A purported oral requirements contract does not satisfy the statute of frauds where there is no written evidence which indicates that the quantity to be delivered under the contract is a party's requirements.

FACTS: Eastern Dental Corp. (EDC) (P) was a manufacturer and retailer of dental products. For four years, Isaac Masel Co. (Masel) (D) supplied certain products to EDC (P) it wished to sell but did not manufacture. During the period of the parties' relationship, several purchase orders and confirmations were exchanged, but no long-term contract was ever signed. Masel (D) finally unilaterally terminated the relationship, and EDC (P) sued for breach of contract, alleging that the parties had a requirements contract that Masel (D) breached, as well as bringing claims for violation of the antitrust law. Masel (D) moved for summary judgment on the breach of contract cause of action, alleging noncompliance with the statute of frauds.

ISSUE: Does a purported oral requirements contract satisfy the statute of frauds where there is no written evidence that indicates that the quantity to be delivered under the contract is a party's requirements?

HOLDING AND DECISION: (Luongo, J.) No. A purported oral requirements contract does not satisfy the statute of frauds where there is no written evidence that indicates that the quantity to be delivered under the contract is a party's requirements. Under the statute of frauds, any contract for the sale of goods over $500 must be in writing, and this requirement applies to both output and requirements contracts. While a requirements contract, by its nature, is indefinite as to price, this does not obviate the necessity for compliance with the statute as to the quantity term. Thus, while the quantity term in requirements contracts need not be numerically stated, there must be some writing which indicates that the quantity to be delivered under the contract is a party's requirements or output. Here, none of the writings between the parties offered such evidence. While certain documents, such as invoices of individual transactions, or letters related to products not at issue in this case, may have indicated that the parties had an ongoing business relationship, they did not, expressly or by implication, reflect that the contract between the parties was for the supply of EDC's (P) requirements of Masel's (D) products. Invoices that solely reflect the terms of individual transactions do not indicate that quantity is to be measured by requirements and, accordingly, do not satisfy the quantity term requirement of the statute of frauds. The remaining documents submitted by the parties also failed to state the requisite quantity term. There were documents concerning credit terms and future shipments of merchandise, but there was no document expressly or impliedly providing that Masel (D) was to supply all of EDC's (P) requirements. Accordingly, the contract failed to satisfy the statute of frauds. Motion granted.

▶ ANALYSIS

A writing which satisfies the requirements of the statute of frauds is only evidence of an agreement and does not necessarily prove the existence or terms of a contract. The implication in this case, therefore, is that since the court failed to find a writing that satisfied the statute's requirements, there was no proof of a requirements contract between the parties. This is in keeping with the purpose of the statute of frauds' writing requirement, which is to "afford a basis for believing that the offered oral evidence rests on a real transaction."

■══■

Quicknotes

REQUIREMENTS CONTRACT An agreement pursuant to which one party agrees to purchase all his required goods or services from the other party exclusively for a specified time period.

STATUTE OF FRAUDS A statute that requires specified types of contracts to be in writing in order to be binding.

SUMMARY JUDGMENT Judgment rendered by a court in response to a motion by one of the parties, claiming that the lack of a question of material fact in respect to an issue warrants disposition of the issue without consideration by the jury.

■══■

Crabtree v. Elizabeth Arden Sales Corp.

Employee (P) v. Employer (D)

N.Y. Ct. App., 305 N.Y. 48, 110 N.E.2d 551 (1953).

NATURE OF CASE: Appeal from affirmance of judgment for plaintiff in action for damages for breach of an employment contract.

FACT SUMMARY: Crabtree (P) was hired by Elizabeth Arden Sales Corp. (D) to be the latter's sales manager. No formal contract was signed but separate writings pieced together showed Crabtree (P) to have been hired for a two-year term with pay raises after the first and second six-month periods. When he did not receive his second pay raise, Crabtree (P) sued for damages for breach.

🏛 RULE OF LAW
Under the statute of frauds, the memorandum expressing the contract that satisfies the statute may be pieced together out of separate writings, connected with one another by their reference to the same subject matter or transaction, with parol evidence permitted to show the connection if it is not obvious.

FACTS: In Sept. 1947, Crabtree (P) began negotiating with Elizabeth Arden Sales Corp. (Arden) (D) for the position of the latter's sales manager. Being unfamiliar with the cosmetics business and giving up a well-paying, secure job, Crabtree (P) insisted upon an agreement for a definite term. He asked for three years at $25,000 per year. But Arden's (D) president, Elizabeth Arden (Miss Arden) (D), offered two years, with $20,000 per year the first six months, $25,000 per year the second six months, and $30,000 per year the second year. This was written down by Miss Arden's (D) personal secretary with the notation "2 years to make good." A few days later, Crabtree (P) telephoned Mr. Johns, Arden's (D) executive vice-president to accept the offer. Crabtree (P) received a "welcome" wire from Miss Arden (D). When he reported for work, a "payroll change" card was made up and initialed by Mr. Johns showing the above pay arrangement with a salary increase noted "as per contractual agreement." Crabtree (P) received his first pay raise as scheduled, but not his second one. Miss Arden (D) allegedly refused to approve the second increase, denying Crabtree (P) had been hired for any specific period. Crabtree (P) sued for damages, which the trial court awarded him, and which the state's intermediate appellate court affirmed. The state's highest court granted review.

ISSUE: Under the statute of frauds, may the memorandum expressing the contract that satisfies the statute be pieced together out of separate writings, connected with one another by their reference to the same subject matter or transaction, with parol evidence permitted to show the connection if it is not obvious?

HOLDING AND DECISION: (Fuld, J.) Yes. Under the statute of frauds, the memorandum expressing the contract that satisfies the statute may be pieced together out of separate writings, connected with one another by their reference to the same subject matter or transaction, with parol evidence permitted to show the connection if it is not obvious. First, as it is alleged that the contract is for a period of two years, there must be written evidence of its terms to be enforceable as the two-year performance places it within the statute of frauds. The payroll cards, one initialed by Arden's (D) executive vice-president and the other by its comptroller, unquestionably constituted a memorandum under the statute. It is enough that they were signed with the intent to authenticate the information contained therein and that such information does evidence the terms of the contract. The cards had all essential terms except for duration. But as the memorandum can be pieced together from more than one document, all that is required between the papers is a connection established simply by reference to the same subject matter or transaction. Parol evidence is permissible in order to establish the connection. As the note prepared by Miss Arden's (D) personal secretary shows, it was made in Miss Arden's (D) presence as well as that of Johns and of Crabtree (P); hence, the dangers of parol evidence were at a minimum. All of the terms must be set out in writing and cannot be shown by parol. That memo, the paper signed by Johns, and the paper signed by the comptroller all refer on their face to the Crabtree (P) transaction. The comptroller's paper shows that it was prepared for the purpose of a "salary increase per contractual arrangements with Miss Arden" (D). That is a reference to more than comprehensive evidence and parol evidence can explain. "[Two] years to make good" probably had no other purpose than to denote the duration of the arrangement and parol evidence may explain its meaning. Affirmed.

▶ ANALYSIS

When there is more than one writing and all are signed by the party to be charged, and it is clear by their contents that they relate to the same transaction, there is little problem. When not all the documents are signed, difficulties obviously crop up. It becomes difficult to say the memorandum has been authenticated to the party to be charged. When the unsigned document is physically attached to the signed writing, the statute of frauds is satisfied. And, as illustrated by this case, this is true when the signed document by its terms expressly refers

Continued on next page.

to the unsigned document. The cases conflict where the papers are not attached or fail to refer to the other. The minority holds that is a failure to show sufficient authentication. The better view is that if the signed document does not expressly refer to the unsigned, it is sufficient if internal evidence refers to the same subject matter or transaction. If so, extrinsic evidence is admissible to help show the connection between the documents.

■═■

Quicknotes

PAROL EVIDENCE RULE Doctrine precluding parties to an agreement from introducing evidence of prior or contemporaneous agreements in order to repudiate or alter the terms of a written contract.

STATUTE OF FRAUDS A statute that requires specified types of contracts to be in writing in order to be binding.

■═■

Wagers v. Associated Mortgage Investors

Real estate buyer (P) v. Mortgage company (D)

Wash. Ct. App., 19 Wash. App. 758, 577 P.2d 622 (1978).

NATURE OF CASE: Appeal from dismissal of action seeking specific enforcement of a land sale contract.

FACT SUMMARY: Wagers (P) contended that a series of letters between his attorney and seller, Associated Mortgage Investors (D), which disagreed over the nature of Wagers's (P) deposit for the purchase of real estate, satisfied the statute of frauds.

🏛 RULE OF LAW

(1) A unilaterally executed earnest money agreement and a series of letters between a buyer and a seller of real estate disagreeing over the nature of that agreement will not satisfy the statute of frauds.

(2) The arrangement by a buyer of real estate of financing for development of the subject of the sale does not constitute sufficient part performance to make the sale an exception to the statute of frauds where this act alone does not unmistakably point to the existence of the claimed agreement.

FACTS: Wagers (P) and Associated Mortgage Investors (AMI) (D) entered into negotiations regarding the former purchasing certain real estate from the latter. Wagers (P) made a supposedly nonrefundable deposit of $10,000. The purchase price was to be $270,000. A series of letters were passed between Wagers's (P) attorney and AMI's (D) agents. Wagers's (P) letters always referred to the sale as already agreed upon, and AMI's letters always referred to the sale as contingent upon clearing title and AMI's (D) board's approval. Title did clear, but AMI (D) backed away from the transaction. Wagers (P) sued for specific performance. AMI (D) invoked the statute of frauds and obtained summary judgment. Wagers (P) appealed. The state's intermediate appellate court granted review.

ISSUE:

(1) Will a unilaterally executed earnest money agreement and a series of letters between a buyer and a seller of real estate disagreeing over the nature of that agreement satisfy the statute of frauds?

(2) Does the arrangement by a buyer of real estate of financing for development of the subject of the sale constitute sufficient part performance to make the sale an exception to the statute of frauds where this act alone does not unmistakably point to the existence of the claimed agreement?

HOLDING AND DECISION: (Dore, J.)

(1) No. A unilaterally executed earnest money agreement and a series of letters between a buyer and a seller of real estate disagreeing over the nature of that agreement will not satisfy the statute of frauds. It is true that, for the statute to be satisfied, it is not necessary that an official "contract of sale," enumerating all terms, be signed. A series of documents may be consolidated to satisfy the statute. However, these documents must show agreement as to essential terms. Here, the letters disagreed over the nature of Wagers's (P) deposit and over whether a sale had actually occurred. This being so, the exchange of documents never indicated agreement over essential terms, and the statute therefore was not satisfied.

(2) No. The arrangement by a buyer of real estate of financing for development of the subject of the sale does not constitute sufficient part performance to make the sale an exception to the statute of frauds where this act alone does not unmistakably point to the existence of the claimed agreement. Part performance is a recognized exception of the requirement of the statute of frauds. One of the requirements of the doctrine of part performance is that the acts relied upon as constituting part performance must unmistakably point to the existence of the claimed agreement. If they may be accounted for by some other hypothesis, they are not sufficient. Generally, there are three principal elements or circumstances involved in determining whether there has been sufficient part performance by a purchaser of real estate under an oral contract otherwise within the statute of frauds: (1) delivery and assumption of actual and exclusive possession of the land; (2) payment or tender of the consideration, whether in money, other property, or services; and (3) the making of permanent, substantial, and valuable improvements, referable to the contract. Each case, however, must be decided on its specific facts. Here, the only act undertaken by Wagers (P) alleged to constitute part performance was his arranging for financing based on conversations that anticipated, but did not confirm, the sale. At best, this arrangement for financing was equally consistent with the earnest money agreement or with the decision to make an offer to increase the purchase price rather than a sale. Thus, none of the three principal elements of part performance were

Continued on next page.

involved, and Wagers's (D) act did not unmistakably point to the existence of the claimed agreement. Affirmed.

▶ ANALYSIS

The Restatement (Second) of Contracts, § 129, provides that a real estate sales contract may be enforced notwithstanding noncompliance with the statute of frauds where the party seeking enforcement, in reasonable reliance on the contract and on the continuing assent of the party against whom enforcement is sought, has so changed his position that injustice can be avoided only by specific enforcement. Under this view, the promisee must act in reasonable reliance on the promise, before the promisor has repudiated it, and the action must be such that the remedy of restitution is inadequate. If these requirements are met, neither taking of possession nor payment of money nor the making of improvements is essential.

■══■

Quicknotes

DETRIMENTAL RELIANCE Action by one party resulting in loss that is based on the conduct or promises of another.

PROMISSORY ESTOPPEL A promise that is enforceable if the promisor should reasonably expect that it will induce action or forbearance on the part of the promisee, and does in fact cause such action or forbearance, and it is the only means of avoiding injustice.

STATUTE OF FRAUDS A statute that requires specified types of contracts to be in writing in order to be binding.

■══■

Thomson Printing Machinery Co. v. B. F. Goodrich Co.

Printing machinery merchant (P) v. Surplus equipment dealer (D)

714 F.2d 744 (7th Cir. 1983).

NATURE OF CASE: Appeal of judgment n.o.v. dismissing action for damages for breach of contract.

FACT SUMMARY: B. F. Goodrich Co. (D) failed to object to a memorandum from surplus equipment buyer Thomson Printing Machinery Co. (P) confirming the sale of a surplus printer.

🏛 RULE OF LAW
A failure by a party selling an item in the regular course of business to object to a memo confirming that sale may result in a waiver of the statute of frauds defense.

FACTS: B. F. Goodrich Co. (Goodrich) (D) sold surplus equipment as a matter of practice. A representative of Thomson Printing Machinery Co. (Thomson) (P) allegedly agreed with Meyers, an agent of Goodrich (D), to purchase a surplus printer for $9,000. The agreement was not signed there, but Thomson (P) sent a confirming letter to Goodrich (D). The letter was not directed to anyone in particular, and Meyers did not see it until weeks later. Goodrich (D) refused to consummate the sale, and Thomson (P) sued. A jury held in favor of Thomson (P), but the district court granted judgment n.o.v., ruling that the action was barred by the statute of frauds. Thomson (P) appealed. The court of appeals granted review.

ISSUE: May a failure by a party selling an item in the regular course of business to object to a memo confirming that sale result in a waiver of the statute of frauds defense?

HOLDING AND DECISION: (Cudahy, J.) Yes. A failure by a party selling an item in the regular course of business to object to a memo confirming that sale may result in a waiver of the statute of frauds. This is the so-called "merchants" exception to the statute. A merchant who makes an oral contract and receives written confirmation of same must object within 10 days after receipt, or the statute of frauds objection is waived. Here, the jury found an oral contract to have been made, and that Goodrich (D) did not object to Thomson's (P) confirmation after receiving it. It does not matter that it was not received by anyone at Goodrich (D) who had reason to know its contents. Had Goodrich's (D) mailroom been exercising reasonable due diligence—which as a matter of law it was not—the confirmation would have reached Meyers in a timely manner. Accordingly, the receipt by Goodrich (D) of the confirmation and its failure to object to it constituted a waiver of the statute, so the district court erred in granting judgment n.o.v. Reversed and remanded.

▶ ANALYSIS

The statute of frauds is found in Uniform Commercial Code (UCC) § 2-201. Subsection (2) codifies the merchants exception. This exception developed at common law and was incorporated into the UCC. It is consistent with the UCC philosophy of promoting valid contracts.

Quicknotes

JUDGMENT N.O.V. A judgment entered by the trial judge reversing a jury verdict if the jury's determination has no basis in law or fact.

MERCHANT'S CONFIRMATORY MEMO A memorandum, the issuance of which gives formal ratification to a prior agreement which was unenforceable, rendering it binding and valid.

STATUTE OF FRAUDS A statute that requires specified types of contracts to be in writing in order to be binding.

McIntosh v. Murphy

Assistant manager (P) v. Employer (D)

Haw. Sup. Ct., 52 Haw. 29, 469 P.2d 177 (1970).

NATURE OF CASE: Appeal from jury verdict for plaintiff in action to enforce an oral employment contract.

FACT SUMMARY: Murphy (D) hired McIntosh (P) as his sales manager, which required relocation to Hawaii, but McIntosh (P), who claimed he had an oral employment contract for a one-year period, was terminated, allegedly without cause, after a little over two months on the job.

🏛 RULE OF LAW
Either part performance or equitable estoppel will remove an oral contract from the statute of frauds to avoid an injustice that would otherwise result from strict adherence to the statute of frauds.

FACTS: Murphy (D) hired McIntosh (P) as his assistant sales manager. The job required McIntosh (P) to move to Hawaii from Los Angeles. After a little over two months on the job, McIntosh (P) was fired. McIntosh (P) brought suit, alleging that he had been given an oral employment contract for a one-year period and had been fired without cause. Murphy (D) alleged that the contract was terminable at will and that even if the contract was for one year, it related from the time of acceptance and would extend for more than one year, hence violating the statute of frauds, which requires a writing for contracts that cannot be completed in one year or less. The contract herein would allegedly have been for one year and one or two days. The judge instructed the jury that substantial detrimental reliance by McIntosh (P) on the oral contract and/or part performance would take the contract out of the statute of frauds. The jury found a one-year contract existed and rendered a verdict for McIntosh (P). The state's supreme court granted review.

ISSUE: Will either part performance or equitable estoppel remove an oral contract from the statute of frauds to avoid an injustice that would otherwise result from strict adherence to the statute of frauds?

HOLDING AND DECISION: (Levinson, J.) Yes. Either part performance or equitable estoppel will remove an oral contract from the statute of frauds to avoid an injustice that would otherwise result from strict adherence to the statute of frauds. It is unnecessary to decide whether the employment contract was for more than one year. Equity provides amelioration from a harsh mechanical application of a rule such as the statute of frauds. Estoppel has been granted where there was substantial reliance on the oral contract. Either part performance of the contract or equitable estoppel will take the contract outside of the application of the statute. The requirements for finding equitable estoppel are: (1) a promise which may reasonably be expected to induce an action or forbearance; (2) injustice resulting from an application of the statute; (3) no other remedy is available. Here, McIntosh (P) moved 2,200 miles in reliance on the promisor, rented an apartment, and was out of work in Hawaii. These facts estop Murphy (D) from pleading the statute as a defense. Affirmed.

DISSENT: (Abe, J.) It was for the jury to determine if the contract came within the statute of frauds, not the trial judge who instructed the jury that the time question was not material. The statute of frauds was enacted by the legislature to handle the kind of disputes this case presents, and the courts should not circumvent that statutory authority by exercising equity powers. The court is limited to interpreting the statute, and if the result is unjust, it is up to the legislature to remedy that injustice, not the courts.

▶ ANALYSIS

Non-application of the statute is based upon a desire to avoid unconscionable results. Most jurisdictions allow equitable exceptions (some of which are codified). Other jurisdictions take the mechanistic approach of the dissent herein, on the ground that it is for the legislature to effectuate equitable changes. The exception of part performance normally is applied to non-divisible contracts to avoid unjust enrichment.

■=■

Quicknotes

AMELIORATE Improve.

EQUITABLE ESTOPPEL A doctrine that precludes a person from asserting a right to which he or she was entitled due to his or her action, conduct or failing to act, causing another party to justifiably rely on such conduct to his or her detriment.

PART PERFORMANCE Exception to the Statute of Frauds rendering a contract enforceable if one party commenced performance in reliance on the existence of a contract and there is no other explanation for the party's conduct.

STATUTE OF FRAUDS A statute that requires specified types of contracts to be in writing in order to be binding.

■=■

CHAPTER 5

The Parol Evidence Rule and Interpretation of the Contract

Quick Reference Rules of Law

Mitchill v. Lath

Property buyer (P) v. Ice house owner (D)

N.Y. Ct. App., 247 N.Y. 377, 160 N.E. 646 (1928).

NATURE OF CASE: Appeal from affirmance of grant of specific performance.

FACT SUMMARY: Mitchill (P) bought some property from Lath (D) pursuant to a full and complete written sales contract. She sought to compel Lath (D) to perform on his parol agreement to remove an ice house on neighboring property.

🏛 RULE OF LAW
An oral agreement is permitted to vary a written contract only if it is collateral in form, does not contradict express or implied conditions of the written contract, and consists of terms that the parties could not reasonably have been expected to include in the written contract.

FACTS: Mitchill (P), through a contract executed by her husband, bought some property from Lath (D). The written contract of sale was completely integrated. Lath (D) then made an oral agreement with Mitchill (P) that in consideration of her purchase of the property, he would remove an ice house which he maintained on neighboring property and which Mitchill (P) found objectionable. After Mitchill (P) bought the property, Lath (D) refused to honor the oral agreement. Mitchill (P) sued for specific performance, which the trial court granted, and which the state's intermediate appellate court affirmed. The state's highest court granted review.

ISSUE: Is an oral agreement permitted to vary a written contract only if it is collateral in form, does not contradict express or implied conditions of the written contract, and consists of terms that the parties could not reasonably have been expected to include in the original writing?

HOLDING AND DECISION: (Andrews, J.) Yes. An oral agreement is permitted to vary a written contract only if it is collateral in form, does not contradict express or implied conditions of the written contract, and consists of terms that the parties could not reasonably have been expected to include in the original writing. Here, the oral agreement does not meet all these requirements since, although it is collateral in form, it is closely related to the subject of the written contract and one reasonably would have expected its terms to have been included in the written agreement. The oral agreement can also be said to contradict the conditions of the written contract. The fact that the written contract was made with her husband while the oral agreement was made with Mitchill (P) herself is not determinative since the deed was given to her and it is evident that she, and not her husband, was the principal in the transaction. Reversed.

DISSENT: (Lehman, J.) The general rule formulated by the majority is correct, but the majority misapplies it to the facts at bar. All of the elements necessary to permit an oral agreement to vary a written one are present in this case. First, there is no dispute that the oral agreement is collateral in form. Second, all the terms of the written contract were fulfilled, so that Lath's (D) obligation to remove the ice house is not inconsistent with the written contract unless the written contract itself contains a provision, express or implied, that Lath (D) is not to do anything not expressed in the written contract. However, there is no such expression provision in the written contract, and such a provision may be implied only if the additional obligation is "so clearly connected with the principal transactions as to be part and parcel of it," and is not "one that the parties would not ordinarily be expected to embody in the writing"—i.e., the issue is reduced to whether the third condition of the test is met. Here, that condition was met. The written contract, which was one for the conveyance of land, was complete on its face, and the obligation to remove a building on other property that was not part of the conveyance was not connected with the obligation to convey. The only connection is that one agreement would not have been made had the other not been made. Accordingly, the second and third conditions of the test are met.

▶ ANALYSIS

Uniform Commercial Code § 2-202 provides, "Terms with respect to which the writings of the parties agree or which are set forth in a writing intended by the parties as a final expression of their agreement may not be contradicted by evidence of any prior agreement or of a contemporaneous oral agreement but may be explained or supplemented by course of dealing or usage of trade, or by course of performance, and by evidence of consistent additional terms unless the court finds the writing to have been intended as a complete and exclusive statement of the terms of the agreement." The section, according to the official commentator, conclusively rejects any assumption that, because a writing is final in some respects, it is to be interpreted as including all matters agreed upon by the parties.

■━■

Continued on next page.

Quicknotes

COLLATERAL AGREEMENT An agreement that is made prior to or contemporaneous with a written agreement, which is admissible in evidence as long as it is consistent with the written document.

EXPRESS CONDITION A condition that is expressly stated in the terms of a written instrument.

IMPLIED CONDITION A condition that is not expressly stated in the terms of an agreement, but which is inferred from the parties' conduct or the type of dealings involved.

PAROL EVIDENCE RULE Doctrine precluding parties to an agreement from introducing evidence of prior or contemporaneous agreements in order to repudiate or alter the terms of a written contract.

■≡■

Betaco, Inc. v. Cessna Aircraft Co.

Airplane purchaser (P) v. Seller (D)

32 F.3d 1126 (7th Cir. 1994).

NATURE OF CASE: Appeal from partial summary judgment in favor of plaintiff in suit alleging breach of an express warranty.

FACT SUMMARY: Betaco, Inc. (P) contracted to buy a new jet airplane advertised to have a greater range than its predecessor, but later became convinced that it would not have a greater range and canceled the purchase, alleging breach of an express warranty.

🏛 **RULE OF LAW**
Under Uniform Commercial Code (UCC) § 2-202 (the parol evidence rule), in ascertaining whether the parties intended their contract to be completely integrated, a court looks beyond the four corners of the document to the circumstances surrounding the transaction, including the words and actions of the parties.

FACTS: Betaco, Inc. (P) agreed to purchase a Citation-Jet from Cessna Aircraft Co. (Cessna) (D) based in part on Cessna's (D) representation in a cover letter accompanying the purchase agreement that the new jet was much faster, more efficient, and had more range than an earlier model. After advancing $150,000, Betaco (P) became convinced that the CitationJet did not have a greater range. It canceled the purchase. When Cessna (D), however, refused to return the $150,000 deposit, Betaco (P) sued for breach of an express warranty. The district court rejected Cessna's (D) contention that the purchase agreement was a fully integrated document that precluded Betaco's (P) attempt to rely on this warranty, notwithstanding the agreement contained an integration clause. A jury concluded that the cover letter did amount to an express warranty which was breached and Betaco (P) was awarded partial summary judgment on the integration issue and was also awarded damages. Cessna (D) appealed, alleging that the trial court erred in concluding that the contract signed by both parties was not a fully integrated contract containing a complete and exclusive statement of the parties' agreement. The court of appeals granted review.

ISSUE: Under UCC § 2-202 (the parol evidence rule), in ascertaining whether the parties intended their contract to be completely integrated, does a court look beyond the four corners of the document to the circumstances surrounding the transaction, including the words and actions of the parties?

HOLDING AND DECISION: (Rovner, J.) Yes. Under UCC § 2-202 (the parol evidence rule), in ascertaining whether the parties intended their contract to be

completely integrated, a court looks beyond the four corners of the document to the circumstances surrounding the transaction, including the words and actions of the parties. Absent an ambiguity, the intent of the parties is to be determined from the face of the contract, without resort to extrinsic evidence. As a threshold matter, because the issue reviewed is whether the district court erred in granting summary judgment on the integration issue, review is de novo. As to whether the parties intended the purchase agreement to be fully integrated, first, the warranty limitation clause of the purchase agreement expressly provides that Cessna (D) made no warranties beyond those included in the agreement itself. However, if in fact Cessna (D) had made an express warranty in its cover letter, the disclaimer in the purchase agreement would be insufficient to disclaim it if it was found to be unreasonable. On the other hand, this limitation is subject to UCC § 2-202, so that if the signed contract is deemed fully integrated, the plaintiff is precluded from attempting to establish any express warranty outside the signed contract. Second, although not dispositive, the presence of a merger clause is strong evidence that the parties intended the writing to be the complete and exclusive agreement between them. The integration clause in the purchase agreement was straightforward and was not hidden in any way. Therefore, it is strong evidence that the parties intended the agreement to be fully integrated. Third, the district court focused on another circumstance that courts frequently consider in assessing the degree to which a contract is integrated: is the term contained in a purported warranty outside the contract one that the parties would have included in the contract itself had they intended it to be part of the agreement? Here, the district thought that the representation as to the relative range of the CitationJet was not such a term, partly because it was not a central term of the contract. However, as a matter of law, it cannot be said that that the range of the aircraft was not something that certainly would be included in the agreement. On the contrary, the specifications made part of the contract did contain an express representation as to the range of the CitationJet. Thus, the extraneous reference to the range of the aircraft is less like a supplemental term about which the contract is otherwise silent, and more like a potentially conflicting term that would be excluded from admission into evidence. The fact that this representation was presented in a cover letter does not change that conclusion. On the one hand, it can be argued that because the reference was informal, it was without language that might alert the reader that the contract should include a comparable provision. On the other hand, however, one might just as readily

Continued on next page.

CASENOTE® LEGAL BRIEFS **105**
Contracts

infer from this that the contents of the letter were not meant to supplement the purchase agreement—especially given that other specifications of the plane that did supplement the agreement were very detailed. In sum, the circumstances identified by the district court did not establish, as a matter of law, that the purchase agreement was not fully integrated and that extrinsic evidence of additional, consistent terms was therefore admissible. Reversed and remanded; jury verdict vacated.

▶ ANALYSIS

The court, sua sponte, referred to an affidavit that implied that the purchase agreement was the culmination of discussions between the parties as to the jet's specifications. In this regard, the court remarked that "If, in fact, there were substantial discussions preceding Betaco's commitment to the purchase of the CitationJet focusing specifically on the range of the new jet vis-à-vis the Citation I, one might infer that the signed agreement did not, ultimately, embody the complete agreement between the parties." While the court warned that it was not saying the evidence should be interpreted that way, it took pains to explain that it was merely giving Betaco (P) every benefit of any reasonable inference that could be drawn from the record. The court also added that "We express no opinion as to the appropriate outcome of this hearing; that is a matter for the district court to decide based on the totality of the circumstances and the resolution of the competing inferences that the evidence permits." The district court found, on remand, that the contract was not integrated, and that the express warranty was therefore admissible. However, on appeal, notwithstanding the hands-off posture it purported to take in its opinion, the Seventh Circuit Court of Appeals nevertheless rendered a directed verdict in Cessna's (D) favor. Arguably, the Court of Appeals—which seemingly had made up its mind that the purchase agreement was integrated—should have rendered summary judgment for Cessna (D) on the first go-round and spared the parties the time and expense of the further proceedings on remand and appeal therefrom.

■■■

Quicknotes

EXTRINSIC EVIDENCE Evidence that is not contained within the text of a document or contract but which is derived from the parties' statements or the circumstances under which the agreement was made.

INTEGRATION CLAUSE A provision in a contract stating that the document represents the total and final expression of the parties' agreement.

■■■

Luria Bros. & Co. v. Pielet Bros. Scrap Iron

Scrap iron buyer (P) v. Supplier (D)

600 F.2d 103 (7th Cir. 1978).

NATURE OF CASE: Appeal of award of damages for breach of contract.

FACT SUMMARY: Pielet Bros. Scrap Iron (D) attempted to introduce testimony that a contract calling for an unconditional sale of goods was in fact contingent upon their receipt of the goods from a particular source.

> ### 🏛 RULE OF LAW
> Where writings intended by the parties to be a final expression of their agreement call for an unconditional sale of goods, parol evidence that the seller's obligations are conditioned upon receiving the goods from a particular supplier is inconsistent so that it must be excluded.

FACTS: Pielet Bros. Scrap Iron (Pielet Bros.) (D) signed an agreement to supply Luria Bros. & Co. (Luria) (P) with iron. The contract contained no conditions. When Pielet Bros. (D) failed to deliver, Luria (P) sued for breach. Pielet Bros. (D) attempted to introduce evidence that the contract was in fact conditioned upon its being able to obtain the iron from a particular source. The district court refused to admit the testimony, and Luria Bros. (P) recovered damages. Pielet Bros. (D) appealed. The court of appeals granted review.

ISSUE: Where writings intended by the parties to be a final expression of their agreement call for an unconditional sale of goods, is parol evidence that the seller's obligations are conditioned upon receiving the goods from a particular supplier inconsistent so that it must be excluded?

HOLDING AND DECISION: (Fairchild, C.J.) Yes. Where writings intended by the parties to be a final expression of their agreement call for an unconditional sale of goods, parol evidence that the seller's obligations are conditioned upon receiving the goods from a particular supplier is inconsistent so that it must be excluded. The parol evidence rule, codified at Uniform Commercial Code (UCC) § 2-202, prohibits testimony which contradicts a writing intended to memorialize the final intent of the parties. "Contradiction" may be defined as the absence of reasonable harmony in terms of the language and respective obligations of the parties. Here, Pielet's (D) proffered testimony would substantially change its obligations and, therefore, constitutes a contradiction, rather than a supplementation or explanation of the agreement. Accordingly, the parol evidence rule was properly invoked. Affirmed.

▶ ANALYSIS

The parol evidence rule arose at early common law. It has since been codified in many states, as well as the UCC. The parol evidence rule, while making inadmissible evidence inconsistent with a final writing, does permit evidence which explains a writing. The distinction can sometimes be elusive; however, an explanation supposedly should not contradict a reasonable reading of the terms of the agreement.

■══■

Quicknotes

CONTRADICTION Evidence that substantially changes the obligations of the parties.

PAROL EVIDENCE RULE Doctrine precluding parties to an agreement from introducing evidence of prior or contemporaneous agreements in order to repudiate or alter the terms of a written contract.

■══■

Lee v. Joseph E. Seagram & Sons

Seagram employee (P) v. Company (D)

552 F.2d 447 (2d Cir. 1977).

NATURE OF CASE: Appeal of award of damages for breach of oral contract.

FACT SUMMARY: Lee (P) agreed in writing to sell his interest in a distributorship to Seagram & Sons (Seagram) (D), and Lee (P) claimed Seagram (D) had orally agreed to offer Lee's sons (P) another distributorship.

RULE OF LAW

Where the parties have a written agreement, the parol evidence rule does not bar proof of a contemporaneous oral agreement that is not of a type which would be expected to be included in the writing.

FACTS: Lee (P) had worked for Joseph E. Seagram & Sons (Seagram) (D) for 36 years. In 1958, Lee (P) and his sons (P) acquired 50 percent of a distributorship from Seagram (D). In 1970, the Lees (P) and their co-owners agreed in writing to sell the distributorship back to Seagram (D). The writing contained no integration clause. Lee (P) alleged that he and Yogman, a long-time friend and executive vice president of Seagram (D), orally conditioned the sale on Seagram's (D) placing Lee's sons (P) in a new distributorship of their own. In 1972, the Lees (P) sued Seagram (D) for breaching the oral agreement by failing to get the sons (P) a distributorship. Seagram (D) argued that the oral agreement either induced the sale or was part of consideration for the sale. Failure to include it in the writing meant proof of the oral agreement was barred by the parol evidence rule. The district court held that the parties did not intend the written sales agreement to be a complete integration of all mutual promises. Thus, the oral agreement was collateral and the jury could hear evidence of its existence. The jury awarded the Lees (P) $400,000, and Seagram (D) appealed. The court of appeals granted review.

ISSUE: Where the parties have a written agreement, does the parol evidence rule bar proof of a contemporaneous oral agreement that is not of a type which would be expected to be included in the writing?

HOLDING AND DECISION: (Gurfein, J.) No. Where the parties have a written agreement, the parol evidence rule does not bar proof of a contemporaneous oral agreement that is not of a type which would be expected to be included in the writing. In such a case the oral agreement is independent and may be proven, like any oral contract, by parol evidence. Here, the oral agreement would not be expected to be part of the writing. Employ-

ment agreements which survive the closing of a sale of corporate assets normally are not included in the written sales agreement. The close relationship between Lee (P) and Yogman makes it very possible they could have struck a handshake deal for Lee's sons (P) which the men would not have felt was integrated with the written sales agreement. The writing contained no integration clause. The oral agreement does not contradict the terms of the written agreement. Affirmed.

ANALYSIS

Restatement (Second) of Contracts § 216 and Uniform Commercial Code § 2-202 provide that a written contract may be explained or supplemented by consistent additional terms found in a contemporaneous oral agreement if under the circumstances such terms might naturally be omitted from the writing. If the terms naturally would be included, the writing is "completely integrated," and the oral agreement is not "collateral." In such circumstances, the parol evidence rule bars the admission of evidence of the oral terms.

Quicknotes

CONTEMPORANEOUS At the same time.

INTEGRATION CLAUSE A provision in a contract stating that the document represents the total and final expression of the parties' agreement.

PAROL EVIDENCE RULE Doctrine precluding parties to an agreement from introducing evidence of prior or contemporaneous agreements in order to repudiate or alter the terms of a written contract.

Pym v. Campbell

Inventor (P) v. Buyer of invention (D)

Q.B., 6 Ellis & Blackburn 370 (1856).

NATURE OF CASE: Rule nisi for new trial on ground of misdirection.

FACT SUMMARY: Subject to an oral understanding that his engineer had to approve Pym's (P) invention, Campbell (D) agreed in writing to purchase the patent on Pym's (P) invention.

🏛 RULE OF LAW
Parol evidence may be admitted to show that the parties to a written agreement also orally agreed that no performance would be due until a certain condition was satisfied.

FACTS: Pym (P) invented a machine he wished to sell to Campbell (D). Pym (P) and Campbell (D) agreed on a purchase price and set up a meeting for Pym (P) to explain his invention to Campbell's (D) two engineers. Because Pym (P) arrived late, only one engineer heard Pym (P) and approved the machine. To avoid further trouble, Pym (P) and Campbell (D) agreed to sign an agreement which would be effective if Campbell's (D) second engineer approved. He did not approve it. Pym (P) sued Campbell (D) for breach of the agreement to purchase the patent. At trial, the jury found for Campbell (D) on the grounds that the oral condition was not fulfilled and no agreement was reached.

ISSUE: May parol evidence be admitted to show that the parties to a written agreement also orally agreed that no performance would be due until a certain condition was satisfied?

HOLDING AND DECISION: (Erle, J.) Yes. Parol evidence may be admitted to show that the parties to a written agreement also orally agreed that no performance would be due until a certain condition was satisfied. Generally evidence extraneous to the written contents of an agreement is not competent to vary the terms contained therein. However, parol evidence may be admitted to show no agreement would exist at all until an orally discussed condition is fulfilled. Here Pym (P) and Campbell (D) signed the memorandum of terms as a convenience; they did not intend to enter an agreement until Campbell's (D) second engineer approved the invention. Evidence of this oral condition was properly introduced at trial. As the condition was not met, no contract arose. Rule discharged.

DISSENT: (Serjt, J.) When a contract is reduced to writing, oral terms not included in the writing are outside of the purview of the contract.

CONCURRENCE: (Crompton, J.) No rule prevents a party to a contract from demonstrating that the contract was signed in error or that there would be no agreement until a certain condition was fulfilled. The parties may not vary a written agreement, but may show they never came to an agreement at all.

CONCURRENCE: (Lord Campbell, C.J.) Evidence to the fact that an agreement was never entered into is admissible as parol evidence.

▶ ANALYSIS

Restatement (Second) of Contracts § 217 is not in accord with this holding, i.e., that the approval of Campbell's (D) engineer was a condition to the very formation of the contract. It would hold that this approval would not be necessary to render the contract void but would merely make Campbell's (D) duty to pay Pym (P) conditional on the approval. The modern theory behind the Restatement is to find methods to support the creation of contracts and fulfillment of their terms.

■═■

Quicknotes

CONDITION Requirement; potential future occurrence upon which the existence of a legal obligation is dependent.

PAROL EVIDENCE RULE Doctrine precluding parties to an agreement from introducing evidence of prior or contemporaneous agreements in order to repudiate or alter the terms of a written contract.

RULE NISI Motion by one party to make a final ruling against the opponent, unless the opponent can show cause as to why such ruling should not be ordered.

■═■

Eichengreen v. Rollins, Inc.

Homeowner (P) v. Contractor (D)

Ill. Ct. App., 25 Ill. App. 3d 517, 757 N.E.2d 952 (2001).

NATURE OF CASE: Appeal from a grant of summary judgment in action for breach of contract and negligence.

FACT SUMMARY: Eichengreen (P) brought suit alleging breach of contract and negligence against Rollins, Inc. (D), f/k/a Apollo Central Protection, Inc., resulting from a fire on his property. Rollins (D) moved for summary judgment on both counts. The district court granted Rollins's (D) motion, and Eichengreen (P) appealed.

🏛 RULE OF LAW
The parol evidence rule excludes extrinsic evidence where a letter operating as a complete integration of the parties' agreement exists.

FACTS: In August of 1988, Eichengreen (P) entered into a contract with Rollins, Inc. (D) f/k/a Apollo Central Protection, Inc., to install a security system on his property. Rollins (D) submitted a letter with an estimate of work to be done. Eichengreen (P) did not sign the letter, but made several handwritten modifications and additions to it, including a provision that the system "be in good working order and guaranteed for at least 12 months." In September of 1995, a fire occurred in Eichengreen's (P) house, originating in the bath house (a separate fixture on the property) in the area of the grill. Eichengreen (P) brought suit alleging breach of contract and negligence against Rollins (D) resulting from this fire. Eichengreen (P) contended that the parties' intent had been for Rollins (D) to protect the entire premises, including the bath house, but the trial court excluded evidence of the parties' prior negotiations, which Eichengreen (P) would have introduced to show such intent. Rollins (D) moved for summary judgment on both counts. The trial court granted Rollins's (D) motion, and Eichengreen (P) appealed. The state's intermediate appellate court granted review.

ISSUE: Does the parol evidence rule exclude extrinsic evidence where a letter operating as a complete integration of the parties' agreement exists?

HOLDING AND DECISION: (Gallagher, J.) Yes. The parol evidence rule excludes extrinsic evidence where a letter operating as a complete integration of the parties' agreement exists. The August letter submitted by Rollins (D) to Eichengreen (P) did not make mention of any outside proposal nor did it contain references to any additional discussions relating to smoke sensors in the bathhouse. Notwithstanding that the letter did not contain an integration clause it was a complete integration of the parties' agreement. Any interpretation of that agreement that only Eichengreen (P) had (subjectively) and that was not part of the letter, is immaterial to an analysis of their agreement. The letter did not require Rollins (D) to install smoke detectors in the bathhouse or to provide security for the entire premises. Thus, Eichengreen (P) has failed to demonstrate a breach of contract, and the trial court properly granted summary judgment to Rollins (D) on this count. Affirmed as to this count. [The court also dismissed the negligence count.]

▶ ANALYSIS

Where a contract is integrated and unambiguous on its face, any evidence of "private understanding" should be excluded.

Quicknotes

BREACH OF CONTRACT Unlawful failure by a party to perform its obligations pursuant to contract.

NEGLIGENCE Conduct falling below the standard of care that a reasonable person would demonstrate under similar conditions.

PAROL EVIDENCE RULE Doctrine precluding parties to an agreement from introducing evidence of prior or contemporaneous agreements in order to repudiate or alter the terms of a written contract.

SUMMARY JUDGMENT Judgment rendered by a court in response to a motion by one of the parties, claiming that the lack of a question of material fact in respect to an issue warrants disposition of the issue without consideration by the jury.

Pacific Gas & Electric Co. v. G. W. Thomas Drayage & Rigging Co.

Electric company (P) v. Contractor (D)

Cal. Sup. Ct., 69 Cal. 2d 33, 442 P.2d 641 (1968).

NATURE OF CASE: Appeal from judgment for plaintiff in action for damages for breach of an indemnity contract.

FACT SUMMARY: G. W. Thomas Drayage & Rigging Co. (Thomas) (D) contracted to repair Pacific Gas & Electric Co.'s (Pacific) (P) steam turbine and to perform work at its own risk and expense and to indemnify Pacific (P) against all loss and damage. Thomas (D) also agreed not to procure less than $50,000 insurance to cover liability for injury to property. But when the turbine rotor was damaged, Pacific (P) claimed it was covered under that policy, while Thomas (D) said it was only to cover injury to third persons.

> 🏛 **RULE OF LAW**
> The test of admissibility of extrinsic evidence to explain the meaning of a written instrument is not whether the writing appears to the court to be plain and unambiguous on its face but whether the offered evidence is relevant to prove a meaning to which the language of the instrument is reasonably susceptible.

FACTS: G. W. Thomas Drayage & Rigging Co. (Thomas) (D) contracted to replace the upper metal cover on Pacific Gas & Electric Company's (Pacific) (P) steam turbine and agreed to perform all work "at [its] own risk and expense" and to "indemnify" Pacific (P) against all loss, damage, expense, and liability resulting from injury to property arising out of or in any way connected with performance of the contract. Thomas (D) agreed to obtain not less than $50,000 insurance to cover liability for injury to property. Pacific (P) was to be an additional named insured, but the policy was to contain a cross-liability clause extending the coverage of Pacific's (P) property. During the work, the cover fell, damaging the exposed rotor in the amount of $25,144.51. Thomas (D) during trial offered to prove that its conduct and, under similar contracts entered into by Pacific (P), the indemnity clause was meant to cover injury to third person's property only, not to Pacific's (P).

ISSUE: Is the test of admissibility of extrinsic evidence to explain the meaning of a written instrument not whether the writing appears to the court to be plain and unambiguous on its face but whether the offered evidence is relevant to prove a meaning to which the language of the instrument is reasonably susceptible?

HOLDING AND DECISION: (Traynor, C.J.) Yes. The test of admissibility of extrinsic evidence to explain the meaning of a written instrument is not whether the writing appears to the court to be plain and unambiguous on its face but whether the offered evidence is relevant to prove a meaning to which the language of the instrument is reasonably susceptible. While the trial court admitted that the contract was "the classic language for a third party indemnity provision," it held that the plain language of the contract would give a meaning covering Pacific's (P) damage. However, this admission by the court clearly shows the ambiguous nature of the agreement and the need for extrinsic evidence in order to clarify the intentions of the parties. Extrinsic evidence for the purpose of showing the intent of the parties could be excluded only when it is feasible to determine the meaning of the words from the instrument alone. Rational interpretation requires at least an initial consideration of all credible evidence to prove the intention of the parties. Accordingly, the trial court erroneously refused to consider extrinsic evidence offered to show that the indemnity clause in the contract was not intended to cover injuries to Pacific's (P) property. Reversed.

▶ ANALYSIS

This case strongly disapproves of the "plain meaning rule," which states that if a writing appears clear and unambiguous on its face, the meaning must be determined from "the four corners" of the writing without considering any extrinsic evidence at all. The trial court applied this rule. However, the rule, while generally accepted but widely condemned, would exclude evidence of trade usage, prior dealings of the parties, and even circumstances surrounding the creation of the agreement. Uniform Commercial Code § 2-202 expressly throws out the plain meaning rule. Instead, it allows use of evidence of a course of performance or dealing to explain the writing "unless carefully negated." Here, Judge Traynor greatly expanded the admission of extrinsic evidence to show intent. When he says it should not be admitted only when it is feasible "to determine the meaning the parties gave to the words from the instrument alone," he is saying in all practicality that extrinsic evidence to show intent should be admissible in just about any case, that rarely will the instrument be so exact as to clearly show intent.

■=■

Quicknotes

EXTRINSIC EVIDENCE Evidence that is not contained within the text of a document or contract, but which is derived

Continued on next page.

from the parties' statements or the circumstances under which the agreement was made.

UCC § 2-202 Provides that terms of a writing cannot be contradicted by evidence of prior or contemporaneous oral agreements.

■■■■■

Nanakuli Paving and Rock Co. v. Shell Oil Co.

Paving contractor (P) v. Asphalt seller (D)

664 F.2d 772 (9th Cir. 1981).

NATURE OF CASE: Appeal of judgment n.o.v. setting aside a jury verdict and damage award for breach of contract.

FACT SUMMARY: Nanakuli Paving and Rock Co. (Nanakuli) (P) entered into long-term supply contracts with Shell Oil Co. (Shell) (D) to buy asphalt and objected when Shell (D) raised the price from $44 to $76.

🏛 RULE OF LAW
Under the Uniform Commercial Code, an agreement goes beyond the written words to mean the bargain of the parties in fact, as found in their language or by implication from other circumstances, including course of dealing, usage of trade, and course of performance.

FACTS: Nanakuli Paving and Rock Co. (Nanakuli) (P) was a large asphaltic paving contractor in Hawaii. It had been purchasing all its asphalt requirements from Shell Oil Co. (Shell) (D) under two long-term contracts. Nanakuli (P) incorporated the price of asphalt into bids. However, on 7,200 tons of committed asphalt, Shell (D) suddenly raised the price from $44 to $76, costing Nanakuli (P) $220,800 on the committed asphalt. Nanakuli (P) argued, with substantial support, that price protection was the convention of the asphalt paving trade in Hawaii. Price protection required that the price of committed asphalt be held constant so that contracts would remain at the same profit level as initially negotiated. During the time in question, the management structure of Shell (D) was completely altered. Prior to this time, Shell (D) had always price protected Nanakuli (P). Nanakuli (P) filed a breach of contract action and was awarded $220,800 by a jury. But the court set aside the verdict, and Nanakuli (P) appealed the judgment n.o.v. The court of appeals granted review.

ISSUE: Under the Uniform Commercial Code, does an agreement go beyond the written words to mean the bargain of the parties in fact, as found in their language or by implication from other circumstances, including course of dealing, usage of trade, and course of performance?

HOLDING AND DECISION: (Hoffman, J.) Yes. Under the Uniform Commercial Code, an agreement goes beyond the written words to mean the bargain of the parties in fact, as found in their language or by implication from other circumstances, including course of dealing, usage of trade, and course of performance. Several factors must be analyzed to determine if a trade usage is implied in a contract. First, the breadth of the trade must be examined to determine if the practice in question was sufficiently

widespread to place a party to a contract on notice. Second, the course of dealing or trade usage must be reasonably consistent with the express terms of the contract before a party will be bound beyond the writing. In this case, the appropriate trade in question is the asphalt paving trade on the island of Oahu. Since government agencies in Hawaii refused to accept escalation clauses, the entire asphalt industry practiced price protection. Shell (D) should have been on notice that everyone in the trade assumed this practice was normal. The express term at issue is the term that allowed Shell (D) to charge its posted price at the time of delivery. However, the trade practice modified the term, through a regular course of dealing, to include price protection for committed asphalt. This implied term, while modifying the writing, could reasonably have been found to be incorporated into the contract. Reversed and remanded.

▶ ANALYSIS

The Uniform Commercial Code acknowledges that an agreement is the bargain in fact, and it may extend beyond the written words. Such a consideration is due in part to the fact that certain industries use language in a way peculiar to the trade. Unfortunately, members of a trade may not even be aware that their turns of phrase are incomprehensible to others, and they may not draft a contract accordingly.

■══■

Quicknotes

JUDGMENT NOTWITHSTANDING THE VERDICT A judgment entered by the trial judge reversing a jury verdict if the jury's determination has no basis in law or fact.

■══■

Zell v. American Seating Co.

Contract procurer (P) v. Company (D)

138 F.2d 641 (2d Cir. 1943).

NATURE OF CASE: Appeal from dismissal on summary judgment of action for breach of contract.

FACT SUMMARY: Zell (P) contended that oral agreements he had with American Seating Co. (American) (D) for commissions should be admitted to contradict the terms of a written contract between the parties because, although the writing seemed on its face to embody the parties' complete agreement, the parties had a secret understanding that the contract was deliberately misleading as to their true agreement.

RULE OF LAW

The parol evidence rule should be imposed only in the relatively rare situation where it is quite obvious that the parties intended the writing to solely evidence their agreement and no ambiguities in that writing exists.

FACTS: Zell (P) offered to procure defense contracts for American Seating Co. (American) (D), whereby he would be paid $1,000 per month, and, if he was successful, American (D) would pay him a commission of between 3 and 8 percent on the value of the contracts he procured. Allegedly, American's (D) president orally agreed to these terms, with the understanding between the parties that the exact percentage of any commissions would be fixed after the value of procured contracts was determined. Thereafter, the parties executed a written agreement that embodied the terms of their agreement, except that the writing was silent as to commissions, saying instead that American (D), at its option, could pay Zell (P) a bonus. However, at the time when they executed this writing, the parties orally agreed that the previous oral agreement was still their actual contract, that the writing was deliberately erroneous with respect to Zell's (P) commissions, and that the misstatement in that writing was made solely in order to "avoid any possible stigma which might result" from putting such a provision "in writing." Allegedly, American's (D) president was afraid that Congress would somehow penalize his company for entering into a contingent-fee arrangement during wartime. Zell (P) was very successful, procuring defense contracts worth around $5,950,000. American (D), however, failed to pay him any commissions based on the oral agreements, and Zell (P) sued for damages. The district court granted summary judgment for American (D), and the court of appeals granted review.

ISSUE: Should the parol evidence rule be imposed only in the relatively rare situation where it is quite obvious that the parties intended the writing to solely evidence their agreement and no ambiguities in that writing exists?

HOLDING AND DECISION: (Frank, J.) Yes. The parol evidence rule should be imposed only in the relatively rare situation where it is quite obvious that the parties intended the writing to solely evidence their agreement and no ambiguities in that writing exists. Historically, the parol evidence rule was strictly applied to prevent the introduction of extrinsic evidence to vary the plain meaning of contract terms, and the most important motive for perpetuation of the rule was distrust of juries, coming from the fear that they could not adequately cope with, or would be unfairly prejudiced by, conflicting "parol" testimony. Numerous exceptions riddling the rule, however, have rendered it ineffective to promote this goal. Courts attempted to use the rule to ensure an objective approach in interpreting the meaning of contract terms by asking whether a man of reasonable intelligence acquainted with all operative facts/usage/circumstances prior to and contemporaneous with the making of the contract would interpret its terms to include the meaning ascribed to them by one of the parties? Under such an approach, custom of the trade, prior dealings between the parties, etc. are also to be considered. The difficulty with such a technique, however, is that the fact finder must use its subjective processes to arrive at an "objective" third person, reasonable person viewpoint. Moreover, the rule, contrary to assertions by its supporters, is not essential to business stability; the recognized exceptions to the rule demonstrate strikingly that business can endure even when oral testimony competes with written instruments. Parties to a contract cannot reasonably rely on the sanctity of the written word when it is guarded by so leaky a rule. It should be imposed only in the relatively rare situation where it is quite obvious that the parties intended the writing to solely evidence their agreement and no ambiguities in that writing exists. Reversed and remanded.

ANALYSIS

The holding in this case was short-lived; the United States Supreme Court reversed (322 U.S. 709 (1944), with some of the Justices finding the contract contrary to public policy and some finding Zell's (P) parol evidence validly precluded by the parol evidence rule. Most state courts give greater deference to the parol evidence rule than Judge Frank did in this case, but that is to be expected since he essentially said the rule is almost useless.

Continued on next page.

Quicknotes

PAROL EVIDENCE RULE Doctrine precluding parties to an agreement from introducing evidence of prior or contemporaneous agreements in order to repudiate or alter the terms of a written contract.

■═■

Avoidance of the Contract

Quick Reference Rules of Law

Raffles v. Wichelhaus

Cotton seller (P) v. Buyer (D)

Ct. of Exchequer, 159 Eng. Rep. 375 (1864).

NATURE OF CASE: Action for damages for breach of a contract for the sale of goods.

FACT SUMMARY: Raffles (P) contracted to sell cotton to Wichelhaus (D) to be delivered from Bombay at Liverpool on the ship "Peerless." Unknown to the parties was the existence of two different ships carrying cotton, each named "Peerless" arriving at Liverpool from Bombay, but at different times.

🏛 RULE OF LAW
Where neither party knows or has reason to know of an ambiguity in their contract or, where both know or have reason to know, the ambiguity is given the meaning that each party intended it to have.

FACTS: Raffles (P) contracted to sell Wichelhaus (D) 125 bales of Surrat cotton to arrive from Bombay at Liverpool on the ship "Peerless." Wichelhaus (D) was to pay 17 percent pence per pound of cotton within an agreed-upon time after the arrival of the goods in England. Unknown to the parties, there were two ships called "Peerless" each of which was carrying cotton from Bombay to Liverpool. One ship was to sail in October by Wichelhaus (D) for delivery of the goods while Raffles (P) had expected the cotton to be shipped on the "Peerless" set to sail in December. As Wichelhaus (D) could not have the delivery he expected, he refused to accept the later delivery. Raffles (P) brought suit, and his barrister, Milward, argued that since the contract was for delivery of cotton on a shipped called the Peerless, it was immaterial on which such named ship the cotton arrived. Moreover, he argued that the words "to arrive ex 'Peerless'" meant that the contract would terminate if the ship itself were lost, and that a jury would have to decide if both parties had the same ship named "Peerless" in mind only if the contract had been for the sale of a ship. Milward also argued that Wichelhaus (D) could not use parol evidence to contradict a contract that was unambiguous on its face, and that Wichelhaus's (D) subjective intent is immaterial as that was not made part of the original contract. Moreover, he argued that the timing of sailing was also not part of the original contract. Wichelhaus's (D) barrister, Mellish, made the points adopted by the court, per curiam, in its opinion.

ISSUE: Where neither party knows or has reason to know of an ambiguity in their contract or, where both know or have reason to know, is the ambiguity given the meaning that each party intended it to have?

HOLDING AND DECISION: (Per curiam) Yes. Where neither party knows or has reason to know of an ambiguity in their contract or, where both know or have reason to know, the ambiguity is given the meaning that each party intended it to have. While the contract did not show which particular "Peerless" was intended, the moment it appeared two ships called "Peerless" were sailing from Bombay to Liverpool with a load of cotton, a latent ambiguity arose, and parol evidence was admissible for the purpose of determining that both parties had intended a different "Peerless" to be subject in the contract. When there is an ambiguity, it is given the meaning that each party intended it to have. However, if different meanings were intended there is no contract if the ambiguity relates to a material term. Consequently, there was no meeting of the minds and no binding contract. Judgment for defendants.

▶ ANALYSIS

When there is no integration of the contract, the standard for its interpretation is the meaning that the party making the manifestation should reasonably expect the other party to give it, i.e., a standard of reasonable expectation. This case illustrates an exception to this rule. Where there is an ambiguity, if both parties give the same meaning to it, there is a contract. If the parties each give a different meaning to the ambiguity, then there is no contract, as occurred here. The ambiguity struck at a material term, as payment was to be made within an agreed-upon time after delivery. The parties could not even agree on the time of delivery. The other exception occurs when one party has reason to know of the ambiguity and the other does not, so it will bear the meaning given to it by the latter, that is the party who is without fault. Note that under Uniform Commercial Code § 2-322, delivery ex ship, it would make no difference which ship would be carrier of the goods and the case would have gone the other way. However, Restatement (First) § 71 would appear to follow the general rule of the present case.

■═■

Quicknotes

AMBIGUITY Language that is capable of more than one interpretation.

INTEGRATION OF THE CONTRACT An agreement between two parties to a contract the document represents the total and final expression of their agreement.

PAROL EVIDENCE RULE Doctrine precluding parties to an agreement from introducing evidence of prior or contemporaneous agreements in order to repudiate or alter the terms of a written contract.

■═■

Sherwood v. Walker

Cow buyer (P) v. Seller (D)

Mich. Sup. Ct., 66 Mich. 568, 33 N.W. 919 (1887).

NATURE OF CASE: Appeal from affirmance of judgment for plaintiff in action of replevin for a cow.

FACT SUMMARY: The Walkers (D), having sold a cow to Sherwood (P) in the mistaken belief that it was barren, refused to deliver it.

🏛 RULE OF LAW
A mutual mistake of a material, underlying fact affords a basis for rescission of a contract for the sale of personal property.

FACTS: The Walkers (D) agreed to sell Sherwood (P) a certain cow, "Rose 2nd of Aborlone," for a price of $850. At the time the contract was entered into, the Walkers (D) indicated their belief that the animal was barren. To this, Sherwood (P) replied that he thought she could be made to breed, but that he believed she was not with calf. The cow was not weighed at the time. When the Walkers (D) discovered that the cow was pregnant, and could have been sold for up to $1,000, they refused to deliver it, whereupon Sherwood (P) brought an action of replevin. The trial court rendered judgment for Sherwood (P), and the state's intermediate appellate court affirmed. The state's highest court granted review.

ISSUE: Does a mutual mistake of a material, underlying fact afford a basis for rescission of a contract for the sale of personal property?

HOLDING AND DECISION: (Morse, J.) Yes. A mutual mistake of a material, underlying fact affords a basis for rescission of a contract for the sale of personal property. Where the thing actually delivered or received is different in substance from the thing bargained for and intended to be sold, there is no contract. However, the mutual mistake must not only be as to some material fact, but must also affect the substance of the whole consideration. Here, the mistake was as to a crucial, material fact. The parties would not have made the contract if they knew that the cow was capable of breeding. A barren cow is a different creature than a breeding one. The cow was sold for beef, when in fact she had considerable value as a breeder. As a result, there was no contract formed. Reversed and new trial granted.

DISSENT: (Sherwood, J.) There was no "mutual" mistake here since Sherwood (P) believed the cow would breed and bought her for this purpose, not purely for beef. Merely because neither party could have known for sure at the time they entered their contract whether the cow was barren does not entitle the Walkers (D) to walk away from the deal just because Sherwood's (P) guess was better than

theirs. When a mistaken fact is relied upon as ground for rescission, such fact must not only exist at the time the contract is made, but must have been known to one or both of the parties. Here, neither party could have known whether the cow was in fact barren, so the doctrine of mistake is inapplicable. Regardless, no warranties were attached to the sale by either party.

▶ ANALYSIS

The court's interpretation of the facts in this case suggests the difficulty inherent in ascertaining all the surrounding circumstances in mistaken assumption analysis. As a result, many commentators have suggested an alternative approach. Following the cue of Uniform Commercial Code § 2-615, these commentators have urged that the nondelivery of goods should be excused where, owing to an unexpected occurrence, "the nonoccurrence of which was a basic assumption on which the contract was made," performance has been rendered commercially impracticable.

■══■

Quicknotes

MATERIAL FACT A fact without the existence of which a contract would not have been entered.

MUTUAL MISTAKE A mistake by both parties to a contract, who are in agreement as to what the contract terms should be, but the agreement as written fails to reflect that common intent; such contracts are voidable or subject to reformation.

■══■

Wood v. Boynton

Uncut gem seller (P) v. Jeweler (D)

Wis. Sup. Ct., 64 Wis. 265, 25 N.W. 42 (1885).

NATURE OF CASE: Appeal from directed verdict for defendant in action to recover possession of chattel.

FACT SUMMARY: Boynton (D) purchased an uncut stone from Wood (P) for $1. Neither party realized the stone was a diamond worth $700.

🏛 RULE OF LAW

In the absence of evidence of fraud on the part of the vendee, a mutual mistake as to the nature and value of a thing sold will not afford a basis for rescission of the contract of sale where the thing sold is the same as the thing delivered.

FACTS: Wood (P) sold a stone to the Boynton (D) jewelers for $1. At the time, both parties believed the stone to be a cheap topaz. Later, it was ascertained that the stone was, in fact, an uncut diamond valued at $700. When Wood (P) learned of this, she tendered $1 plus interest for the gem, but the Boyntons (D) refused to deliver it to her. The trial court directed a jury verdict for the Boyntons (D), and the state's highest court granted review.

ISSUE: In the absence of evidence of fraud on the part of the vendee, will a mutual mistake as to the nature and value of a thing sold afford a basis for rescission of the contract of sale where the thing sold is the same as the thing delivered?

HOLDING AND DECISION: (Taylor, J.) No. In the absence of evidence of fraud on the part of the vendee, a mutual mistake as to the nature and value of a thing sold will not afford a basis for rescission of the contract of sale where the thing sold is the same as the thing delivered. The only reasons for rescinding a sale and revesting title in the vendor are that the vendee has committed some fraud in procuring the sale, or that there has been a mistake made by the vendor in delivering an article other than the article sold. In the absence of such circumstances, mutual mistake affords no basis for rescission of a contract of sale. Here, there was no fraud since both parties were ignorant as to the stone's true value. And there was no pretense of any mistake as to the identity of the thing sold. When the sale was made, the stone was open to the investigation of both parties, and since neither knew its intrinsic value, they both supposed that the price paid was adequate. No ground for rescission on the basis of fraud or mistake has here been made out. Affirmed.

▶ ANALYSIS

Since most parties to contracts deal at arm's length, mistakes as to value generally may not be remedied. Each party, as a part of the bargaining process, assumes the risk of his judgment. Some commentators have, however, in focusing on the risk element, distinguished between those cases in which both parties have assumed all risks of value as in the instant case, where neither party knew the stone's true value and those in which the seller has relied on the buyer's expertise in placing a ceiling on the goods negotiated for.

Quicknotes

MUTUAL MISTAKE A mistake by both parties to a contract, who are in agreement as to what the contract terms should be, but the agreement as written fails to reflect that common intent; such contracts are voidable or subject to reformation.

RESCISSION The canceling of an agreement and the return of the parties to their positions prior to the formation of the contract.

Williams v. Glash

Injured passenger (P) v. Other driver (D)

Texas Sup. Ct., 789 S.W.2d 261 (1990).

NATURE OF CASE: Appeal from affirmance of a denial on summary judgment of damages for personal injuries based on a release.

FACT SUMMARY: Although the accident settlement check which Williams (P) accepted for her damaged auto included a release of all claims, Williams (P) sought to recover damages for injuries which she discovered after accepting the check.

🏛 RULE OF LAW
The doctrine of mutual mistake, which allows for the avoidance of contracts where the parties are mistaken about a material assumption of the contract, applies to releases.

FACTS: Williams (P) was involved in a car accident with Glash (D). Although Williams's (P) car was damaged, she appeared to have suffered no personal injuries at the time of the accident. Williams (P) settled the car damage claim with State Farm Insurance, Glash's (D) insurer. There was no discussion or negotiation of any personal injury claim. On the back of the settlement check given to Williams (P) was language which purported to release all claims, including personal injury claims, upon acceptance. Later, Williams (P) was diagnosed with head and neck injuries due to the accident, and she filed suit against Glash (D). The trial court ruled that the suit was barred by the release, and the appeals court affirmed. Williams (P) appealed.

ISSUE: Does the doctrine of mutual mistake, which allows for the avoidance of contracts where the parties are mistaken about a material assumption of the contract, apply to releases?

HOLDING AND DECISION: (Doggett, J.) Yes. The doctrine of mutual mistake, which allows for the avoidance of contracts where the parties are mistaken about a material assumption of the contract, applies to releases. A release is not effective if both parties are mistaken about a material assumption basic to the contract. An unknown injury not contemplated at the time of the release is a material fact basic to the contract. However, parties may intentionally assume the risk of unknown injuries in a release. Consideration of the conduct of the parties is necessary to determine whether this risk was assumed. Although the language of the release signed by Williams (P) was evidence that the risk of unknown injuries was assumed by Williams (P), the settlement of personal injury claims was never discussed or bargained for, and the settlement check equaled the amount of car damage exactly.

Therefore, there is enough evidence to show that the parties were both mistaken about material facts basic to the release. The issue should be determined by a jury, and the summary judgment motion should have been denied. Reversed and remanded.

DISSENT: (Spears, J.) Policy considerations favoring the orderly settlement of disputes override the interest in compensating accident victims. The invalidation of releases poses unreasonable problems for insurers, and here, the majority has effectively rendered useless most releases. By doing so, it will eliminate the reason insurers enter into settlements. The result here is too one-sided in favor of the tort victim.

▶ ANALYSIS

This decision is in accord with the Restatement (Second) of Contracts § 152. This section allows for avoidance of the contract "where a mistake of both parties at the time the contract was made as to a basic assumption on which the contract was made has a material effect on the agreed exchange of performances." A comment to § 152 expressly refers to the conduct of parties to a personal injury release.

■=■

Quicknotes

MATERIAL ASSUMPTION BASIC TO CONTRACT A fact without the existence of which a contract would not have been entered.

MUTUAL MISTAKE A mistake by both parties to a contract, who are in agreement as to what the contract terms should be, but the agreement as written fails to reflect that common intent; such contracts are voidable or subject to reformation.

SUMMARY JUDGMENT Judgment rendered by a court in response to a motion by one of the parties, claiming that the lack of a question of material fact in respect to an issue warrants disposition of the issue without consideration by the jury.

■=■

Bailey v. Ewing

Purchaser of land (P) v. Purchaser of land (D)

Idaho Ct. App., 105 Idaho 636, 671 P.2d 1099 (1983).

NATURE OF CASE: Appeal from decision to quiet title in plaintiff.

FACT SUMMARY: Bailey (P) brought suit to eject Ewing (D) from a disputed piece of land between their properties. Ewing (D) filed a counterclaim against Bailey (P) and third party Erhardt, personal representative of the estate that had sold the properties, to reform the deeds. The trial court found for Bailey (P) and Erhardt. Ewing (D) appealed.

🏛 RULE OF LAW
In the absence of evidence of fraud on the part of the vendee, a mutual mistake as to the nature and value of a thing sold will not afford a basis for rescission of the contract of sale where the thing sold is the same as the thing delivered.

FACTS: Erhardt, the personal representative of decedent Mary Ellen Erhardt, conducted an auction sale of decedent's real and personal property. The real property consisted of two city lots, 5 and 6, plus an additional twenty-foot strip of land adjoining the east side of lot 6. When the bidding was conducted, Ewing (D) purchased lot 5, but no satisfactory bid was received for lot 6. A week after auction, Erhardt sold lot 6 and the adjoining strip to Bailey (P). When selling the properties, Erhardt and the auctioneer informed prospective purchasers that they were unsure of the exact location of the property line, but Erhardt also expressed the belief that the line was at a row of lilac bushes between the properties. During his occupancy of lot 5, Ewing (D) mowed the grass and trimmed the lilac bushes in the strip between what he believed was the boundary line of his property—the lilac bushes—and his house. Later, Ewing (D) erected a fence around this area. Bailey (P) then ordered a survey to be conducted and learned where the "true" line was. The true line, in fact, cut through the eaves of Ewing's (D) house. Bailey (P) asserted his claim to this strip of land and ordered the fence removed. Ewing (D) failed to comply and Bailey (P) brought this quiet title action. Ewing (D) filed a counterclaim against Bailey (P) and third party Erhardt, to reform the deeds, alleging mutual mistake. The trial court found for Bailey (P) and Erhard, concluding that Ewing's (D) mistake as to the location of the boundary line was unilateral. Ewing (D) appealed, and the state's intermediate appellate court granted review.

ISSUE: Is parol evidence admissible both to prove that, by reason of mutual mistake, the parties' true intent was not expressed by the written instrument and to show what that intent was?

HOLDING AND DECISION: (Swanstrom, J.) Yes. Parol evidence is admissible to prove both that, by reason of mutual mistake, the parties' true intent was not expressed by the written instrument and to show what that intent was. Erhardt clearly intended to sell the whole house on Lot 5 and believed the boundary line was somewhere east of its subsequently determined "true" location. Ewing (D) shared this belief. Thus, Ewing (D) and Erhardt made a mutual mistake as to the boundary of lot 5. The presence of mutual mistake does not always favor the party adversely affected by the mistake where that party has "conscious ignorance" of that mistake, i.e., where the party is aware at the time the contract is entered that he has limited knowledge of the facts, but assumes the risk of that limited knowledge. Here, both Ewing (D) and Bailey (P) assumed the risk of uncertainty as to the exact location of the boundary line. However, in this instance, the scope of the risk assumed does not prevent Ewing (D) from prevailing, since both parties reasonably would have assumed that the boundary line was somewhere east of the house—so that the lot would encompass the entire house—but not cutting through the house. Where there is mutual mistake, as here, parol evidence is admissible to show that the written instrument does not reflect the parties' true intent as well as to prove what the true intent was; in this case to deed the whole house on lot 5 to Ewing (D). However, Ewing's (D) deed can only be reformed if such relief will not prejudice the rights of Bailey (P), if Bailey is a bona fide and innocent purchaser. A purchaser must lack notice both of the mistake and of the true intent of the parties, in order to prevent reformation. Reversed and remanded.

▶ ANALYSIS

Despite the fact that the court found mutual mistake in the deeding of lot 5, a reformation of the deed cannot occur without taking into account the rights of the owner of lot 6. If lot 6 had not been sold, the deed to lot 5 could be reformed as only the rights of the Estate and Ewing would be affected.

■══■

Quicknotes

MUTUAL MISTAKE A mistake by both parties to a contract, who are in agreement as to what the contract terms should be, but the agreement as written fails to reflect that common intent; such contracts are voidable or subject to reformation.

PAROL EVIDENCE Evidence given verbally; extraneous evidence.

■══■

First Baptist Church of Moultrie v. Barber Contracting Co.

Church (P) v. Law contract bidder (D)

Ga. Ct. App., 189 Ga. App. 804, 377 S.E.2d 717 (1989).

NATURE OF CASE: Appeal of a denial of cross-motions for summary judgment for breach of contract.

FACT SUMMARY: Barber Contracting Co. (Barber) (D) submitted a construction bid to First Baptist Church of Moultrie (P) which contained a miscalculation, causing Barber (D) to withdraw the bid.

🏛 RULE OF LAW
A contract may be rescinded when one party has entered into the contract based upon an unintentional mistake.

FACTS: First Baptist Church of Moultrie (First Baptist) (P) sought bids for the construction of a recreation building. Barber Contracting Co. (Barber) (D) submitted the lowest bid of $1.86 million and was awarded the contract. As part of the agreement, Barber (D) had issued a bid bond of $93,000 payable to First Baptist (P) if Barber (D) failed to execute the contract. The following day, Barber (D) discovered that an error had been made in calculating the bid price. The error caused the bid to be $143,120 lower than it should have been. Barber (D) informed First Baptist (P) of the error and its withdrawal of the bid. First Baptist (P) brought suit against Barber (D) to recover the $93,000 bid bond when Barber (D) refused to have it paid to First Baptist (P). Each party filed summary judgment motions which were denied by the trial court. Both sides appealed. The state's intermediate appellate court granted review.

ISSUE: May a contract be rescinded when one party has entered into the contract based upon an unintentional mistake?

HOLDING AND DECISION: (McMurray, J.) Yes. A contract may be rescinded when one party has entered into the contract based upon an unintentional mistake. The mistake must involve a fact material to the contract and must be an unintentional act, omission, or error. Even if the mistake was caused by negligence, the contract may be avoided if the opposing party would not be prejudiced. Barber's (D) miscalculation in computing the bid price was an unintentional clerical error about a fact material to the contract. Therefore, it was a unilateral mistake which allows for rescission of the contract. Even if the error could be considered negligent, First Baptist (P) was not prejudiced since they stood to lose only the advantage of Barber's (D) mistake. Barber's (D) summary judgment motion should have been granted. Reversed as to Barber's (D) summary judgment motion.

▶ ANALYSIS

The court's decision conflicts with the general rule that unilateral mistakes do not make a contract voidable. However, the decision is in accord with other decisions, providing equitable relief where mistaken bids are caught promptly, and with the Restatement (Second) of Contracts § 153.

■■■

Quicknotes

MATERIAL FACT A fact without the existence of which a contract would not have been entered.

RESCISSION The canceling of an agreement and the return of the parties to their positions prior to the formation of the contract.

SUMMARY JUDGMENT Judgment rendered by a court in response to a motion by one of the parties, claiming that the lack of a question of material fact in respect to an issue warrants disposition of the issue without consideration by the jury.

UNILATERAL MISTAKE When only one party to a contract is mistaken as to its terms, which does not render the agreement unenforceable.

■■■

Beynon Building Corp. v. National Guardian Life Insurance Co.

Building company (P) v. Mortgage company (D)

III. App. Ct., 118 III. App. 3d 754, 455 N.E.2d 246 (1983).

NATURE OF CASE: Appeal from dismissal of complaint for release from mortgage, and appeal from reformation of that mortgage.

FACT SUMMARY: National Guardian Life Insurance Co. (D) discovered that when Beynon Building Corp. (P) proferred a final payment on a mortgage and note the monthly payment amount reflected on the original note had been miscalculated.

RULE OF LAW

A written agreement, which does not conform with the true intentions of the parties and as to which there is strong, clear, and convincing evidence of mutual mistake of fact, will be reformed in equity.

FACTS: In 1964, Beynon Building Corp. (Beynon) (P) executed a mortgage and note for $85,000 with Rockford Mortgage Co. (Rockford). The note provided for 180 monthly installments of $649, at an interest rate of 5.5 percent, with a final payment due in 1979. Rockford assigned the mortgage and note to National Guardian Life Insurance Co. (National) (D). In 1965, National (D) sent Beynon (P) a new amortization schedule, reflecting that with payments of $649, a longer term of 200 payments ending in 1981, would be needed to amortize the loan at 5.5 percent; this longer loan term was acknowledged by Beynon (P) in 1973 in a letter to National (D). In 1979, after making 178 payments, Beynon (P) attempted to make its final two installment payments. National (D) refused to accept them, replying that it had just discovered that an error had been made in calculating the monthly payment, which at 5.5 percent should have been $694, not $649. Beynon (P) sued for release from the mortgage, and National (D) counterclaimed for reformation. National (D) prevailed, and Benyon (P) appealed. The state's intermediate appellate court granted review.

ISSUE: Will a written agreement, which does not conform with the true intentions of the parties and as to which there is strong, clear, and convincing evidence of mutual mistake of fact, be reformed in equity?

HOLDING AND DECISION: (Unverzagt, J.) Yes. A written agreement, which does not conform with the true intentions of the parties and as to which there is strong, clear, and convincing evidence of mutual mistake of fact, will be reformed in equity. Reformation is warranted where actual good-faith agreement is reached but due to error is not expressed in the written reduction of the agreement. However, there must be strong, clear, and convincing evidence of mutual mistake of fact. Parol evidence, normally inadmissible when an instrument is unambiguous on its face, may be used to meet this standard. Here, Beynon (P) and Rockford had agreed on a 5.5 percent interest rate which was not accurately reflected by the $649 monthly payment. Reformation of the note and mortgage to reflect the proper amount of $694 will effectuate the parties' true intentions. Although Beynon's (P) cause of action accrued in 1964, when the mortgage and note documents were drawn and executed, Beynon (P) is estopped from asserting the 10-year statute of limitations because in 1973 it acknowledged the correct amortization period in a letter to National (D). This is akin to the situation where a new promise to pay has been made in writing within or after the 10-year period, which also permits bringing of the action within 10 years from the new promise. The statute of frauds and laches also do not bar the reformation. Affirmed.

ANALYSIS

Reformation is also appropriate to correct a written instrument when there has been a mistake of law, such as a misunderstanding about the legal meaning of a term which is used to incorporate the previous agreement of the parties. Also, while negligence by a plaintiff in a reformation action (such as forgetting to read the contract in question) is not a defense, sale of the subject matter of the agreement at issue to a bona fide purchaser for value may well constitute a defense.

■==■

Quicknotes

MISTAKE OF FACT A mistake as to a factual assumption upon which an action or contract is based, and which may be an adequate defense to a criminal prosecution or a cause for voiding or reforming a contract.

MUTUAL MISTAKE A mistake by both parties to a contract, who are in agreement as to what the contract terms should be, but the agreement as written fails to reflect that common intent; such contracts are voidable or subject to reformation.

PAROL EVIDENCE RULE Doctrine precluding parties to an agreement from introducing evidence of prior or contemporaneous agreements in order to repudiate or alter the terms of a written contract.

REFORMATION OF CONTRACT An equitable remedy whereby the written terms of an agreement are altered in order to reflect the true intent of the parties; reformation requires a demonstration by clear and convincing evidence of mutual mistake by the parties to the contract.

■==■

Vokes v. Arthur Murray, Inc.

Dance student (P) v. Dance instruction company (D)

Fla. Dist. Ct. App., 212 So. 2d 906 (1968).

NATURE OF CASE: Appeal from dismissal of action for cancellation of contracts.

FACT SUMMARY: Vokes (P) was continually cajoled into purchasing thousands of hours of dancing lessons at Arthur Murray, Inc.'s (D) school of dance, even though it was apparent that she did not have the dance potential the school's employees told her she had.

🏛 RULE OF LAW

A party to a contract may reasonably rely on opinions as assertions of fact when given by a party of superior knowledge on the subject, so as to be entitled to seek rescission of the contract when those opinions turn out to be fraudulent or misleading.

FACTS: Vokes (P), at age 51, decided she wished to become an accomplished dancer to give purpose to her life. Over a period of years, by flattery, cajolery, awards, etc., Vokes (P) was convinced to sign up, under a number of contracts, for $31,000 worth of dancing lessons from an Arthur Murray, Inc. (D) dancing school franchise. Vokes (P) was repeatedly informed that she was a promising student who was quickly becoming sufficiently skilled to pursue a career as a professional dancer. Vokes (P) subsequently brought an action to cancel the unused portion of approximately 2,302 hours of lessons to which she had subscribed. Vokes (P) alleged that she had attained little or no skill as a dancer and obviously had no such aptitude. Vokes (P) alleged that Arthur Murray (D) employees had purposefully misrepresented her skills and had taken unconscionable advantage of her. Vokes (P) alleged that she had relied on Arthur Murray (D) employees' superior knowledge as to her ability and the skills necessary to become a professional dancer. The trial court dismissed, and the state's intermediate appellate court granted review.

ISSUE: May a party to a contract reasonably rely on opinions as assertions of fact when given by a party of superior knowledge on the subject, so as to be entitled to seek rescission of the contract when those opinions turn out to be fraudulent or misleading?

HOLDING AND DECISION: (Pierce, J.) Yes. A party to a contract may reasonably rely on opinions as assertions of fact when given by a party of superior knowledge on the subject, so as to be entitled to seek rescission of the contract when those opinions turn out to be fraudulent or misleading. Normally, the party to a contract has no reasonable right to rely on opinions expressed by the other party to the contract. Misrepresentations of opinion are normally not actionable. However, a statement made by a party having superior knowledge may be regarded as a statement of fact even though it would be regarded as opinion if the parties were dealing on the basis of equal knowledge. Where a party undertakes to make representations based on its superior knowledge, it is under a duty to act honestly and to disclose the entire truth. Vokes (P) has stated a valid cause of action. Reversed.

▶ ANALYSIS

Basically, *Vokes* is concerned with reliance and credibility. One has a right to rely on opinions of attorneys, doctors, etc. *Vokes* extends such reasonable reliance to experts or those highly knowledgeable in a field in which plaintiff is generally unfamiliar. *Ramel v. Chasebrook Construction Company*, 135 So. 2d 876 (1961). To be actionable, the misrepresentation must be material and there must be some overreaching in cases such as *Vokes*.

■■■

Quicknotes

MISREPRESENTATION A statement or conduct by one party to another that constitutes a false representation of fact.

■■■

Stambovsky v. Ackley

Home buyer (P) v. Seller of haunted house (D)

N.Y. Sup. Ct., App. Div., 169 App. Div. 2d 254, 572 N.Y.S.2d 672 (1991).

NATURE OF CASE: Appeal of dismissal of action for rescission of contract.

FACT SUMMARY: Ackley (D), when selling his home, failed to tell the buyer, Stambovsky (P), that they believed that the house was haunted, and Stambovsky (P) sought to rescind the contract for nondisclosure.

🏛 RULE OF LAW
Where a condition which has been created by the seller materially impairs the value of the contract and is peculiarly within the knowledge of the seller or unlikely to be discovered by a prudent purchaser exercising due care with respect to the subject transaction, nondisclosure constitutes a basis for rescission as a matter of equity.

FACTS: Ackley (D), the seller of a home, failed to inform the buyer, Stambovsky (P), that the house was believed by Ackley (D), and widely known in the community, to be haunted. This reputation had been fostered by Ackley (D), who had claimed to have seen ghosts in the house in the years prior to the sale. This reputation reduced the house's value and its ability to be resold. After discovering this reputation, Stambovsky (P) sought to recover the down payment and rescind the contract when Ackley (D) made this information known while the agreement was negotiated. The trial court dismissed Stambovsky's (P) claim, and this appeal followed. The state's intermediate appellate court granted review.

ISSUE: Where a condition which has been created by the seller materially impairs the value of the contract and is peculiarly within the knowledge of the seller or unlikely to be discovered by a prudent purchaser exercising due care with respect to the subject transaction, does nondisclosure constitute a basis for rescission as a matter of equity?

HOLDING AND DECISION: (Rubin, J.) Yes. Where a condition which has been created by the seller materially impairs the value of the contract and is peculiarly within the knowledge of the seller or unlikely to be discovered by a prudent purchaser exercising due care with respect to the subject transaction, nondisclosure constitutes a basis for rescission as a matter of equity. Ordinarily, absent a special legal relationship between the parties, the doctrine of caveat emptor prevents nondisclosure from being actionable where a material fact can be discovered by the reasonably prudent purchaser, and the law does not provide for damages in such situations of nondisclosure. Where a condition created by the seller materially impairs the value of the contract and cannot be discovered by the buyer through reasonable inspection, the seller must inform the buyer. Here, Ackley (D) deliberately advanced the belief that the home was haunted, which reduced the value of the house, and Stambovsky (P) had no reasonable means of discovering the presence of ghosts or the reputation of the house in the community. Moreover, Ackley's (D) contention that the merger or "as is" clause in the contract for sale bars recovery of Stambovsky's (P) deposit is unavailing, since even an express disclaimer will not be given effect where the facts are peculiarly within the knowledge of the party invoking it. Therefore, Ackley (D) took unfair advantage of Stambovsky (P) and may not insist on enforcement of the contract. Reversed.

DISSENT: (Smith, J.) Mere silence of a party to an arm's-length transaction, without some act or conduct, does not amount to fraud by nondisclosure.

▶ ANALYSIS

Restatement (Second) of Contracts § 161 states the instances in which nondisclosure acts as an assertion: (1) where disclosure is necessary to prevent a previous assertion from being a misrepresentation; (2) where nondisclosure amounts to failure to act in good faith; (3) where disclosure would correct a mistake of the other party; and (4) where there is a relationship of trust between the parties.

Quicknotes

MATERIAL FACT A fact without the existence of which a contract would not have been entered.

RESCISSION The canceling of an agreement and the return of the parties to their positions prior to the formation of the contract.

Cousineau v. Walker

Gravel business owner (P) v. Seller of land (D)

Alaska Sup. Ct., 613 P.2d 608 (1980).

NATURE OF CASE: Appeal of action seeking to rescind a land sale contract.

FACT SUMMARY: Walker (D) made certain misrepresentations regarding his property, the accuracy of which buyer Cousineau (P) did not investigate.

🏛 RULE OF LAW
A purchaser of land is entitled to: rely on material representations made by the seller; is not obligated to ascertain whether such representations are truthful; and, if relying on an innocent misrepresentation, is not barred from recovery if his acts in failing to discover the truth are not wholly irrational, preposterous, or in bad faith.

FACTS: Walker (D) owned certain undeveloped land. He listed it for sale. The land was advertised as having 80,000 cubic yards of gravel, and certain road access. Cousineau (P), who worked in the gravel business, negotiated to purchase the land. He did not investigate the accuracy of Walker's (D) representations. A sale was made. The land turned out to have only 6,000 cubic yards of gravel and less road access than advertised, although it appeared that Walker's (D) misrepresentations were innocent. Cousineau (P) brought an action for rescission. The trial court found that Cousineau's (P) reliance on the misstatements was not justified and awarded a defense verdict. Cousineau (P) appealed. The state's highest court granted review.

ISSUE: Is a purchaser of land entitled: to rely on material representations made by the seller; not obligated to ascertain whether such representations are truthful; and, if relying on an innocent misrepresentation; not barred from recovery if his acts in failing to discover the truth are not wholly irrational, preposterous, or in bad faith?

HOLDING AND DECISION: (Boochever, J.) Yes. A purchaser of land is entitled to: rely on material representations made by the seller; is not obligated to ascertain whether such representations are truthful; and, if relying on an innocent misrepresentation, is not barred from recovery if his acts in failing to discover the truth are not wholly irrational, preposterous, or in bad faith. At common law, the doctrine of caveat emptor was the rule regarding land sale contracts. In recent times, however, the rule has evolved that a buyer is entitled to rely on assertions made regarding the property, regardless of examination by the buyer. While this most often occurs in instances of fraud, it has also been applied to negligent misrepresentation as well. Thus, only when a buyer's acts in failing to discover

defects are wholly irrational or in bad faith is he barred from recovering. Here, while Cousineau's (P) acts were lacking in sound business judgment, they cannot be called irrational or in bad faith. The trial court erred in concluding that Cousineau (P) did not rely on Walker's (D) false statements. The court also erred in concluding that those statements were not material. The statements regarding highway frontage and gravel content were material, as a reasonable person would be likely to consider the existence of gravel deposits an important consideration in developing a piece of property. Reversed and remanded.

▶ ANALYSIS

Whether reliance was justifiable is one of three elements necessary to rescind a land contract. The threshold question is whether there were false statements. Next, it must be found that the statements were material. Whether there was justifiable reliance is the final issue.

■══■

Quicknotes

CAVEAT EMPTOR Let the buyer beware; doctrine that a buyer purchases something at his own risk.

MISREPRESENTATION A statement or conduct by one party to another that constitutes a false representation of fact.

RESCISSION The canceling of an agreement and the return of the parties to their positions prior to the formation of the contract.

■══■

Totem Marine Tug & Barge v. Alyeska Pipeline Service Co.

Shipper (P) v. Pipeline company (D)

Alaska Sup. Ct., 584 P.2d 15 (1978).

NATURE OF CASE: Appeal from denial of damages for breach of contract.

FACT SUMMARY: Totem Marine Tug & Barge (Totem) (P) claimed that Alyeska Pipeline Service Co. (Alyeska) (D) had used economic duress to get Totem (P) to sign a binding release of all claims it had against Alyeska (D) after Alyeska (D) terminated a contract with Totem (P).

🏛 **RULE OF LAW**
A contract can be voided if it was entered into as the result of economic duress.

FACTS: Totem Marine Tug & Barge (Totem) (P) had contracted to transport pipeline construction materials from Houston, Texas, to a designated port in southern Alaska for Alyeska Pipeline Service Co. (Alyeska) (D). According to Totem (P), Alyeska's (D) failure to proceed in accordance with the terms and specifications in the contract caused considerable delays and occasioned the hiring of a second tug to handle the extra tonnage in materials that were waiting to be loaded when Totem (P) arrived in Houston. Alyeska (D) eventually terminated the contract without reason. When Totem (P) submitted invoices of around $300,000 and began pressing for payment, it was in a serious cash-flow crisis and faced the possibility of bankruptcy. This, it maintained, led it to accept Alyeska's (D) offer of $97,500 in cash for settlement of all claims by Totem (P). Later, Totem (P), claiming economic duress, sought to recover in a contract action. A summary judgment was granted in favor of Alyeska (D). The state's highest court granted review.

ISSUE: Can a contract be voided if it was entered into as the result of economic duress?

HOLDING AND DECISION: (Burke, J.) Yes. A contract can be voided if it was entered into as the result of economic duress. Avoidance of a contract on the ground that it was entered into as a result of economic duress is widely recognized. According to Professor Williston, the party alleging economic duress must show that he has been the victim of a wrongful or unlawful act or threat and that such act or threat deprived him of his unfettered will. Thus, Totem (P) would have to show that wrongful acts or threats by Alyeska (D) intentionally caused Totem (P) to involuntarily enter into the settlement agreement. This would mean showing that Totem (P) had no reasonable alternative to agreeing to Alyeska's (D) settlement terms. Certainly, the facts of this case are such as would lend themselves to such proof. It is up to Totem (P) to prove its allegations, but there are sufficient disputed facts that

rendered summary judgment improper. Reversed and remanded.

▶ **ANALYSIS**

Section 492 of the Restatement of Contracts focused on the exercise of "free will and judgment" in defining duress, while the revised Restatement looks to the victim's having "no reasonable alternative." At early common law, avoidance of a contract on the ground of duress was available only if a party could show that it was entered into for fear of loss of life or limb, mayhem, or imprisonment.

■═■

Quicknotes

DURESS Unlawful threats or other coercive behavior by one person which causes another to commit acts he would not otherwise do.

SUMMARY JUDGMENT Judgment rendered by a court in response to a motion by one of the parties, claiming that the lack of a question of material fact in respect to an issue warrants disposition of the issue without consideration by the jury.

■═■

Kase v. French

Administrator of estate (P) v. Caretakers (D)

S.D. Sup. Ct., 325 N.W.2d 678 (1982).

NATURE OF CASE: Appeal from denial of recovery in administrator's action to vacate real estate contract.

FACT SUMMARY: Mr. and Mrs. French (D) delivered groceries and developed a close relationship with Kase's (P) testator, Mrs. McWilliams, who sold the Frenches (D) her home at a very low price.

🏛 RULE OF LAW
The dominant party in a confidential relation must exercise the utmost good faith and refrain from obtaining an advantage at the expense of the confiding party.

FACTS: Mr. and Mrs. French (D) regularly delivered groceries to Kase's (P) testator, Mrs. McWilliams. After McWilliams injured herself in a fall, the Frenches (D) began to visit her daily and to do chores for her. McWilliams offered to sell her home to the Frenches (D) if they would fix an apartment for her in it. They had the home appraised, and McWilliams sold it to them against the advice of her attorney for $5,000 more than the appraised value. The interest rate she gave them was 1 percent per annum, and the Frenches (D) agreed to allow McWilliams to live there rent-free for two years. McWilliams had a previous offer on the house of over twice the appraisal value, and the prevailing market interest rate was 6-8 percent. Even though the Frenches (D) knew this was the market rate of interest, they did not apprise Mrs. McWilliams of this fact. The trial court upheld the validity of McWilliam's deed to the Frenches (D), after Kase (P), McWilliams's administrator, sought to vacate the real estate sales contract on the ground that it had been obtained by the Frenches (D) through undue influence. The state's highest court granted review.

ISSUE: Must the dominant party in a confidential relation exercise the utmost good faith and refrain from obtaining an advantage at the expense of the confiding party?

HOLDING AND DECISION: (Wollman, J.) Yes. The dominant party in a confidential relation must exercise the utmost good faith and refrain from obtaining an advantage at the expense of the confiding party. A confidential relationship here existed by the time McWilliams sold her home to the Frenches (D). By then, she had fully reposed her trust in their integrity and fidelity. This required the Frenches (D) to exercise the utmost good faith toward McWilliams and to refrain from obtaining any advantage at her expense. Whether undue influence was exercised is shown by a susceptible subject; opportunity to exert undue influence and to effect a wrongful purpose; disposition to do so; and clear result showing undue influence. Here, it appeared that McWilliams was strong-willed and independent, received the favorable term of living in the house she formerly owned for two years, and received the advice of an attorney concerning the sale. The Frenches (D) did pay a price greater than the appraisal value and did take care of McWilliams as promised. They did not exert undue influence. Affirmed.

DISSENT: (Henderson, J.) Inasmuch as the Frenches (D) handled McWilliams's financial affairs, they stood in a fiduciary relationship to her. They both breached this duty and exercised undue influence by appropriating McWilliams's bank accounts and using them for their own purpose and by hiding the market interest rate at the time they bought McWilliams's home. They patently took advantage of a lonely elderly woman and acted unconscionably. Therefore, equity demands that the sale contract should be voided and the Frenches (D) directed to return McWilliams's inter vivos "gifts" to them.

▶ ANALYSIS

Elements tending to show undue influence are discussing or completing a transaction at an unusual place or time; insistence that the bargain be struck at once with an emphasis on the risks of delay; several persons "ganging up" on the weaker party; and the absence of independent third party advisors to the weaker party, such as lawyers or accountants.

■=■

Quicknotes

FIDUCIARY RELATIONSHIP Person holding a legal obligation to act for the benefit of another.

INTER VIVOS Between living persons.

UNDUE INFLUENCE Influence exerted by one party over the other such that the latter's will is so dominated that he acts in accordance with the will of the party exerting the force.

■=■

Odorizzi v. Bloomfield School District

Teacher (P) v. School district (D)

Cal. Dist. Ct. App., 246 Cal. App. 2d 123 (1964).

NATURE OF CASE: Appeal from dismissal of action to rescind resignation based on undue influence.

FACT SUMMARY: Odorizzi (P), a teacher with the Bloomfield School District (District) (D), was arrested on homosexual charges. Immediately after his release from custody, the superintendent of the District (D) and the principal of his school came to his apartment and convinced him to resign. He subsequently sought to rescind the resignation, claiming it had been obtained, inter alia, through undue influence.

> 🏛 **RULE OF LAW**
> Where a party's physical and emotional condition is such that excessive persuasion leads to his own will being overborne, he can charge undue influence so as to rescind a resignation or contract.

FACTS: Odorizzi (P) was arrested for criminal homosexual activities. At the time, he was under contract as a teacher for the Bloomfield School District (District) (D). Immediately after he was released on bail, the District's (D) superintendent and the principal of his school came to his apartment and convinced him to resign. Odorizzi (P) was subsequently acquitted of the charges, but was refused reemployment by the District (D). He brought suit to rescind his resignation. He charged duress, menace, fraud, and undue influence. He claimed that on the day he resigned, he had not slept in nearly 40 hours and was under severe emotional and physical stress. He was told that if he did not immediately resign the District (D) would be forced to suspend him and then dismiss him. This would occasion embarrassing and humiliating publicity. However, if he resigned, the matter would be kept quiet and his chance for future jobs would not be impaired. The trial court found nothing wrong with these actions, no confidential relationship existed, and the District (D) would have been forced by law to suspend Odorizzi (P). Accordingly, the trial court dismissed, and the state's intermediate appellate court granted review.

ISSUE: Where a party's physical and emotional condition is such that excessive persuasion leads to his own will being overborne, can he charge undue influence so as to rescind a resignation or contract?

HOLDING AND DECISION: (Fleming, J.) Yes. Where a party's physical and emotional condition is such that excessive persuasion leads to his own will being overborne, he can charge undue influence so as to rescind a resignation or contract. While none of Odorizzi's (P) other claims have merit, he has made out a prima facie case of undue influence. In essence the charge involves the use of excessive pressures to persuade one vulnerable to such pressures to decide a matter contra to his judgment. It can involve an application of excessive strength by a dominant subject against a servient object. Extreme weakness or susceptibility is an important factor in establishing undue influence. It is normally found in cases of extreme youth or age or sickness. While it normally involves fiduciary or other confidential relationships, they are not necessary to the action. Here, extreme pressures were leveled against Odorizzi (P). He had just gone through an arrest, booking, and interrogation procedure for a crime which, if well publicized, would subject him to public humiliation. He was threatened with such publicity if he did not immediately resign. He was approached at his apartment immediately after his release. He was not given the opportunity to think the matter over or to consult outside advice or obtain legal counsel. He was told that in any event he would be suspended and dismissed. These factors present a jury issue. If Odorizzi (P) can establish that he wouldn't have resigned but for these pressures and the jury finds that they were unreasonable and overbore his will, Odorizzi (P) could rescind his resignation. Reversed.

▶ ANALYSIS

Many types of contracts may be rescinded for undue influence. Mortmain statutes are in effect in some states. These hold that bequests made to churches shortly before death and after a visit by religious leaders are void and unenforceable. Wills may be declared invalid where they were procured through undue influence. Contracts to sell land for far less than its value and transfers made in fear of civil or criminal prosecution are other examples.

■══■

Quicknotes

DURESS Unlawful threats or other coercive behavior by one person which causes another to commit acts he would not otherwise do.

MORTMAIN STATUTE Statutes prohibiting the alienation of lands to religious institutions without first meeting certain requirements.

RESCISSION The canceling of an agreement and the return of the parties to their positions prior to the formation of the contract.

UNDUE INFLUENCE Influence exerted by one party over the other such that the latter's will is so dominated he acts in accordance with the will of the party exerting the force.

■══■

Bennett v. Hayes

Repair shop owner (P) v. Automobile owner (D)

Cal. Ct. App., 53 Cal. App. 3d 700 (1975).

NATURE OF CASE: Appeal from denial of damages for breach of contract.

FACT SUMMARY: Hayes (D) brought his automobile to Bennett's (P) shop for repairs, but Bennett (P) performed work without providing written or oral price estimates as required by statute.

🏛 **RULE OF LAW**
A contract for services will be rendered unenforceable on grounds of illegality if a party violates a statute during the performance of the contract.

FACTS: Hayes (D) brought his Jaguar automobile to Bennett's (P) repair shop for brake work and installation of a radio. When he arrived for pick-up, Bennett (P) informed him his brakes were inoperable. Hayes (D) left the car with Bennett (P), who did not provide Hayes (D) with an estimate of the cost of repairs, in violation of Cal. Bus. & Prof. Code § 9884.9. When Hayes (D) refused to pay $500 on delivery (he had authorized only $200), Bennett (P) sued to recover the charge for repairs. The trial court ruled for Hayes (D), and the state's intermediate appellate court granted review.

ISSUE: Will a contract for services be rendered unenforceable on grounds of illegality if a party violates a statute during the performance of the contract?

HOLDING AND DECISION: [Judge not listed in casebook excerpt.] Yes. A contract for services will be rendered unenforceable on grounds of illegality if a party violates a statute during the performance of the contract. State law requires that automotive repair dealers give customers written estimated prices for labor and parts necessary to perform repairs; under the statute, dealers cannot charge for work done or parts supplied in excess of the estimated price without the oral or written consent of the customer. Here, Bennett (P) gave Hayes (D) no estimates. His failure to do so was a violation of a consumer protection statute enacted for the benefit of his customers. To allow him to recover $500 against Bennett (P) would encourage practices forbidden by law. There are insufficient equitable considerations present to permit Bennett (P) to recover notwithstanding his statutory violation. Affirmed.

► **ANALYSIS**

Whether illegality will preclude formation of a contract, discharge obligations already assumed based on a theory of excusable non-performance, or render the attempted bargain void depends upon whether the illegality existed prior to the attempted formation or arose afterwards.

Courts also look to the nature or subject matter of the illegality, distinguishing between malum in se (where the subject matter is intrinsically evil, such as violation of a penal statute) or malum prohibitum (where there is a violation of a statute which regulates matters for the convenience of society, such as the child labor laws). In the latter case but not the former, courts may intervene to allow an innocent or protected party to recover in quasi-contract.

■═■

Quicknotes

ILLEGALITY Not in accordance with law.

MALUM IN SE An act that is wrong in accordance with natural law, without respect to whether it is prohibited by statute.

MALUM PROHIBITUM An action that is not inherently wrong, but which is prohibited by law.

QUASI-CONTRACT An implied contract created by law to prevent unjust enrichment.

■═■

Carnes v. Sheldon

Separated woman (P) v. Father cohabitor (D)

Mich. Ct. App., 109 Mich. App. 204, 311 N.W.2d 747 (1981).

NATURE OF CASE: Appeal from denial of request for equitable distribution of defendant's property and of custody of the defendant's child.

FACT SUMMARY: Carnes (P) cohabited with Sheldon (D), who allegedly promised to marry her once her divorce was final, but after Sheldon (D) ended the relationship short of marriage, Carnes (P) sued for half of Sheldon's (D) property and custody of Sheldon's (D) minor daughter.

🏛 RULE OF LAW

Courts will not find implied-in-fact contracts for the accumulation or division of property between cohabitants when the underlying circumstances reveal a meretricious relationship.

FACTS: After his wife left him, Sheldon (D) allowed a separated woman, Carnes (P), to move in with him and his four children. Carnes (P) alleged Sheldon (D) promised to marry her once her divorce was final, but the evidence did not support this. Although Carnes (P) was known at the children's school as "Mrs. Sheldon," all her personal and financial matters were conducted in her own name. Income from Carnes's (P) employment helped pay household expenses. When the relationship ended, Carnes (P) sued for custody of one of Sheldon's (D) own children and an equitable distribution of Sheldon's (D) property based on an express or implied-in-fact agreement which allegedly divided property accumulated between them during cohabitation. The trial court denied both claims. The state's intermediate appellate court granted review.

ISSUE: Will courts find implied-in-fact contracts for the accumulation or division of property between cohabitants when the underlying circumstances reveal a meretricious relationship?

HOLDING AND DECISION: (Riley, J.) No. Courts will not find implied-in-fact contracts for the accumulation or division of property between cohabitants when the underlying circumstances reveal a meretricious relationship. Generally contracts in consideration of a meretricious relationship will not be enforced. However, an express agreement to accumulate or transfer property following a relationship of some permanence and independent consideration such as money or services will be enforced. Here, Carnes (P) did not show there was such an express agreement between her and Sheldon (D). Nor will such an agreement be implied from the facts. The presumption that the provision of services to Sheldon's (D) household was gratuitous cannot be overcome because Carnes's (P) services were of a household, not commercial, nature. To imply a contract here would raise these types of relationships to the legal status of abolished common law marriage, which is a public policy issue better left to the legislature. Affirmed as to this issue. [Remanded on other grounds].

▶ ANALYSIS

Other courts have followed this rule, i.e., that recovery for domestic services will be denied as inextricably linked to and deriving from the illegal cohabitation. See, e.g., *Schwegman v. Schwegman*, 441 So. 2d 316 (La. App. 1983). However, some have disagreed, noting the origin of this rule in an age when nonmarital cohabitation was considered akin to prostitution, and arguing that the prevalence of cohabitation today reflected a change in social mores which warranted rejection of the unlawfulness of the meretricious relationship.

Quicknotes

COHABITANTS Persons living together as husband and wife.

GRATUITOUS Something that is given without consideration received therefore.

MERETRICIOUS An unlawful sexual relationship.

White v. Fletcher/Mayo/Associates

Vice-president (P) v. Ad agency (D)

Ga. Sup. Ct., 251 Ga. 203, 303 S.E.2d 746 (1983).

NATURE OF CASE: Appeal from injunction enforcing judicially-edited covenant not to compete.

FACT SUMMARY: When Fletcher/Mayo/Associates (FMA) (D) was acquired by a New York company, White (P) signed an employment contract which in part prevented him from competing with FMA (D) after termination, and then, shortly after the merger, White (P) was fired.

🏛 RULE OF LAW
If an overbroad covenant not to compete is ancillary to an employment contract rather than to the sale of a business, it is unenforceable in its entirety, so that even judicial "blue-lining" to limit its time and territorial effect cannot save it.

FACTS: White (P) was a senior vice-president in charge of the Atlanta office of Fletcher/Mayo/Associates (FMA) (D), an advertising agency. FMA (D) merged with a New York ad company. At the time of the merger, White (P) traded his 7,114 shares of FMA (D) common stock worth about $85,000 (4.6 percent of the company) for DDB stock worth $145,000. He also was one of only three FMA (D) employees to sign an employment agreement containing a restrictive covenant which precluded him from post-termination competition with FMA (D). Shortly after the merger, White (P) was fired. White (P) sued for a determination of the enforceability of the covenant, which the trial court found overbroad but nevertheless "blue-lined" to limit its time and territorial scope. The trial court enjoined White (P) from violating the covenant as judicially rewritten. The state's highest court granted review.

ISSUE: If an overbroad covenant not to compete is ancillary to an employment contract rather than to the sale of a business, is it unenforceable in its entirety, so that even judicial "blue-lining" to limit its time and territorial effect cannot save it?

HOLDING AND DECISION: (Bell, J.) Yes. If an overbroad covenant not to compete is ancillary to an employment contract rather than to the sale of a business, it is unenforceable in its entirety, so that even judicial "blue-lining" to limit its time and territorial effect cannot save it. A covenant not to compete ancillary to an employment contract is enforceable only when it is strictly limited in time and territorial effect and is otherwise reasonable considering the business interest of the employer sought to be protected and the effect on the employee. If such a covenant as read in its entirety is unenforceable, it cannot be judicially rewritten, or "blue-lined," so as to sever the objectionable portion, because to do so would violate public policy. Severability is allowed, however, if the covenant is contained in an agreement to sell a business because in such a case the seller receives consideration for it. Here, notwithstanding that White (P) was a minority shareholder, White (P) entered the covenant not to compete in his capacity as an employee and had no control over FMA (D) management generally. The profit he made on his stock swap was no greater than that made by any other shareholder. Therefore, White's (P) status in terms of bargaining power was that of an employee only, and his noncompetition covenant cannot be enforced at all. To rule otherwise and to permit blue lining in a situation such as the one at bar would encourage a purchaser of an existing business to genteelly coerce an employee of the acquired business to agree to an employment contract which contains noncompetition covenants and which appears to be the result of a true bargain but is actually a contract of adhesion. Reversed.

▶ ANALYSIS

Courts scrutinize employment covenants very carefully and will uphold them if they were written to accomplish one or both of two aims: (1) to stop the worker from revealing or using the employer's confidential information or trade secrets; or (2) to stop him from profiting from his contacts with the employer's customers. However, some states prohibit covenants not to compete by employers entirely. See, e.g., Cal. Bus. & Prof. Code §§ 16600-16607.

■▬■

Quicknotes

COVENANT NOT TO COMPETE A provision, typically contained in an employment contract or a contract for the sale of a business, pursuant to which the promisor agrees not to compete with the promisee for a specified time period and/or within a particular geographic area.

INJUNCTION A remedy imposed by the court ordering a party to cease the conduct of a specific activity.

RESTRICTIVE COVENANT A promise contained in a deed to limit the uses to which the property will be made.

■▬■

Valencia v. White

Hauling business owner (P) v. Repair shop owner (D)

Ariz. Ct. App., 134 Ariz. 139, 654 P.2d 287 (1982).

NATURE OF CASE: Appeal of order rescinding a contract and awarding damages.

FACT SUMMARY: Valencia (P), a minor engaged in a business, disaffirmed a contract from which he had been conferred certain benefits.

🏛 RULE OF LAW
A minor who disaffirms a contract may be held liable for nonnecessary benefits even if the benefits cannot be returned in kind.

FACTS: Valencia (P), a minor, operated a small hauling enterprise. He took a truck to White's (D) repair shop for certain work. The engine had to be replaced at a cost of $10,700. Valencia (P) agreed to this. The engine did not work properly, and Valencia (P) refused to pay more than the $7,100 he initially paid and sued for return of these monies. The trial court, finding Valencia (P) to have been able to disaffirm the contract, ordered the $7,100 returned to Valencia (P), even though it found that the lack of care by Valencia (P) had led to the engine's failure. The court, to return the parties to the status quo, placed title to the engine in White (D). White (D) appealed, and the state's intermediate appellate court granted review.

ISSUE: May a minor who disaffirms a contract be held liable for nonnecessary benefits even if the benefits cannot be returned in kind?

HOLDING AND DECISION: (Birdsall, J.) Yes. A minor who disaffirms a contract may be held liable for nonnecessary benefits even if the benefits cannot be returned in kind. While a minor is entitled to disaffirm a contract which provides for that other than what is characterized as necessaries of life, a small but growing number of jurisdictions permit the minor to be held liable for the value of the benefits received by him, even if he cannot return the benefits in kind. Here, Valencia (P) received benefits of time and labor from White (D), which obviously cannot be returned in kind and for which White (D) should be entitled to compensation. Given that White (D) did not take advantage of Valencia's (P) being a minor, and that the contract was fair to Valencia (P), White (D) is entitled to damages equivalent to the value rendered (around 20,000) minus the money received on account ($7,100) for a total of around $12,900. Reversed and remanded.

▶ ANALYSIS

The minor-incapacity rule is one of longstanding duration. An increasing number of commentators view it disfavorably, citing the increasing sophistication of older minors. Nonetheless, the rule is virtually universal.

■═■

Quicknotes

MINOR A person who has not yet reached legal age.

■═■

Williams v. Walker-Thomas Furniture Co.

Debtor (D) v. Creditor (P)

350 F.2d 445 (D.C. Cir. 1965).

NATURE OF CASE: Appeal from affirmance of judgment for creditor in action in replevin.

FACT SUMMARY: Williams (D) made a series of purchases, on credit, from Walker-Thomas Furniture Co. (Walker-Thomas) (P), but defaulted on her payments, after which Walker-Thomas (P) sought to repossess all the items she had bought on credit.

🏛 RULE OF LAW
Where in light of the general commercial background of a particular case it appears that gross inequality of bargaining power between the parties has led to the formation of a contract on terms to which one party has had no meaningful choice a court should refuse to enforce such a contract on the ground that it is unconscionable.

FACTS: Beginning about 1957, Walker-Thomas Furniture Co. (Walker-Thomas) (P), a retail furniture company, began using a standard form contract for all credit transactions which contained, inter alia, a clause by which the company (P) reserved the right, upon default by a purchaser, to repossess all items contemporaneously being purchased by the buyer at the time of the repossession. This clause was accompanied by one which stated that all credit purchases made from Walker-Thomas (P) were to be handled through one account, with each installment payment spread pro-rata over all items purchased (even where purchased separately and at different times), until all items were paid for. Williams (D) began purchasing items from Walker-Thomas (P) in 1957. In 1962, she bought a stereo set there. When she defaulted on a payment soon thereafter, Walker-Thomas (P) filed this action to replevin (i.e., repossess) all items she had purchased (and was still paying for) since 1957. Determining that it did not have the authority to refuse to enforce an unconscionable contract, the trial court for the District of Columbia held for Walker-Thomas (P), and the District's appellate court affirmed. The D.C. Circuit court granted further review.

ISSUE: Where in light of the general commercial background of a particular case it appears that gross inequality of bargaining power between the parties has led to the formation of a contract on terms to which one party has had no meaningful choice, should a court refuse to enforce such a contract on the ground that it is unconscionable?

HOLDING AND DECISION: (Wright, J.) Yes. Where in light of the general commercial background of a particular case it appears that gross inequality of bargaining power between the parties has led to the formation of a

contract on terms to which one party has had no meaningful choice, a court should refuse to enforce such a contract on the ground that it is unconscionable. It is true that the common law, operating by the caveat emptor rationale, refused to look into the essential fairness of a contract absent evidence of out and out fraud. The Uniform Commercial Code (UCC), however, notably § 2-302, as adopted in this jurisdiction, has accepted the rule that courts should seek to prevent overreaching in contracts of adhesion such as the one at bar. Williams (D) and other consumers similarly situated come from a socioeconomic class for whom credit is difficult to obtain. To permit Walker-Thomas (P) to exploit this condition with provisions such as those in Walker-Thomas's (P) credit contract arguably would be unconscionable. However, whether those terms were in fact unconscionable is a matter of fact to be determined from the particular circumstances. Unconscionability has generally been recognized to include an absence of meaningful choice on the part of one of the parties together with contract terms which are unreasonably favorable to the other party. Whether a meaningful choice is present in a particular case can only be determined by consideration of all the circumstances surrounding the transaction. In many cases the meaningfulness of the choice is negated by a gross inequality of bargaining power. The manner in which the contract was entered is also relevant to this consideration. A court must ask whether each party to the contract, considering his obvious education or lack of it, have a reasonable opportunity to understand the terms of the contract, or were the important terms hidden in a maze of fine print and minimized by deceptive sales practices. Because the lower courts did not believe they had authority to void an unconscionable contract, they did not make findings as to these factors. On remand, the trial court must determine whether, in light of the general commercial background and commercial needs of the parties, Walker-Thomas's (P) credit contract was unconscionable; if it was, the trial court must not enforce it. Reversed and remanded.

DISSENT: (Danaher, J.) It is up to Congress, not the courts, to protect the public from exploitive contracts such as the one at bar. The court ignores many policy considerations in its decision. For one, the high risk of granting credit to the poor for companies like Walker-Thomas (P) is not even addressed. A more cautious approach is warranted.

Continued on next page.

▶ *ANALYSIS*

This case points up the major application which the UCC § 2-302 concept of unconscionability has had to date: adhesion (i.e., form) contracts. Note that the general common law rule regarding such contracts remains the general rule today. That rule is that a person who signs a contract will be held responsible for any clauses or conditions which a reasonable man making a reasonable inspection would have discovered. The UCC rule merely qualifies this to say that, where one party to a form contract has no real choice over whether to accept the terms because of his relative economic position, then the fact he knows of the terms will not be enough to constitute a "meeting of the minds" on his part necessary to form a valid contract.

■══■

Quicknotes

ADHESION CONTRACT A contract, usually in standardized form, that is prepared by one party and offered to another, whose terms are so disproportionately in favor of the drafting party that courts tend to question the equality of bargaining power in reaching the agreement.

CAVEAT EMPTOR Let the buyer beware; doctrine that a buyer purchases something at his own risk.

INTER ALIA Among other things.

REPLEVIN An action to recover personal property wrongfully taken.

UNCONSCIONABILITY Rule of law whereby a court may excuse performance of a contract, or of a particular contract term, if it determines that such term(s) are unduly oppressive or unfair to one party to the contract.

■══■

AT&T Mobility v. Concepcion

Cell phone service provider (D) v. Consumer (P)

131 S. Ct. 1740 (2011).

NATURE OF CASE: Appeal from affirmance of denial of motion to compel arbitration in a consumer class action.

FACT SUMMARY: AT&T Mobility LLC (AT&T) (D) contended that the enforceability of the arbitration provision in its cell phone service agreement could not be conditioned by the states on the availability of classwide arbitration procedures, since the states were preempted by the Federal Arbitration Act (FAA) from so doing.

> **RULE OF LAW**
> The Federal Arbitration Act (FAA) prohibits states from conditioning the enforceability of arbitration agreements on the availability of classwide arbitration procedures.

FACTS: The cell phone service contract between the Concepcions (P) and AT&T Mobility LLC (AT&T) (D) provided for arbitration of all disputes, but did not permit classwide arbitration. After the Concepcions (P) were charged sales tax on the retail value of phones provided free under their service contract, they sued AT&T (D) in a California federal district court. Their suit was consolidated with a class action alleging, inter alia, that AT&T (D) had engaged in false advertising and fraud by charging sales tax on "free" phones. The district court denied AT&T's (D) motion to compel arbitration under the Concepcions' (P) contract. Relying on the California Supreme Court's decision in *Discover Bank v. Superior Court,* 36 Cal. 4th 148, 30 Cal. Rptr. 3d 76, 113 P. 3d 1100 (2005), it found the arbitration provision unconscionable because it disallowed classwide proceedings and AT&T had failed to show that bilateral arbitration adequately substituted for the deterrent effects of class actions. The court of appeals agreed that the provision was unconscionable under California law and held that the Federal Arbitration Act (FAA), which in Section 2 makes arbitration agreements "valid, irrevocable, and enforceable, save upon such grounds as exist at law or in equity for the revocation of any contract," did not preempt its ruling. The United States Supreme Court granted certiorari.

ISSUE: Does the Federal Arbitration Act (FAA) prohibit states from conditioning the enforceability of arbitration agreements on the availability of classwide arbitration procedures?

HOLDING AND DECISION: (Scalia, J.) Yes. The Federal Arbitration Act (FAA) prohibits states from conditioning the enforceability of arbitration agreements on the availability of classwide arbitration procedures. The

FAA's Section 2 reflects a "liberal federal policy favoring arbitration and the "fundamental principle that arbitration is a matter of contract. Thus, courts must place arbitration agreements on an equal footing with other contracts and enforce them according to their terms. Section 2's saving clause permits agreements to be invalidated by "generally applicable contract defenses," but not by defenses that apply only to arbitration or derive their meaning from the fact that an agreement to arbitrate is at issue. Under *Discover Bank,* class waivers in consumer arbitration agreements are unconscionable if the agreement is in an adhesion contract, disputes between the parties are likely to involve small amounts of damages, and the party with inferior bargaining power alleges a deliberate scheme to defraud. The Concepcions (P) claim that the *Discover Bank* rule is a ground that "exist[s] at law or in equity for the revocation of any contract" under FAA § 2. When state law prohibits outright the arbitration of a particular type of claim, the FAA displaces the conflicting rule. But the inquiry is more complex when a generally applicable doctrine is alleged to have been applied in a fashion that disfavors or interferes with arbitration. Although § 2's saving clause preserves generally applicable contract defenses, it does not suggest an intent to preserve state-law rules that stand as an obstacle to the accomplishment of the FAA's objectives. The FAA's overarching purpose is to ensure the enforcement of arbitration agreements according to their terms so as to facilitate informal, streamlined proceedings. Parties may agree to limit the issues subject to arbitration, to arbitrate according to specific rules, and to limit with whom they will arbitrate. Class arbitration, to the extent it is manufactured by *Discover Bank* rather than consensual, interferes with fundamental attributes of arbitration. The switch from bilateral to class arbitration sacrifices arbitration's informality and makes the process slower, more costly, and more likely to generate procedural morass than final judgment. Also, class arbitration greatly increases risks to defendants. The absence of multilayered review makes it more likely that errors will go uncorrected. That risk of error may become unacceptable when damages allegedly owed to thousands of claimants are aggregated and decided at once. Arbitration is poorly suited to these higher stakes. In litigation, a defendant may appeal a certification decision and a final judgment, but FAA § 10 limits the grounds on which courts can vacate arbitral awards. Reversed and remanded.

CONCURRENCE: (Thomas, J.) the FAA requires that an agreement to arbitrate be enforced unless a party

Continued on next page.

successfully challenges the formation of the arbitration agreement, such as by proving fraud or duress. Under such an interpretation, a court cannot follow both the FAA and the *Discover Bank* rule, which does not relate to defects in the making of an agreement. Arguably, the language of § 2's savings clause does not include all defenses applicable to any contract but rather some subset of those defenses. Since the section's exception pertains only to grounds for "revocation" of a contract, presumably Congress intended to limit those grounds to defects in the formation of the contract. *Discover Bank's* holding was premised on public policy, not on whether there were defects in contract formation. Therefore, *Discover Bank* is preempted.

DISSENT: (Breyer, J.) The rule enunciated by *Discover Bank* does not conflict with the FAA and is consistent with its language and primary objective. Where the circumstances articulated by that rule are met, class action waivers are unconscionable under state law. The rule thus sets forth a general principle of unconscionability that does not apply to all class action waivers in the consumer context. Because it applies equally to class action litigation waivers in contracts without arbitration agreements as it does to class arbitration waivers in contracts with such agreements, the rule falls directly within the scope of the FAA's exception permitting courts to refuse to enforce arbitration agreements on grounds that exist "for the revocation of any contract." The majority is wrong, however, in finding that the *Discover Bank* rule stands as an obstacle to achievement of the FAA's objectives, and it does not provide support for its belief that individual, rather than class, arbitration is a fundamental attribute of arbitration. Because California applies the same legal principles to address the unconscionability of class arbitration waivers as it does to address the unconscionability of any other contractual provision, the merits of class proceedings should not factor into our decision. Moreover, class proceedings have well-known countervailing advantages, such as encouraging the bringing of small claims—and the acceptance of them by attorneys. Under our federalist system, states are considered sovereigns; here, California is entitled to weigh the pros and cons of all class proceedings alike, and its law should be upheld, not preempted.

▶ ANALYSIS

Since almost all class actions occur between parties who are in transactional relationships with one another, such as shareholders and corporations, consumers and merchants, employees and employers, etc., it is arguable that this decision will permit the party with greater bargaining power in any particular transaction to force the weaker parties to accept class waivers with no recourse—other than not entering into the transaction at all.

■≡■

Quicknotes

ARBITRATION AGREEMENT A mutual understanding entered into by parties wishing to submit to the decision making authority of a neutral third party, selected by the parties and charged with rendering a decision.

CLASS ACTION A suit commenced by a representative on behalf of an ascertainable group that is too large to appear in court, who shares a commonality of interests and who will benefit from a successful result.

UNCONSCIONABLE A situation in which a contract, or a particular contract term, is unenforceable if the court determines that such term(s) are unduly oppressive or unfair to one party to the contract.

■≡■

Weaver v. American Oil Co.

Lessee (D) v. Lessor (P)

Ind. Sup. Ct., 257 Ind. 458, 276 N.E.2d 144 (1971).

NATURE OF CASE: Appeal from declaratory judgment holding defendant liable for damages incurred by negligence.

FACT SUMMARY: American Oil Co. (P) sued Weaver (D) for indemnification for damages that occurred on premises leased by Weaver (D) from American Oil (P), pursuant to certain clauses contained in a standard form contract.

🏛 **RULE OF LAW**
When a party can show that a contract is in fact an unconscionable one, the unconscionable contract provision, or the contract as a whole if the provision is not separable, should be unenforceable on the grounds that the provision is contrary to public policy.

FACTS: Weaver (D), a high school dropout, leased a gas station from American Oil Co. (P). The lease contained certain clauses that required Weaver (D) to hold harmless and indemnify American Oil (P) for any damages arising on the premises due to anyone's negligence. These clauses were in fine print and contained within a standard form contract. Weaver (D) signed the leases year after year as a mere formality, allegedly without ever reading the clauses. An employee of American Oil (P) came to the gas station and negligently sprayed Weaver (D) and his assistant with gasoline, burning them and causing injuries. Pursuant to the standard form contract, American Oil (P) sued Weaver (D) for indemnification for the injuries. Weaver (D) argued that the clauses were invalid and unconscionable, but the trial court ruled for American Oil (P). On appeal, the state's appellate court ruled that the exculpatory clause was invalid, but the indemnification clause was valid. Weaver (D) appealed, and the state's highest court granted review.

ISSUE: When a party can show that a contract is in fact an unconscionable one, should the unconscionable contract provision, or the contract as a whole if the provision is not separable, be unenforceable on the grounds that the provision is contrary to public policy?

HOLDING AND DECISION: (Arterburn, C.J.) Yes. When a party can show that a contract is in fact an unconscionable one, the unconscionable contract provision, or the contract as a whole if the provision is not separable, should be unenforceable on the grounds that the provision is contrary to public policy. Here, the clauses in the contract must be read together, and when read as such, are unconscionable given the facts of this case. Weaver (D) was an unsophisticated businessman who was presented with a form lease on a take-it-or-leave-it basis.

He never read the clauses in question, nor was he savvy enough in business to know to look out for such clauses. His bargaining power in comparison to American Oil's (P) was minimal. The indemnification clause was unfair. To enforce such a clause would be to circumvent the theory of proper contracting, in that all parties should come to a meeting of the minds with equal bargaining power. Parties may only bargain away such rights knowingly and voluntarily. The party seeking to enforce such a contract has the burden of showing that such provisions were adequately explained and that the contract was signed voluntarily and knowingly. Such was not the case here. Reversed and remanded.

DISSENT: (Prentice, J.) Weaver (D) had every opportunity to review the document or to seek legal counsel with respect to the lease. The general rule is that a person who signs a contract without having read it will still be bound by the terms of the contract. By allowing Weaver (D) to escape the terms of his contract, the majority is unfairly attempting to make certain that all parties are of equal bargaining power.

▶ **ANALYSIS**

This case demonstrates the importance of the bargaining power of the parties to a contract. Historically, courts did not actively involve themselves in leveling the playing field of the parties, thereby allowing the more powerful party to extend its power unchecked. Now, courts are more likely to take an active role in protecting all of the parties' rights.

■══■

Quicknotes

DECLARATORY JUDGMENT A judgment of the court establishing the rights of the parties.

INDEMNIFICATION Reimbursement for losses sustained or security against anticipated loss or damages.

UNCONSCIONABLE A situation in which a contract, or a particular contract term, is unenforceable if the court determines that such term(s) are unduly oppressive or unfair to one party to the contract.

■══■

Taylor v. Caldwell

Entertainer (P) v. Hall owners (D)

Q.B., 3 B.&S. 826, 122 Eng. Rep. 309 (1863).

NATURE OF CASE: Action for damages for breach of a contract for letting of premises.

FACT SUMMARY: Taylor (P) contracted to let Caldwell's (D) hall and gardens for four fetes and concerts, for four days, for £100 per day. Taylor (P) expended money in preparation and for advertising, but Caldwell (D) could not perform when the hall burned down without his fault.

> **RULE OF LAW**
> In contracts in which the performance depends on the continued existence of a given person or thing, a condition is implied that the impossibility of performance arising from the perishing of the person or thing shall excuse the performance.

FACTS: By written agreement, Caldwell (D) agreed to let the Surrey Gardens and Musical Hall at Newington, Surrey for four days for giving four "Grand Concerts" and "Day and Night Fetes." Taylor (P) was to pay £100 at the end of each day. Before any concerts were held, the hall was completely destroyed by fire without any fault of either of the parties. Taylor (P) alleged that the fire and destruction of the hall was a breach and that it resulted in his losing large sums in preparation and advertising for the concerts and fetes.

ISSUE: In contracts in which the performance depends on the continued existence of a given person or thing, is a condition implied that the impossibility of performance arising from the perishing of the person or thing shall excuse the performance?

HOLDING AND DECISION: (Blackburn, J.) Yes. In contracts in which the performance depends on the continued existence of a given person or thing, a condition is implied that the impossibility of performance arising from the perishing of the person or thing shall excuse the performance. Caldwell (D) was excused from performance. First, the agreement was not a lease but a contract to "let." The entertainments that were planned could not be made without the existence of the hall. Ordinarily, when there is a positive contract to do something that is not unlawful, the contractor must perform or pay damages for not doing it even if an unforeseen accident makes performance unduly burdensome or even impossible. This is so when the contract is absolute and positive and not subject to either express or implied conditions and that it appears that the parties must have known from the beginning that the contract could not be fulfilled unless a particular, specified thing continued to exist; and when there is no express or implied warranty that the thing shall exist, the contract is not positive and absolute. It is subject to the implied condition that the parties shall be excused in case, before breach, performance becomes impossible from the perishing of the thing without fault of the contractor. This appears to be within the intention of the parties when they enter into a contract. The excuse from the contract's performance is implied in law because from the nature of the contract it is apparent it was made on the basis of the continued existence of the particular, specified thing. Verdict for defendants.

ANALYSIS

It was important for J. Blackburn not to find the agreement to be a lease; otherwise, the decision would come within direct conflict of *Paradine v. Jane*, K.B., 82 Eng. Rep. 897 (1647), which held that a lease must be performed to the letter despite unforeseen hardship or good fortune. Next, performance is excused only if the destruction of the specified thing is without fault. Had Caldwell (D) been shown to be guilty of arson in the destruction of the hall, he would not have been excused. If there is impossibility of performance due to no one's fault, the one seeking to enforce performance takes the risk. It might be said that the court was actually apportioning the loss if the contract was, in effect, a joint venture with Taylor (P) paying Caldwell (D) £100 out of each day's admission fees to the concerts (Caldwell (D) was supplying the band). The view of this case is found in Uniform Commercial Code § 2-613, where for total destruction of the specified thing, the contract is avoided, or, if the specified thing is goods which have so deteriorated as to no longer conform, the contract can be avoided or the goods can be accepted with an allowance for their lesser value. Note that there is not a satisfactory distinction between a contract to let and a lease.

Quicknotes

IMPOSSIBILITY A doctrine relieving the parties to a contract from liability for nonperformance of their duties thereunder, if the subject matter of the contract ceases to exist, a person essential to the performance of the contract is deceased, or the service or goods contracted for has become illegal.

Nissho–Iwai Co. v. Occidental Crude Sales

Japanese oil distributor (P) v. Oil sales company (D)

729 F.2d 1530 (5th Cir. 1984).

NATURE OF CASE: Appeal from award of damages for breach of contract and fraud.

FACT SUMMARY: Occidental Crude Sales (Occidental) (D), an oil producer, failed to supply oil drilled in Libya to Nissho-Iwai Co. (Nissho) (P), a Japanese oil distributor, for eight months due to a Libyan embargo on oil exports and a pipeline breakdown.

> 🏛 **RULE OF LAW**
> A party relying on a force majeure clause to excuse nonperformance under a contract must prove it did not exercise reasonable control over the excusing event.

FACTS: In 1965 Occidental Crude Sales (Occidental) (D) obtained concessions from Libya to drill for oil on fields with wells managed by the Libyan government; 51 percent of these concessions were nationalized in 1973 after Colonel Khadafi deposed the Libyan king. In 1971 Occidental (D) agreed with Nissho-Iwai Co. (Nissho) (P), a Japanese distributor, to supply it 750,000 barrels of low sulphur crude for distribution to Japanese power and electric companies. The contract contained a "force majeure" clause, excusing nonperformance by Occidental (D) based on, among other things, acts of the Libyan government or other events not within Occidental's (D) control. During eight months in 1975 and 1976, Occidental (D) did not supply Nissho (P) with any oil; earlier supplies in 1974 and 1975 had been severely reduced as well. At first quantities were low due to the Arab-Israeli war and Nissho's (P) own problems with its shipper; however, the Libyan government also began receiving 81 percent of Occidental's (D) oil production, started ordering production increases and cutbacks at will, and refused to pay as agreed for oil exploration. Occidental (D) objected by withholding $117 million in back taxes and royalties due the Libyan government to which Libya retaliated with a complete embargo on oil exports. Although the embargo was lifted in late 1975, breakdowns in Occidental's (D) oil pipeline stopped the further flow of oil until May 1976. A jury awarded Nissho (P) damages for the breach as well as fraud damage. The court of appeals granted review.

ISSUE: Must a party relying on a force majeure clause to excuse nonperformance under a contract prove it did not exercise reasonable control over the excusing event?

HOLDING AND DECISION: (Goldberg, J.) Yes. A party relying on a force majeure clause to excuse nonperformance under a contract must prove it did not exercise reasonable control over the excusing event. "Force majeure" denotes events beyond the "reasonable control" of the contractor. "Reasonable control" means that the nonperforming party must not have affirmatively caused the excusing event nor have been able to take reasonable steps to prevent it. The performance must have been impossible or unreasonably expensive and the nonperforming party must have exercised skill, diligence, and good faith in taking extra steps to prevent the excusing event, unless to do so would involve extreme and unreasonable difficulty, expense, injury, or loss. The nonperforming party bears the burden of proving to a jury that it did not have "reasonable control." Here the embargo and pipeline problems preventing Occidental's (D) performance were found by the jury under proper instructions from the judge to have been within Occidental's (D) "reasonable control." Occidental (D) could have prevented the embargo by paying Libya what was legitimately owed in back royalties, and any production restriction losses could have been recouped through arbitration. Further, Occidental (D) purposely left the pipeline disconnected and unrepaired until it settled with Libya. Affirmed as to liability. [Reversed as to the amount of damages and as to the fraud verdict.]

▶ ANALYSIS

This case presents an example of alleged impossibility due to the failure of a third party, here Libya, to cooperate with the nonperforming party, here Occidental (D). More generally in buyer/seller situations, this arises when a middleman contracts for the supply of goods from a given source, and the source cannot or will not follow through. If the contract between buyer and middleman does not specify the source of goods to be supplied, then performance is not deemed impossible; however, if the source breaches an already existing and specified contract with the middleman, then impossibility may be found.

■═■

Quicknotes

FORCE MAJEURE CLAUSE Clause, pursuant to an oil and gas lease, relieving the lessee from liability for breach of the lease if the party's performance is impeded as the result of a natural cause that could not have been prevented.

IMPOSSIBILITY A doctrine relieving the parties to a contract from liability for nonperformance of their duties thereunder, if the subject matter of the contract ceases to exist, a person essential to the performance of the contract is deceased, or the service or goods contracted for has become illegal.

NONPERFORMANCE Failure to perform a duty.

■═■

Sunflower Electric Cooperative, Inc. v. Tomlinson Oil Co.

Public utility (P) v. Oil company (D)

Kan. Ct. App., 7 Kan. App. 2d 131, 638 P.2d 963 (1981).

NATURE OF CASE: Appeal of denial of damages for breach of contract.

FACT SUMMARY: Tomlinson Oil Co. (D) contracted to supply natural gas to Sunflower Electric Cooperative, Inc. (P) from an as-yet-unproven gas field.

> 🏛 **RULE OF LAW**
> When a party contracts to supply a certain quantity of product from an unproven source, and that party is in a better position to foresee that the source may not produce the requisite quantity, that party assumes the risk of impossibility if the source fails, absent a disclaimer of such risk.

FACTS: Tomlinson Oil Co. (Tomlinson) (D) had the natural gas rights to a certain gas field. The field had been tapped but was unproven. Tomlinson (D) contracted with Sunflower Electric Cooperative, Inc. (Sunflower) (P) to supply the latter with natural gas from this field. The field turned out to be much less productive than anticipated, and Tomlinson (D) was unable to deliver on the contract. Sunflower (P) purchased elsewhere at higher cost. It sued for the difference. The trial court found Tomlinson (D) to have breached the contract but to have been excused on the basis of impossibility. Sunflower (P) appealed. The state's intermediate appellate court granted review.

ISSUE: When a party contracts to supply a certain quantity of product from an unproven source, and that party is in a better position to foresee that the source may not produce the requisite quantity, does that party assume the risk of impossibility if the source fails, absent a disclaimer of such risk?

HOLDING AND DECISION: (Herd, J.) Yes. When a party contracts to supply a certain quantity of product from an unproven source, and that party is in a better position to foresee that the source may not produce the requisite quantity, that party assumes the risk of impossibility if the source fails, absent a disclaimer of such risk. Generally speaking, impossibility may be invoked by a promisor if the impossibility had not been caused by the promisor, the promisor had no reason to know of the impossibility, and the promisor had not assumed the risk of impossibility. In a situation where a promisor has superior knowledge of the possibility of the event leading to impossibility, the law presumes that the promisor has assumed the risk of impossibility, absent contractual language to the contrary. Here, Tomlinson (D) was much better informed than Sunflower (P) about the condition of the field and was in a better position to assess its potential productivity. There being no contractual disclaimer, Tomlinson (D) must be presumed to have assumed the risk of impossibility. Reversed and remanded.

▶ *ANALYSIS*

Impossibility may be categorized into two types: objective ("It can't be done") and subjective ("I can't do it"). Only the former type permits the defense of impossibility. Sunflower (P) argued this to be a case of subjective impossibility. The court disagreed, because it was clear that no gas could be obtained the field covered by the contract, and reversed on the grounds stated instead.

■=■

Quicknotes

IMPOSSIBILITY A doctrine relieving the parties to a contract from liability for nonperformance of their duties thereunder, if the subject matter of the contract ceases to exist, a person essential to the performance of the contract is deceased, or the service or goods contracted for has become illegal.

■=■

Krell v. Henry

Flat owner (P) v. Coronation watcher (D)

C.A., K.B., 2 K.B. 740 (1903).

NATURE OF CASE: Action for damages for breach of a contract for a license for use.

FACT SUMMARY: Henry (D) paid a deposit of £25 to Krell (P) for the use of his apartment in Pall Mall, London, for the purpose of a viewing sight for King Edward VII's coronation procession. The King became ill, causing a delay of the coronation upon which Henry (D) refused to pay a £50 balance for which Krell (P) sued.

🏛 **RULE OF LAW**
Where the object of one of the parties is the basis upon which both parties contract, the duties of performance are constructively conditioned upon the attainment of that object.

FACTS: In two letters of June 20, 1902, Henry (D) contracted through Krell's (P) agent, Bisgood, to use Krell's (P) flat in Pall Mall, London, to view the coronation procession of King Edward VII which had been advertised to pass along Pall Mall. The contract made no mention of this purpose. The period of use of the flat was the daytime only of June 26, 27, 1902 for £75, £25 paid in deposit with the £50 remainder due on June 24, 1902. Henry (D) became aware of the availability of Krell's (P) flat through an advertisement Krell (P) had made, indicating the availability of his flat for viewing the coronation procession, and this purpose was reiterated by Krell's (P) housekeeper who showed Henry (D) the rooms. When the king became very ill, the coronation was delayed, and Henry (D) refused to pay the £50 balance, for which Krell (P) brought suit.

ISSUE: Where the object of one of the parties is the basis upon which both parties contract, are the duties of performance constructively conditioned upon the attainment of that object?

HOLDING AND DECISION: (Lord Williams, J.) Yes. Where the object of one of the parties is the basis upon which both parties contract, the duties of performance are constructively conditioned upon the attainment of that object. It can be inferred from the surrounding circumstances that the rooms were taken for the purpose of viewing the processions, and that was the foundation of the contract. It was not a lease of the rooms—they could not be used at night—but a license for use for a particular purpose. With the defeat of the purpose of the contract, the performance is excused. Appeal dismissed.

▶ ANALYSIS

This case is an extension of *Taylor v. Caldwell* (Q.B., 3 B.&S. 826, 122 Eng. Rep. 309, 1863), and as in that case it was necessary to remove the roadblock of a lease in order to avoid a conflict with *Paradine v. Jane*, (Aleyn 26, 1647). The rule explained here is "frustration of purpose" or "commercial frustration." It has not been made clear whether this doctrine rests upon the failure of consideration or the allocation of the risks. While there is a frustration, performance is not impossible. No constructive condition of performance has failed as Krell (P) made no promise that the condition would occur. Rather, a constructive condition based upon the attainment of the purpose or object has arisen. Note that the frustration should be total or nearly total, though that is a matter of degree.

■■■

Quicknotes

FRUSTRATION OF PURPOSE A doctrine relieving parties to a contract from liability for nonperformance of their duties thereunder when the purpose of the agreement ceases to exist due to circumstances not subject to either party's control.

■■■

Performance and Breach

Quick Reference Rules of Law

Howard v. Federal Crop Insurance Corp.

Farmer (P) v. Insurance company (D)

540 F.2d 695 (4th Cir. 1976).

NATURE OF CASE: Appeal from dismissal on summary judgment of action for payment of proceeds of an insurance policy.

FACT SUMMARY: Federal Crop Insurance Corp. (FCIC) (D) claimed that Howard's (P) violation of a condition precedent negated its obligation to pay.

🏛 RULE OF LAW
Where it is doubtful whether words create a promise or an express condition, they should be interpreted as creating a promise, thereby avoiding forfeiture.

FACTS: Howard (P) suffered losses to his tobacco crop due to alleged rain damage. He notified the Federal Crop Insurance Corp. (FCIC) (D), with whom he had an insurance policy, of the loss. However, before an FCIC (D) agent was able to come out and inspect the land, Howard (P) plowed under the tobacco field, including the damaged stalks, in order to plant a cover crop of rye, which he claimed was necessary for preservation of the soil. The plowing under of the damaged crop was in violation of a provision in the FCIC (D) insurance policy, but that provision did not purport to be a condition precedent, whereas a different provision in the same policy was expressly a condition precedent. Claiming that the provision constituted a condition precedent to its obligation to pay, FCIC (D) refused to settle the claim. Howard (P) brought suit to recover on the policy, but the trial court found for FCIC (D). Howard (P) appealed, arguing that the subject provision constituted a promise, rather than a condition precedent. The court of appeals granted review.

ISSUE: Where it is doubtful whether words create a promise or an express condition, should they be interpreted as creating a promise, thereby avoiding forfeiture?

HOLDING AND DECISION: (Widener, J.) Yes. Where it is doubtful whether words create a promise or an express condition, they should be interpreted as creating a promise, thereby avoiding forfeiture. It is a well-established maxim that the law abhors forfeiture. Therefore, a provision which does not clearly constitute a condition precedent should be interpreted as creating a mere promise. In such a manner, the imposition of forfeiture is avoided. In the instant case, the offending clause did not specify that Howard's (D) agreement not to destroy evidence of an asserted claim constituted a condition precedent to FCIC'S (D) obligation to pay. However, FCIC (D) had expressly made a different provision of the policy a condition precedent, so it is persuasive that its failure to use the words "condition precedent" in the provision at issue means it

intended for that provision to not be a condition precedent. Under these circumstances, a condition precedent will generally not be found. Accordingly, summary judgment in FCIC's (D) favor was improperly granted. Reversed and remanded.

▶ ANALYSIS

The distinction between a condition and a mere promise, on which the *Howard* decision primarily rests, was described by one court as follows. "A condition is distinguished from a promise in that it creates no right or duty in and of itself but is merely a limiting or modifying factor. . . . If the condition is not fulfilled, the right to enforce the contract does not come into existence." See *Lach v. Cahill*, 138 Conn. 418, 85 A.2d 481 (1951).

■■■

Quicknotes

CONDITION PRECEDENT The happening of an uncertain occurrence, which is necessary before a particular right or interest may be obtained or an action performed.

SUMMARY JUDGMENT Judgment rendered by a court in response to a motion by one of the parties, claiming that the lack of a question of material fact in respect to an issue warrants disposition of the issue without consideration by the jury.

■■■

Jones Associates v. Eastside Properties

Engineering/surveying firm (P) v. Real estate developer (D)

Wash. Ct. App., 41 Wash. App. 462, 704 P.2d 681 (1985).

NATURE OF CASE: Appeal from a dismissal of an action for damages for breach of contract.

FACT SUMMARY: After Jones Associates (Jones) (P) prepared a feasibility study and plat application for Eastside Properties' (D) property, the parties disputed whether payment to Jones (P) was conditioned on approval of the plans by the county.

🏛 RULE OF LAW
Ambiguous contractual language should be construed as a promise rather than a condition where the conditioning event is out of the control of the obligee.

FACTS: Eastside Properties (Eastside) (D), a real estate developer, contracted with Jones Associates (Jones) (P), an engineering, consulting and surveying firm, to provide a feasibility study and plat application for a land parcel owned by Eastside (D). The agreement provided that Jones (P) "shall be responsible for obtaining [county] approval for all platting." Jones (P) completed the necessary work, but the county failed to approve the plans. Eastside (D) refused to pay Jones (P) for the balance due for the work done, claiming that the approval of the county was a condition precedent to Eastside's (D) performance under the contract. Jones (P) filed suit, responding that the agreement was only a promise by Jones (P) to do all the necessary work in order to obtain approval. The trial court ruled for Eastside (D), and Jones (P) appealed. The state's intermediate appellate court granted review.

ISSUE: Should ambiguous contractual language be construed as a promise rather than a condition where the conditioning event is out of the control of the obligee?

HOLDING AND DECISION: (Swanson, J.) Yes. Ambiguous contractual language should be construed as a promise rather than a condition where the conditioning event is out of the control of the obligee. Whether a provision in a contract is a condition or a promise depends upon the intent of the parties, as ascertained from a reasonable construction of the language, circumstances surrounding the contract's formation, the parties' subsequent conduct, and the reasonableness of the parties' respective interpretations. Here an examination of all these factors indicates that the parties intended Jones's (P) assumption of responsibility for obtaining county approval to be a duty under the contract but not a condition precedent to payment. Interpretations which reduce the obligee's risk of forfeiture are preferred, unless the event is within the obligee's control or the circumstances indicate that the obligee has assumed this risk. The language of the agreement between Jones (P) and Eastside (D) is ambiguous. The approval of the county was out of the control of both of the parties. Therefore, since there was no evidence that Jones (P) assumed the risk of disapproval, and nonperformance by Eastside (D) would result in forfeiture to Jones (P), the provision should be interpreted as a promise. Jones (P) is entitled to performance under the contract as long as it can prove that the necessary requirements were performed. However, Jones (P) may be liable in damages to Eastside (D) for failing to obtain plat approval, and on remand the parties will have to prove their respective positions in that regard. Reversed and remanded.

▶ ANALYSIS

The court's decision is in accord with the Restatement (Second) of Contracts § 227(1). Comment b to this section defines forfeiture as the denial of compensation, after substantial reliance by the performance of a party, following the nonoccurrence of the conditioning event.

■═■

Quicknotes

CONDITION Requirement; potential future occurrence upon which the existence of a legal obligation is dependent.

■═■

Bright v. Ganas

Executor of employer (D) v. Personal assistant (P)

Md. Ct. App., 171 Md. 493, 189 A. 427 (1937).

NATURE OF CASE: Appeal from partial enforcement of testamentary contract.

FACT SUMMARY: Ganas (P) was to have received $20,000 under a testamentary contract with his employer, Darden, conditioned on Ganas's (P) serving the employer faithfully until Darden's death. Upon Darden's death his executor, Bright (D), refused to award Ganas (P) the $20,000 on the theory that Ganas (P) had not served Darden faithfully.

> ### 🏛 RULE OF LAW
> A breach of an implied condition in a contract between master and servant may, as a matter of law, justify voiding the contract.

FACTS: Ganas (P), a native of Greece, was employed by Col. Darden, a picturesque and colorful character, for approximately four years before Darden's death. Darden agreed to leave $20,000 to Ganas (P) in his will if he served Darden faithfully and continuously until Darden's death. Prior to his death, Darden was ill for several months, and so far as he knew, Ganas (P) was serving him faithfully and assisted in nursing him. Approximately two or three months prior to Darden's death, Mrs. Darden received a strange "love letter" from Ganas (P). She showed the letter to Darden's doctor, who advised her against telling her husband about it. Ganas (P) continued in Darden's employ until Darden's death. Just after Darden's funeral, Mrs. Darden showed Ganas's (P) letter to Bright (D), Darden's executor, telling Bright (D) that Ganas (P) must leave the Darden house. Ganas (P) left the house and his claim under the will was subsequently rejected by Bright (D). Ganas (P) sued, and the jury awarded him $8,999. The state's highest court granted review.

ISSUE: May a breach of an implied condition in a contract between master and servant, as a matter of law, justify voiding the contract?

HOLDING AND DECISION: (Sloan, J.) Yes. A breach of an implied condition in a contract between master and servant may, as a matter of law, justify voiding the contract. If an act of unfaithfulness by a servant is such as to warrant his immediate discharge, had his employer known of the disloyalty, then the servant's right to compensation is also forfeited. Every servant impliedly stipulates that both his words and behavior in regard to his master and master's family shall be respected and free from insolence. In this case, it cannot be assumed that Darden would not have immediately discharged Ganas (P) had Darden known of the letter. Where the facts are disputed, it is for the jury to say upon all the evidence whether there were sufficient grounds to warrant discharge, but there are cases so flagrant and manifestly contrary to the implied conditions arising from the relationship between master and servant that they can be decided by the court as matters of law. This is such a case. Reversed.

▶ ANALYSIS

Ganas's (P) letter was strange and subject to interpretation. There is no indication as to why the jury awarded Ganas (P) the sum of $8,999. Perhaps they felt that Ganas's (P) behavior toward Mrs. Darden did not constitute sufficient infidelity to Mr. Darden to justify voiding the entire devise of $20,000. The appeals court obviously found Ganas's (P) behavior sufficiently unfaithful to constitute a material breach of contract.

Quicknotes

IMPLIED CONDITION A condition that is not expressly stated in the terms of an agreement, but which is inferred from the parties' conduct or the type of dealings involved.

MATERIAL BREACH Breach of a contract's terms by one party that is so substantial as to relieve the other party from its obligations pursuant therefore.

Gray v. Gardner

Oil seller (P) v. Oil buyer (D)

Mass. Sup. Jud. Ct., 17 Mass. 188 (1821).

NATURE OF CASE: Appeal from judgment for plaintiff in action for breach of contract.

FACT SUMMARY: Gardner (D) promised to pay an extra 25 cents a gallon for whale oil if a certain amount of oil failed to arrive at Nantucket's port by October 1.

🏛 RULE OF LAW
The party attempting to escape contractual liability has the burden of proving that a condition has or has not occurred.

FACTS: Gardner (D) entered into a contract with Gray (P) for the purchase of whale oil. The price was to be 85 cents per gallon if no more oil was received in Nantucket and New Bedford than had been received there the previous year. If more oil was received there from whaling ships, then the price for the oil was only to be 60 cents. At midnight on the last day of the period a whaling ship entered Nantucket harbor. It had not docked prior to the expiration of the period specified in the contract. Gardner (D) argued that this ship's oil should be included in the total and that, with the addition of this oil he should only have to pay 60 cents per gallon. The trial court ruled that the agreement called for the docking of the vessel and Gardner (D) had the burden of the proof to show that the vessel had arrived on the last day of the period since he was seeking to escape contractual obligations. Gardner (D) claimed that this was a condition precedent and that Gray (P) had to establish that the condition did not occur before he could enforce the promise. The state's highest court granted review.

ISSUE: Does the party attempting to escape contractual liability have the burden of proving that a condition has or has not occurred?

HOLDING AND DECISION: (Parker, C.J.) Yes. The party attempting to escape contractual liability has the burden of proving that a condition has or has not occurred. Because Gardner (D) was going to be able to avoid some of his duties under the contract if more whale oil came into port this year than in the previous year, he had the burden of proof to show the happening of that event. Gardner (D) was bound by his promise to pay 85 cents a gallon for the whale oil unless a subsequent condition occurred, and that promise remained in force until he could show the happening of the condition. It was necessary for Gardner (D) to show that the vessel in question had come to anchor or had been moored, and since he could only show that the vessel was coming toward the port on October 1, he didn't sustain his burden of proof. Affirmed.

▶ ANALYSIS

It is usually unnecessary, in terms of substantive law, to distinguish between condition precedents and condition subsequent. However, from a procedural point of view, the distinction has great significance. As this famous case illustrates, the party to whom a duty is owed, as a rule, must prove the occurrence of a condition precedent which has discharged his obligation of counter-performance. On the other hand, the party who owes the duty usually has the burden of showing that he has been released from his obligation by the occurrence of a condition subsequent.

■■■

Quicknotes

ASSUMPSIT An oral or written promise by one party to perform or pay another.

CONDITION PRECEDENT The happening of an uncertain occurrence which is necessary before a particular right or interest may be obtained or an action performed.

CONDITION SUBSEQUENT Potential future occurrence that extinguishes a party's obligation to perform pursuant to the contract.

■■■

Chodos v. West Publishing Co.

Author (P) v. Publishing company (D)

292 F.3d 992 (9th Cir. 2002).

NATURE OF CASE: Appeal from a grant of summary judgment in an action for quantum meruit.

FACT SUMMARY: Chodos (P) sued West Publishing Co. (West) (D) for breach of contract for failure to publish his manuscript. Later, Chodos (P) amended his complaint and sued in quantum meruit. The district court held that West's (D) decision not to publish was within its discretion and granted summary judgment in West's (D) favor. Chodos (P) appealed.

> ## 🏛 RULE OF LAW
> A publisher does not retain the right to reject an author's manuscript written pursuant to a standard industry contract if the manuscript is of a quality contemplated by both parties.

FACTS: Chodos (P) entered into a standard author agreement with Bancroft-Whitney Publishing Co. under which he agreed to write a treatise on the law of fiduciary duty. Chodos (P) spent a number of years fulfilling this agreement and submitted the completed manuscript to Bancroft-Whitney's successor, West Publishing Co. (D). Chodos (P) significantly limited the time spent on his law practice during these years. After several rounds of editorial comments and direction to which Chodos (P) timely responded, West Publishing Co. (D) declined to publish the treatise, citing sales and marketing reasons. The decision not to publish was made by Carole Gamble, who joined West Publishing Co. (D) the same year Chodos (P) completed the manuscript and was based on criteria developed after Chodos (P) submitted his treatise. Chodos (P) sued West Publishing Co. (D) for breach of contract for failure to publish his manuscript. Later, Chodos (P) amended his complaint and sued in quantum meruit. The district court held that West Publishing Co.'s (D) decision not to publish was within its discretion and granted summary judgment in West's (D) favor. Chodos (P) appealed. The court of appeals granted review.

ISSUE: Does a publisher retain the right to reject an author's manuscript written pursuant to a standard industry agreement if the manuscript is of a quality contemplated by both parties?

HOLDING AND DECISION: (Reinhardt, J.) No. A publisher does not retain the right to reject an author's manuscript written pursuant to a standard industry contract if the manuscript is of a quality contemplated by both parties. As a threshold matter, the contract at issue is not illusory because West's (D) right to exercise its discretion is not absolute, but is limited by the duty to exercise good

faith. In determining whether Chodos's (P) manuscript was satisfactory as to form and content under the standard agreement, it was improper for West Publishing Co. (D) to consider the likelihood of the commercial success of the book. Nothing in the contract suggests that the ordinary meaning of "form and content" was not intended, and nothing suggests that the publisher may terminate the agreement if it changes its management structure or its marketing strategy, or if it revises its business or economic forecasts, all matters unrelated to "form and content." Such a reading is supported by the fact that the contract afforded Chodos (P) an opportunity to cure any deficiency West (D) found unacceptable; Chodos (P) would not be able to cure a matter not within his control. Chodos (P) worked for many years on this manuscript, to the detriment of his practice, and in cooperation with West's (D) editors. It is inequitable and unconscionable to allow West (D) to escape its contractual obligations based upon the vagaries of the market, its change in management, or its failure to plan appropriately when entering into this standard author agreement. Because damages cannot be readily calculated, as the determination of what 15 percent of revenues on sales of the book has been foreclosed by West (D), Chodos (P) is entitled to sue for restitution for the time and effort he reasonably invested in writing the manuscript. The district court's decision is reversed and remanded.

▶ ANALYSIS

This case recognizes that a publishing company using a standard writer's contract cannot simply change its mind in regard to publishing a manuscript that was diligently researched and written in good faith by a writer who had every expectation it would be published, especially when the manuscript was undertaken after a proposal was submitted and accepted by the publisher.

■═■

Quicknotes

BREACH OF CONTRACT Unlawful failure by a party to perform its obligations pursuant to contract.

QUANTUM MERUIT Equitable doctrine allowing recovery for labor and materials provided by one party, even though no contract was entered into, in order to avoid unjust enrichment by the benefitted party.

■═■

Gulf Construction Co. v. Self

Construction company (D) v. Subcontractors (P)

Tex. App. Ct., 676 S.W.2d 624 (1984).

NATURE OF CASE: Consolidated appeal of award-ing of damages for breach of contract.

FACT SUMMARY: Gulf Construction Co. (Gulf) (D), a general contractor, entered into subcontracting agreements with Self (P) and another subcontractor, which provided that the general contractor would not be obligated to pay the subcontractors until he had been paid by the owner. When the owner failed to pay Gulf (D) and Gulf (D) refused to pay the subcontractors, Self (P) sued.

🏛 RULE OF LAW
When the finding of a contractual condition precedent will result in forfeiture, and another rea-sonable reading of the contract will avoid such forfeiture, the condition precedent is to be disfavored.

FACTS: Gulf Construction Co. (Gulf) (D), a general contractor, entered into contracts with Good Hope Chem-ical Corporation (Good Hope) for construction of buildings at Good Hope's plant site. Gulf (D) then entered into subcontracting agreements with Self (P) and another subcontractor, which Gulf (D) authored. The agreements each carried a paragraph nine which contained the follow-ing language: "Under no circumstances shall the general contractor be obligated or required to advance or make payments to the subcontractor until the funds have been advanced or paid by the owner . . . to the general contrac-tor." Good Hope encountered financial difficulties and ordered the work to cease. Subsequently, it filed for bank-ruptcy. Gulf (D), relying on paragraph nine, refused to pay the subcontractors, arguing that it had not been paid by Good Hope. Self (P) and the other subcontractor sued Gulf (D) and its surety. The trial court ruled for the subcontrac-tors (P) and Gulf (D) appealed. The state's intermediate appellate court granted review.

ISSUE: When the finding of a contractual condition precedent will result in forfeiture, and another reasonable reading of the contract will avoid such forfeiture, is the condition precedent to be disfavored?

HOLDING AND DECISION: (Utter, J.) Yes. When the finding of a contractual condition precedent will result in forfeiture, and another reasonable reading of the contract will avoid such forfeiture, the condition prece-dent is to be disfavored. The law does not favor forfeiture. When a contract reasonably can be read to avoid a condi-tion precedent which would result in forfeiture, the alternative reading is preferred. The risk of nonpayment by an owner should fall with the general contractor and should not be shifted to the subcontractor unless there is a

clear, unequivocal and expressed agreement between the contractor and the subcontractor to do so. The ninth paragraph does not state that Gulf (D) shall be liable to the subcontractors if the money is not received from the owner, but that the Gulf (D) shall not be obligated to make payments until the money has been received. As such, the ninth paragraph is merely a covenant dealing with the manner of payment and not a condition prece-dent. As the contracts do not clearly and unequivocally express intent to the subcontractors, Gulf (D) is liable to Self (P) for payment. Affirmed.

▶ ANALYSIS

In this case, the balance appears to turn on the word "until," a term modifying a time provision. The court appar-ently found that the ninth paragraph, stating that Gulf (D) did not have to pay the subcontractors until Gulf (D) was paid by the owner, did not contemplate a situation where-by Gulf (D) was not paid by the owner. It is unlikely that the subcontractors agreed to forfeit their rights to look at the general contractor for payment in such event, even if Gulf (D) intended such forfeiture. As Gulf (D) was author of the contract, it would be strictly construed against Gulf (D).

■═■

Quicknotes

CONDITION PRECEDENT The happening of an uncertain occurrence, which is necessary before a particular right or interest may be obtained or an action performed.

COVENANT A written promise to do, or to refrain from doing, a particular activity.

FORFEITURE The loss of an interest in property without compensation.

■═■

Kingston v. Preston

Buyer (P) v. Seller of business (D)

K.B., 2 Doug. 689, 99 Eng. Rep. 437 (1773).

NATURE OF CASE: Action to recover damages for breach of contract.

FACT SUMMARY: Preston (D) agreed to sell his business to Kingston (P), and Kingston (P) agreed to, but did not, give security for the payments.

🏛 RULE OF LAW
Breach of a covenant by one party to a contract relieves the other party's obligation to perform another covenant which is dependent thereon, the performance of the first covenant being an implied condition precedent to the duty to perform the second covenant.

FACTS: Preston (D) agreed (among other things) to sell his business to Kingston (P). Kingston (P) agreed (among other things) to give sufficient security for his payments. Kingston's (P) personal worth was negligible. Kingston (P) failed to provide sufficient security, and thereafter Preston (D) refused to sell.

ISSUE: Does breach of a covenant by one party to a contract relieve the other party's obligation to perform another covenant which is dependent thereon, the performance of the first covenant being an implied condition precedent to the duty to perform the second covenant?

HOLDING AND DECISION: [Judge not stated in the casebook excerpt.] Yes. Breach of a covenant by one party to a contract relieves the other party's obligation to perform another covenant which is dependent thereon, the performance of the first covenant being an implied condition precedent to the duty to perform the second covenant. When one party covenants to sell and a second party covenants in return to give sufficient security for his payments, those covenants are dependent. Therefore, Kingston (P) must show that he has provided or is ready and willing to provide sufficient security as a condition precedent to Preston's (D) duty to sell. The dependence or independence of covenants is to be determined from the intention of the parties which in turn will normally be determined by the "order of time in which the intent of the transaction requires their performance." Here, the security was to be given "at and before the sealing and delivery of the deeds" conveying the business. Thus, according to the "temporal sequence" test, Preston's (D) duty to convey his business was dependent on Kingston's (P) giving of sufficient security. Furthermore, "it would be the greatest injustice if the plaintiff [Kingston (P)] should prevail." The giving of sufficient security was the essence of this agreement and "therefore, must necessarily be a condition precedent." Judgment for defendant.

▶ ANALYSIS

Although Lord Mansfield in this famous decision focused on the time sequence of the contract provisions (e.g., a provision to be performed after another provision is dependent on that other provision), he was very likely reacting primarily to the personal poverty of Kingston (P) and the "injustice" that would be done by making Preston (D) go through with his performance and then sue poor Kingston (P) for damages. (Kingston (P), presumably, might run the business into the ground very quickly, leaving Preston's (D) court victory a purely theoretical one.) Note that Lord Mansfield, in determining the time sequence (which he felt was so important), apparently looked not only to the contract itself but also to what he thought must have been the reasonable intentions of the parties.

Quicknotes

CONDITION PRECEDENT The happening of an uncertain occurrence, which is necessary before a particular right or interest may be obtained or an action performed.

DEPENDENT COVENANTS An obligation of one party to perform pursuant to an agreement, which is dependent upon the performance of the other.

IMPLIED CONDITION A condition that is not expressly stated in the terms of an agreement, but which is inferred from the parties' conduct or the type of dealings involved.

Shaw v. Mobil Oil Corp.

Service station lessee (P) v. Oil company/lessor (D)

Or. Sup. Ct., 272 Or. 109, 535 P.2d 756 (1975).

NATURE OF CASE: Appeal of judgment in favor of lessor in action to determine a lessee's obligations in a lease.

FACT SUMMARY: Shaw (P) and Mobil Oil Corp. (Mobil) (D) entered into a service station lease agreement whereby Mobil (D) agreed to sell to Shaw (P) the amount of gasoline ordered by Shaw (P), not to exceed 500,000 gallons per year, and Shaw (P) agreed to pay Mobil (D) as rent, 1.4 cents per gallon delivered, but no less than the $470 per month. Even though Mobil (D) failed to deliver a minimum monthly amount of gasoline, it sought the minimum monthly rental from Shaw (P).

🏛 RULE OF LAW

A party does not have to perform a promise that is conditioned upon the other party's performance when the other party fails to perform, notwithstanding that such failure is excused and not a breach of contract.

FACTS: Shaw (P) entered into a service station lease agreement with Mobil Oil Corp. (Mobil) (D). The agreement required Shaw (P) to purchase no less than 200,000 gallons of gasoline per year, and Mobil (D) to sell Shaw (P) the amount of gasoline he ordered, subject to a maximum of 500,000 gallons per year. The agreement also provided that Shaw (P) pay to Mobil (D) 1.4 cents per gallon of gasoline delivered, as rent, but not less than $470 per month. In order for the rent per gallon to equal the minimum rent, Mobil (D) had to deliver 33,572 gallons per month. In July 1972, Shaw (P) ordered 34,000 gallons, but Mobil (D) delivered only 25,678, claiming that it was complying with a government request that it allocate its existing gasoline supply among its dealers. Nevertheless, Mobil (D) demanded the minimum rent from Shaw (P) for that month. The agreement also had an excuse clause: "Seller shall not be liable for loss, damage or demurrer due to any delay or failure in performance (a) because of compliance with any order, request or control of any governmental authority. . . ." The trial court held that Shaw (P) was obligated to pay the minimum rent for July. The state's highest court granted review.

ISSUE: Does a party have to perform a promise that is conditioned upon the other party's performance when the other party fails to perform, notwithstanding that such failure is excused and not a breach of contract?

HOLDING AND DECISION: (Denecke, J.) No. A party does not have to perform a promise that is conditioned upon the other party's performance when the other

party fails to perform, notwithstanding that such failure is excused and not a breach of contract. The promise to pay a minimum rent and the promise to deliver a minimum amount of gasoline were dependent covenants. As Shaw's (P) promise to pay a minimum rent was dependent on Mobil's (D) promise to deliver a certain amount of gasoline, and as Mobil (D) did not deliver the required amount, Shaw (P) did not have to perform his promise to pay the minimum rent for July, notwithstanding that Mobil's (D) failure to deliver the required amount of gasoline was excused and did not constitute a breach of the contract. Reversed.

⏵ ANALYSIS

Where dependent promises are concerned, even if one of these promises becomes impossible, and therefore excused, this does not justify the excused party's demanding performance by the other party. 6 Corbin, *Contracts* 510–511, § 1363 (1962). Williston is to the same effect. 6 Williston, *Contracts* 131, 139, § 838 (3d ed. 1962).

■■■

Quicknotes

CONCURRENT CONDITIONS Dependent conditions that are to be performed at the same time.

DEPENDENT PROMISES An obligation of one party to perform pursuant to an agreement, which is dependent upon the performance of the other.

■■■

Jacob & Youngs, Inc. v. Kent

Homebuilder (P) v. Buyer (D)

N.Y. Ct. App., 230 N.Y. 239, 129 N.E. 889 (1921).

NATURE OF CASE: Appeal from reversal of verdict for defendant in action for damages for breach of a construction contract.

FACT SUMMARY: Jacob & Youngs, Inc. (P) was hired to build a $77,000 country home for Kent (D). When the dwelling was completed, it was discovered that through an oversight, pipe not of Reading manufacture (though of comparable quality and price), which had been specified in the contract, was used. Kent (D) refused to make final payment of $3,483.46 upon learning of this.

🏛 RULE OF LAW
(1) A dependent condition may be deemed an independent and collateral condition where the condition's breach is trivial and innocent.
(2) Where a construction contract has been substantially performed, and where the cost of replacing an unspecified material is vastly disproportionate to the value to be obtained from such replacement, the measure of damages is the difference between the value of the structure as built and its built-to-specifications value.

FACTS: Jacob & Youngs, Inc. (Jacob) (P) built a country home for $77,000 for Kent (D) and sued for $3,483.46, which remained unpaid. Almost a year after completion, Kent (D) discovered that not all pipe in the home was of Reading manufacture, as specified in the contract. Kent (D) ordered the plumbing replaced, but as it was encased in the walls, except in those spots where it had to remain exposed, Jacob (P) refused to replace the pipe, stating that the pipe used was of comparable price and quality. It appeared that the omission was neither fraudulent nor willful and was due to oversight. Kent (D) refused to pay the balance of the construction cost still due, and Jacob (P) sued for payment. The trial court refused to allow evidence that the pipes used were essentially the same in quality and price as the Reading pipe, and a verdict was directed for Kent (D). The state's intermediate appellate court reversed, and the state's highest court granted review.

ISSUE:
(1) May a dependent condition be deemed an independent and collateral condition where the condition's breach is trivial and innocent?
(2) Where a construction contract has been substantially performed, and where the cost of replacing an unspecified material is vastly disproportionate to the value to be obtained from such replacement, is the measure of damages the difference between the value of the structure as built and its built-to-specifications value?

HOLDING AND DECISION: (Cardozo, J.)
(1) Yes. A dependent condition may be deemed an independent and collateral condition where the condition's breach is trivial and innocent. Where the significance of the default or omission is grievously out of proportion to the oppression of the forfeiture, the breach is considered to be trivial and innocent. What is considered significant vs. trivial, however, is a matter to be determined in each case, and there is no set formula for making such a determination. A change will not be tolerated if it is so dominant and pervasive so as to frustrate the purpose of the contract. The contractor cannot, as a rule, install anything he believes to be just as good. It is a matter of degree judged by the purpose to be served, the desire to be gratified, the excuse for deviation from the letter, and the cruelty of enforced adherence.
(2) Yes. Where a construction contract has been substantially performed, and where the cost of replacing an unspecified material is vastly disproportionate to the value to be obtained from such replacement, the measure of damages is the difference between the value of the structure as built and its built-to-specifications value. Under the circumstances, the measure of damages should not be the cost of replacing the pipe, which would be great. Instead, the difference in value between the dwelling as specified and the dwelling as constructed should be the measure, even though that difference may be nominal or nothing. Usually, the owner is entitled to the cost of completion but not where it is grossly unfair and out of proportion to the good to be obtained. This simply is a rule to promote justice when there is substantial performance with trivial deviation. Affirmed.

DISSENT: (McLaughlin, J.) Jacob (P) failed to perform as specified. It makes no difference why Kent (D) wanted a particular kind of pipe. Failure to use the kind of pipe specified was either intentional or due to gross neglect, which amounted to the same thing. Because Kent (D) expressly agreed to pay only for Reading pipe, he should not be compelled to pay unless that condition is satisfied; the rule, therefore, of substantial performance, with damages for unsubstantial omissions, has no application to the case at bar.

Continued on next page.

▶ *ANALYSIS*

Substantial performance cannot occur where the breach is intentional as it is the antithesis of material breach. The part unperformed must not destroy the purpose or value of the contract. Because here there is an unsatisfied land-owner who stands to retain the defective structure built on his land, there arises the problem of unjust enrichment. Usually, it would appear that the owner would pocket the damages he collected rather than remedying the defect by tearing out the wrong pipe and replacing it with the speci-fied pipe. The owner would have a home substantially in compliance and a sum of money greatly in excess of the harm suffered by him. Note that under the doctrine of de minimis non curat lex, that is, that the law is not concerned with trifles, trivial defects, even if willful, will be ignored. The party which claims substantial performance has still breached the contract and is liable for damages but in a lesser amount than for a willful breach.

∎══∎

Quicknotes

CONDITION Requirement; potential future occurrence upon which the existence of a legal obligation is depen-dent.

DE MINIMUS NON CURAT LEX Not of sufficient significance to invoke legal action.

FRUSTRATION OF PURPOSE A doctrine relieving the parties to a contract from liability for nonperformance of their duties thereunder when the purpose of the agreement ceases to exist, due to circumstances not subject to either party's control.

SUBSTANTIAL PERFORMANCE Performance of all the es-sential obligations pursuant to an agreement.

∎══∎

O. W. Grun Roofing and Construction Co. v. Cope

Roofing company (D) v. Homeowner (P)

Tex. Civ. App., 529 S.W.2d 258 (1975).

NATURE OF CASE: Suit to recover damages and to set aside a mechanic's lien.

FACT SUMMARY: O. W. Grun Roofing and Construction Co. (Grun) (D) contracted to install a new roof on Cope's (P) house but used shingles that were not of uniform color. As a result, Cope (P) refused to pay Grun (D) for the new roof.

🏛 **RULE OF LAW**
A party to a contract may not claim substantial performance where he has breached the agreement in a material respect.

FACTS: O. W. Grun Roofing and Construction Co. (Grun) (D) agreed to install a new roof on Cope's (P) house at a cost of $648. The roof was to be brown in color, but some of the shingles used by Grun (D) were yellow. When Cope (P) complained, Grun (D) removed at least some of the yellow shingles, but the roof still was not uniformly brown. Cope (P), therefore, refused to pay Grun (D) and ultimately sued for damages and to set aside a mechanic's lien which Grun (D) had filed. Grun (D) cross-claimed for foreclosure of the mechanic's lien and for recovery of the contract price. The trial court set aside the lien and awarded Cope (P) damages in an amount equal to the difference between the price of having a proper roof installed and the contract price. On appeal, Grun (D) claimed that it had substantially performed the agreement. The state's intermediate appellate court granted review.

ISSUE: May a party to a contract claim substantial performance where he has breached the agreement in a material respect?

HOLDING AND DECISION: (Cadena, J.) No. A party to a contract may not claim substantial performance where he has breached the agreement in a material respect. In order to establish that he has substantially performed a contract, a party must demonstrate that he intended in good faith to comply with his obligations and that any omissions or deviations which did occur were unintentional and comparatively insignificant. While it is impossible to articulate a universal test for determining whether or not substantial performance has occurred, it is obvious that a party has not substantially performed as long as the other party's general plan and purpose in entering into the contract remains unfulfilled. In this case, Cope's (P) general purpose included having a roof of uniform color, and since she can have such a roof only by having Grun's (D) work completely redone, it cannot be said that Grun (D) has substantially performed the contract. Nor may Grun (D) recover on a quantum meruit theory because Cope (P) has received no real benefit from Grun's (D) work. Therefore, the judgment of the trial court must be affirmed.

▶ **ANALYSIS**

The doctrine of substantial performance is most frequently invoked in building construction cases. In this context, the contract in question usually involves materials which ultimately are affixed to real estate. Since it is usually impractical, if not impossible, under such a circumstance, to return the parties to their previous status quo by ordering the return of all money and materials expended, courts are anxious to reach a compromise in such cases.

■═■

Quicknotes

MECHANICS LIEN A lien enforceable pursuant to statute in structures and/or improvements constructed in order to secure payment for the value of labor performed or materials furnished.

QUANTUM MERUIT Equitable doctrine allowing recovery for labor and materials provided by one party, even though no contract was entered into, in order to avoid unjust enrichment by the benefited party.

SUBSTANTIAL PERFORMANCE Performance of all the essential obligations pursuant to an agreement.

■═■

Carter v. Sherburne Corp.

Construction contractor (P) v. Company (D)

Vt. Sup. Ct., 132 Vt. 88, 315 A.2d 870 (1974).

NATURE OF CASE: Appeal of judgment in favor of contractor.

FACT SUMMARY: Sherburne Corp. (D) failed to make full payments to Carter (P) under several construction contracts, claiming that Carter's (P) performance was defective, and, in particular, that Carter (P) failed to comply with completion schedules.

> 🏛 **RULE OF LAW**
> Unless time is made of the essence in a construction contract, failure to complete the work within a specified time will not terminate the contract.

FACTS: Carter (P) entered into four written agreements with Sherburne Corp. (D) for performance of various construction projects. Two of the contracts called for completion dates and forfeitures for noncompletion on schedule. Carter (P) also performed work for Sherburne (D) outside of the contracts, without compensation, under a promise for additional work which was never fulfilled by Sherburne (D). Sherburne (D) eventually terminated the contracts on the basis of delay and withheld approximately $10,000, or 20 percent of the amount billed to it by Carter (P), and Carter (P) sued for payment. The trial court found that many of the delays were occasioned by acts of Sherburne (D) and that Carter (P) has substantially performed and was due the entire invoiced amount. The trial court also held that Carter (P) could recover for work performed without compensation on a quantum meruit basis. The state's highest court granted review.

ISSUE: Unless time is made of the essence in a construction contract, will failure to complete the work within a specified time terminate the contract?

HOLDING AND DECISION: (Shangraw, C.J.) No. Unless time is made of the essence in a construction contract, failure to complete the work within a specified time will not terminate the contract. Ordinarily, in contracts where time is not of essence, a failure to complete the work within the specified time will not terminate the contract but will subject the contractor to damages for delay. While two of the contracts called for completion dates and forfeitures for noncompletion on schedule, the inclusion of dates in construction contracts does not make time of the essence. Since most of the delays in this case were due to the actions of Sherburne (D), it was not proper for Sherburne (D) to withhold payment. Additionally, with respect to the recovery granted Carter (P), Sherburne's (D) failure to perform gives rise to several remedies, one of which is quantum meruit. Affirmed.

▶ **ANALYSIS**

In general, performance at the agreed time by the contractor is not of essence. Construction contracts are subject to many delays for innumerable reasons, the blame for which may be difficult to assess. Delays are generally foreseen as probable; and the risks thereof are discounted. 3A A. Corbin, *Contracts* § 720, at 377 (1960).

■══■

Quicknotes

FORFEITURE The loss of an interest in property without compensation.

QUANTUM MERUIT Equitable doctrine allowing recovery for labor and materials provided by one party, even though no contract was entered into, in order to avoid unjust enrichment by the benefitted party.

TIME IS OF THE ESSENCE Contract provision specifying that the time period in which performance is rendered constitutes an essential term of the agreement.

■══■

Printing Center of Texas, Inc. v. Supermind Publishing Co.

Printer (D) v. Publishing company (P)

Tex. Ct. App., 669 S.W.2d 779 (1984).

NATURE OF CASE: Appeal from award of refund of deposit in breach of contract action.

FACT SUMMARY: In Supermind Publishing Co.'s (Supermind) (P) action against Printing Center of Texas, Inc. (Printing Center) (D) for refund of a deposit made under a written contract to print 5,000 books, Supermind (P) contended that it rightfully rejected the books upon delivery because the books failed in all respects to conform to the contract.

RULE OF LAW

Under the Uniform Commercial Code, a buyer has a right to reject goods if the goods fail to conform to either the express or implied terms of the contract between buyer and seller.

FACTS: Supermind Publishing Co., Inc. (Supermind) (P) contracted with Printing Center of Texas, Inc. (Printing Center) (D) to print 5,000 books. The written contract between the parties covered essential terms such as quantity, trim size, and type of paper and cover. The type of paper specified was 30-pound white newsprint. Supermind's (P) witness, at trial, testified that he was shown a sample of the newsprint to be used, and that the tendered books were not the same color as the sample. Other nonconformities alleged were off-center cover art, wrinkled pages, and inadequate perforation on a pull-out page. Supermind (P) sued Printing Center (D) for refund of a deposit made under the contract and contended that it rightfully rejected the books upon delivery because the books failed in all respects to conform to the contract. Publishing Center (D) argued that if nonconformities existed, they were minor, and that Supermind (P) rejected the books in bad faith. The trial court, on the verdict of the jury, awarded Supermind (P) a refund of its deposits and attorney's fees. Publishing Center (D) appealed. The state's intermediate appellate court granted review.

ISSUE: Under the Uniform Commercial Code, does a buyer have a right to reject goods if the goods fail to conform to either the express or implied terms of the contract between buyer and seller?

HOLDING AND DECISION: (Cannon, J.) Yes. Under the Uniform Commercial Code, a buyer has a right to reject goods if the goods fail to conform to either the express or implied terms of the contract between buyer and seller. Although it is doubtful that this case should have proceeded under the legal theory that the contract was governed by Chapter 2 of the state's version of the Uniform Commercial Code (UCC), since that statute deals with sales of goods and since a contract for the printing of books involves predominantly the provision of services, because Publishing Center (D) failed to object to proceeding under this theory, the court will entertain the dubious assumption that Chapter 2 of the UCC applies. It should be noted, however, that under the common law, if delivered goods failed in any respect to conform to the contract, the purchaser would not have the right—as purchasers do under the UCC—to reject and recover a refund of the purchase price. Under the UCC, evidence first must be reviewed to determine if a contract exists between the parties and if the right goods were tendered at the right time and place. If the evidence does establish nonconformity in some respect, the buyer is entitled to reject if he rejects in good faith. If the seller alleges that the buyer rejected in bad faith, the seller has the burden of proof on this issue. Here, Printing Center (D) contended that if nonconformities existed, they were minor, and that Supermind (P) rejected in bad faith. Printing Center (D) has failed to carry its burden to prove that Supermind (P) rejected the books in bad faith. Printing Center's (D) contentions that the alleged nonconformities should be classified as minor are inappropriate. A jury could reasonably conclude that books with crooked or wrinkled pages, off-center cover art, and inadequate perforation are not fit for sale to the public. Evidence is sufficient to support the jury's finding that the books did not conform to the contract. Affirmed.

▌ *ANALYSIS*

If a seller alleges that a buyer rejected goods contracted for in bad faith, the seller has the burden of proof on this issue. Evidence of circumstances which indicate that the buyer's motivation in rejecting goods was to escape the bargain would support a finding of rejection in bad faith. Thus, evidence of rejection of goods because of a minor defect in a falling market would in some instances be sufficient to support a finding that the buyer acted in bad faith when he rejected the goods.

Quicknotes

BAD FAITH Conduct that is intentionally misleading or deceptive.

NONCONFORMING GOODS Goods tendered pursuant to a contract for sale that do not conform to the contract's requirements or which are otherwise defective in some way.

Capitol Dodge Sales v. Northern Concrete Pipe, Inc.

Truck seller (P) v. Pipe company (D)

Mich. Ct. App., 131 Mich. App. 149, 346 N.W.2d 535 (1983).

NATURE OF CASE: Appeal from award of damages for breach of contract.

FACT SUMMARY: Northern Concrete Pipe, Inc. (D) took possession from Capitol Dodge Sales (Capitol) (P) of a truck, but stopped payment on the check for the purchase price a few days later when, after repositioning the snowplow attachment as directed and having the truck serviced by Capitol (P), the truck continued to overheat.

🏛 **RULE OF LAW**
Under the Uniform Commercial Code, a buyer may possess goods for a period reasonably necessary to inspect them without being said to have accepted them.

FACTS: Northern Concrete Pipe, Inc. (Northern) (D) wished to buy a truck with a snowplow attachment from Capitol Dodge Sales (Capital) (P). During a test drive of the truck, the engine overheated; however Capitol's (P) representative assured Northern's (D) agent that this was due to the incorrect positioning of the snowplow. Northern (D) was willing to buy the truck if this was correct, and Capitol (P) assured that it was. The following day, agents of Northern (D) came to Capitol (P) to pick up the truck. They were instructed by Capitol (P) in the correct positioning of the plow, and it was so positioned before leaving Capitol (P). Nevertheless, before arriving at Northern's (D) place of business, the truck again overheated. Northern (D) called Capitol (P) and was told by an employee in the service department to recheck the blade and refill the radiator, which Northern (D) did. The truck again overheated and was taken to Capitol (P) for service. When Northern (D) again picked the truck up from Capitol (P), Capitol (P) stated that a radiator cap had been replaced. Once again, by the time the truck was driven to Northern's (D) place of business it overheated. Northern (D) then called Capitol (P) to say that Northern (D) was not taking the truck, that payment was being stopped on the check, and that Capitol (P) should come and get the truck. Capitol (P) sent a wrecker that evening and towed the truck back to its lot. Title to the truck was issued in Northern's (D) name shortly thereafter. Northern (D) tendered the title to Capitol (P), but Capitol (P) rejected it on the theory that the transaction was complete, and it sued for payment. The trial court held that Northern (D) had accepted the truck and entered judgment for Capitol (P). The state's intermediate appellate court granted review.

ISSUE: Under the Uniform Commercial Code, may a buyer possess goods for a period reasonably necessary to inspect them without being said to have accepted them?

HOLDING AND DECISION: (Peterson, J.) Yes. Under the Uniform Commercial Code, a buyer may possess goods for a period reasonably necessary to inspect them without being said to have accepted them. The Uniform Commercial Code provides that acceptance of goods occurs if the buyer, after a reasonable time to inspect them, signifies to the seller that they are conforming or that he will retain them despite their nonconformity. The evidence shows that Northern (D) did not signify to Capitol (P) that the truck conformed, or that it would accept the truck despite its nonconformance. Reversed and remanded.

▶ **ANALYSIS**

The opinion of the trial judge contained no findings of fact, discussion, or conclusion as to an acceptance of the truck by Northern (D). The conclusion that acceptance was deemed to have occurred was inferred from the trial court's statement of issues. Had the decision turned on what constituted a "reasonable opportunity," this would have been an issue of fact for the trier of fact.

■━■

Quicknotes

ACCEPTANCE OF GOODS In a contract for the sale of goods, the buyer's taking of possession of the goods that are the subject matter of the offer constitute acceptance by the recipient.

INSPECTION The examination of goods, which are the subject matter of a contract for sale, for the purpose of determining whether they are satisfactory.

■━■

[handwritten notes: 2-606; 2-601 buyer may reject if goods fail in any respect to conform to K]

Colonial Dodge, Inc. v. Miller

Auto seller (P) v. Buyer (D)

Mich. Sup. Ct., 420 Mich. 452, 362 N.W.2d 704 (1984).

NATURE OF CASE: Appeal of judgment awarding damages to seller.

FACT SUMMARY: Miller (D), who bought a car from Colonial Dodge, Inc. (P), renounced the sale the following day upon discovering that the car had no spare tire, and that no spare tire was available.

🏛 RULE OF LAW
Under the Uniform Commercial Code, a buyer may revoke his acceptance of goods whose nonconformity substantially impairs their value to him.

FACTS: Miller (D), whose occupation required extensive driving, purchased a station wagon from Colonial Dodge, Inc. (Colonial) (P). Miller (D) ordered the car with a special package including extra wide tires. The day Miller (D) took possession of the car he discovered that the spare tire was missing. The next day, Miller (D) called Colonial (P) and insisted on having the spare tire immediately. When told that no spare tire was then available, Miller (D) informed Colonial (P) that he would stop payment on the checks made in payment for the car, and Colonial (P) could pick up the vehicle from in front of Miller's (D) home. The car was parked in front of Miller's (D) home until the ten-day temporary registration sticker expired, whereupon the car was towed by the police. Colonial (P) applied for license plates, registration, and title in Miller's (D) name. Miller (D) refused the license plates when they were delivered to him. According to Colonial (P), the spare tire was not included in the delivery of the vehicle due to a nationwide shortage caused by a strike. Miller (D) contended that the spare was important to him because he was afraid of having a flat tire on a Detroit freeway during the early morning hours. Some months later, Miller (D) was informed that the spare tire was available. Colonial (P) sued Miller (D) for the purchase price of the car. The trial court held for Colonial (P), finding that Miller (D) had wrongfully revoked acceptance of the vehicle. The court of appeals reversed. On rehearing, the court of appeals, noting the trial court found the parties had agreed there was a valid acceptance, affirmed the trial court's decision. The state's highest court granted review.

ISSUE: Under the Uniform Commercial Code, may a buyer revoke his acceptance of goods whose nonconformity substantially impairs their value to him?

HOLDING AND DECISION: (Kavanagh, J.) Yes. Under the Uniform Commercial Code, a buyer may revoke acceptance of goods whose nonconformity substantially impairs their value to him. Colonial (P) argues that the missing spare tire did not constitute a substantial impairment in the value of the car; however, the relevant statute provides that a buyer may revoke acceptance of goods whose nonconformance impairs their value to him. In this case, Miller's (D) concern with safety is evidenced by his ordering a special package which included special tires. Miller's (D) occupation required that he travel extensively, and Miller (D) testified that he was afraid of a flat tire on a Detroit freeway during the early morning hours. Since the nonconformity substantially impaired the value of the vehicle to Miller (D), his timely revocation of acceptance was proper. Reversed.

DISSENT: (Ryan, J.) The nonconformity must be substantial. It is not enough that the nonconformity be worrisome, aggravating, or even potentially dangerous.

DISSENT: (Boyle, J.) The trial judge's determination that the temporarily missing spare tire did not constitute substantial impairment in value under either a subjective or objective test was not clearly erroneous.

▌ *ANALYSIS*

Whether there was a substantial impairment in the value of the car is a question of fact to be determined by the factfinder. It seems that in making that determination, the trial court may have used an objective standard, which the Michigan Supreme Court found to be an error of law, given that the statute uses the words "value to him"—implying that a subjective standard needs to be applied.

■=■

Quicknotes

NONCONFORMING GOODS Goods tendered pursuant to a contract for sale that do not conform to the contract's requirements or which are otherwise defective in some way.

REVOCATION The cancellation or withdrawal of some authority conferred; or of destruction or making void an instrument drafted.

■=■

Sullivan v. Bullock

Homeowner (P) v. Construction contractor (D)

Idaho Ct. App., 124 Idaho 738, 864 P.2d 184 (1993).

NATURE OF CASE: Appeal from jury verdict awarding damages to cross-plaintiff in a breach of contract suit.

FACT SUMMARY: When Sullivan (P) sued for damages for Bullock's (D) nonperformance on a construction contract, Bullock (D) counter-sued, alleging that he had been prevented from completing the work because of Sullivan's (P) refusal to let him enter the home.

🏛 RULE OF LAW
To excuse a party's nonperformance, the conduct of the party preventing performance must be outside what was permitted in the contract or outside the reasonable contemplation of the parties when the contract was executed.

FACTS: Sullivan (P) hired Bullock (D) to remodel her kitchen, hallway, utility room, bathroom, and sewing room. The written contract lacked detail and Sullivan (P) claimed that Bullock's (D) work was grossly defective, and that he had been unresponsive to requests to improve his product. Sullivan (P) told Bullock (D) she would not be at home on a certain day, but when a workman entered the home through a window to complete some work, Sullivan (P) became very upset and told Bullock (D) that he and his workmen were never to set foot in her house again. Sullivan (P) sued for damages to completely redo the work Bullock (D) had started and return of the amount she had already paid him. Bullock (D) filed a counter-claim, alleging that his work was satisfactory or repairable, but that Sullivan (P) has prohibited him from finishing the project or fixing defects. Bullock (D) requested damages for the work he had performed. The jury returned a special verdict finding that Bullock (D) had not substantially performed under the contract, but that he had been prevented or substantially hindered from performing by Sullivan (P). The jury awarded Bullock (D) damages, costs and attorney fees as provided by the contract. Sullivan (P) moved for judgment notwithstanding the verdict or new trial. Her motion was denied and she appealed. The state's intermediate appellate court granted review.

ISSUE: To excuse a party's nonperformance, must the conduct of the party preventing performance be outside what was permitted in the contract or outside the reasonable contemplation of the parties when the contract was executed?

HOLDING AND DECISION: (Walters, C.J.) Yes. To excuse a party's nonperformance, the conduct of the party preventing performance must be outside what was permitted in the contract or outside the reasonable

contemplation of the parties when the contract was executed. There was substantial evidence from which the jury could conclude that Bullock's (D) failure to complete performance on the contract was to be excused by Sullivan's (P) act of denying access to her home. When Sullivan (P) denied any further access to her home she acted in a manner that was outside the contemplation of the contract or the parties when they executed the contract. The denial of Sullivan's (P) motions is affirmed insofar as the decision below holds that Sullivan (P) prevented Bullock's (D) complete performance. However, the decision is reversed and remanded to the extent it approved an erroneous measure of damages in favor of Bullock (D). The award of attorney fees is vacated and remanded.

▶ ANALYSIS

The court mentioned that implied in every contract there is a condition to cooperate. There is generally in a contract subject to either an express or implied condition, an implied promise not to prevent or hinder performance. Some authorities state that the conduct of the party preventing performance must be wrongful or unjustified.

■═■

Quicknotes

IMPLIED PROMISE A promise inferred by law from a document as a whole and the circumstances surrounding its implementation.

■═■

Burger King Corp. v. Family Dining, Inc.

Restaurant franchisor (P) v. Exclusive franchisee (D)

426 F. Supp. 485 (E.D. Pa. 1977), *aff'd*, 566 F.2d 1168 (3d Cir. 1977).

NATURE OF CASE: Action to declare a contract unenforceable.

FACT SUMMARY: Burger King Corp. (P) sued to have an exclusivity franchise contract declared unenforceable due to Family Dining, Inc.'s (D) failure to meet a development schedule.

🏛 RULE OF LAW
The determination of whether words in a contract constitute a condition or a promise is a matter of the intention of the parties to be ascertained from a reasonable construction of the language used and the surrounding circumstances.

FACTS: Burger King Corp. (P) granted Family Dining, Inc. (Family) (D) an exclusive territory within which to operate franchised restaurants. The contract allowed such exclusivity for as long as 80 years so long as Family (D) kept up with a development schedule requiring it to construct one restaurant a year for 10 years. Family (D) fell behind in its construction schedule yet ultimately built all 10. A controversy arose over the building of the final restaurant as Burger King (P) contended the failure to begin construction on one restaurant per year breached the contract and allowed it to cancel the exclusivity clause. Family (D) defended on the basis that the development schedule was a mere condition and not a promise.

ISSUE: Is the determination of whether words in a contract constitute a condition or a promise a matter of the intention of the parties to be ascertained from a reasonable construction of the language used and the surrounding circumstances?

HOLDING AND DECISION: (Hannum, J.) Yes. The determination of whether words in a contract constitute a condition or a promise is a matter of the intention of the parties to be ascertained from a reasonable construction of the language used and the surrounding circumstances. In this case, it is clear from the record of dealings between the parties that the main focus of concern was the development of the restaurants and not the literal compliance with the schedule. Burger King (P) on several occasions waived the schedule. Therefore, it is clear that the intent was that the schedule be a condition subsequent and not a promise. As such, its breach did not give rise to cancellation of the exclusivity provision, which would amount to forfeiture. Judgment for Family (D).

▶ ANALYSIS

The court in this case also took into consideration the fact that to interpret the contract in a way so as to declare the schedule a promise, and its breach grounds for cancellation, would cause Family (D) to suffer forfeiture. As courts generally follow the maxim that the law of equity abhors forfeiture, this result was avoided.

■=■

Quicknotes

CONDITION PRECEDENT The happening of an uncertain occurrence, which is necessary before a particular right or interest may be obtained or an action performed.

PROMISE The expression of an intention to act, or to forbear from acting, granting a right to the promisee to expect and enforce its performance.

■=■

Inman v. Clyde Hall Drilling Co.

Employee (P) v. Drilling company (D)

Alaska Sup. Ct., 369 P.2d 498 (1962).

NATURE OF CASE: Appeal from summary judgment for defendant in action for damages for breach of an employment contract.

FACT SUMMARY: Clyde Hall Drilling Co. (the Company) (D) employed Inman (P) under a contract which provided that a thirty-day written notice of claim had to be given to the Company (D) as an express condition precedent to a remedy.

🏛 RULE OF LAW
Where there is an express condition precedent to filing suit in a contract, such has to be fulfilled before suit is filed.

FACTS: Inman (P) worked for Clyde Hall Drilling Co. (the Company) (D) under a contract that provided for a thirty-day written notice of claim to be given to the Company (D) as an express condition precedent to a remedy, and barred any action on the contract unless such notice was given. Inman (P) sued the Company (D) for breach of contract but failed to give the requisite notice. Inman (P) alleged that the notice of the suit served as adequate notice within the thirty-day period, and that the Company (D) had repudiated the contract by anticipatory breach which gave him an excuse from performing the condition. The Company (D) moved for summary judgment, which the trial court granted to it. The state's highest court granted review.

ISSUE: Where there is an express condition precedent to filing suit in a contract, does such have to be fulfilled before suit is filed?

HOLDING AND DECISION: (Dimond, J.) Yes. Where there is an express condition precedent to filing suit in a contract, such has to be fulfilled before suit is filed. It is the function of the judiciary to allow parties to contract as freely as the law will allow, and the court will maintain and enforce contracts absent a showing that the court is used as an instrument of inequity or the contract is unconscionable. In this case, there is nothing to suggest that the contract was unconscionable or unfair. Inman (P) showed knowledge of its terms—particularly the notice provision. To hold that filing a complaint was effective notice under the provision would be to ignore the express provision of the contract. There was no anticipatory breach by the Company (D) which would have entitled Inman (P) to conclude the contract had been repudiated. Also, there is no showing that the Company (D) prevented Inman (P)

in some way from performing the condition precedent. Affirmed.

▶ ANALYSIS

It is rare for a court to excuse a condition simply because of hardship to the promisee or lack of a substantial interest which the promisor seeks to promote. Here, there was no showing of the actual purpose of the notice provision, nor prejudice to the drilling Company (D) by not having notice, yet the court not only upheld the provision, but barred an action on the contract because of Inman's (P) failure to abide by it. This case represents the general trend of courts to uphold express conditions precedent where there is no fraud, bad faith, illegality, or other inequitable circumstances brought on by the promisor.

■■■

Quicknotes

ANTICIPATORY REPUDIATION Breach of a contract subsequent to formation but prior to the time performance is due.

CONDITION PRECEDENT The happening of an uncertain occurrence, which is necessary before a particular right or interest may be obtained or an action performed.

EXPRESS CONDITION A condition that is expressly stated in the terms of a written instrument.

SUMMARY JUDGMENT Judgment rendered by a court in response to a motion by one of the parties, claiming that the lack of a question of material fact in respect to an issue warrants disposition of the issue without consideration by the jury.

UNCONSCIONABLE A situation in which a contract, or a particular contract term, is unenforceable if the court determines that such term(s) are unduly oppressive or unfair to one party to the contract.

■■■

Moe v. John Deere Co.

Buyer (P) v. Seller (D)

S.D. Sup. Ct., 516 N.W.2d 332 (1994).

NATURE OF CASE: Appeal from summary judgment in favor of defendant in suit alleging wrongful repossession.

FACT SUMMARY: Moe (P) bought a farm tractor from John Deere Co. (D), which repossessed it after accepting several late payments.

🏛 RULE OF LAW
Repeated acceptance of late payments by a creditor who has the contractual right to repossess the property imposes a duty on the creditor to notify the debtor that strict compliance with the contract terms will be required before the creditor can lawfully repossess the collateral.

FACTS: Moe (P) purchased a farm tractor from John Deere Co. (John Deere) (D), by trading in two old tractors and agreeing to pay five annual installments. When Moe (P) was late in paying his first two installments, John Deere (D) waived full payment and extended the time in which Moe (P) was to make payment. When Moe (P) was late in making a partial payment on the third installment, John Deere (D) repossessed the tractor. Moe (P) was out of state at the time of the repossession and had not received any notice of the repossession. Moe (P) sued for wrongful repossession, fraudulent repossession, commercially unreasonable sale, and failure to account for the surplus. The trial court granted John Deere's (D) motion for summary judgment. Moe (P) appealed. The state's highest court granted review.

ISSUE: Does repeated acceptance of late payments by a creditor who has the contractual right to repossess the property impose a duty on the creditor to notify the debtor that strict compliance with the contract terms will be required before the creditor can lawfully repossess the collateral?

HOLDING AND DECISION: (Moses, J.) Yes. Repeated acceptance of late payments by a creditor who has the contractual right to repossess the property imposes a duty on the creditor to notify the debtor that strict compliance with the contract terms will be required before the creditor can lawfully repossess the collateral. Modification of a written contract may be effected either through subsequent conduct or oral agreements. A secured party, who has not insisted upon strict compliance in the past, must, before he can declare a default and effect repossession, give notice to the debtor that strict compliance of the terms of the contract will be demanded henceforth if repossession is to be avoided. John Deere (D) was required to give pre-possession notice upon modification of the contract. The dispositive issue in this case was whether Moe (P) was in default. There is a question of fact here. Did the oral statements and conduct of the parties modify the written agreement? Whether a default exists is a factual question not properly resolved on a motion for summary judgment. Reversed and remanded.

▶ ANALYSIS

The parties' actions in this case could be dealt with under several theories. Waiver, the intentional relinquishment of a known right, may have been indicated. Courts usually do not apply the doctrine of estoppel to such cases, however. The implied covenant of good faith may also be asserted.

■══■

Quicknotes

ESTOPPEL An equitable doctrine precluding a party from asserting a right to the detriment of another, who justifiably relied on the conduct.

WAIVER The intentional or voluntary forfeiture of a recognized right.

■══■

Anticipatory Repudiation

Quick Reference Rules of Law

Hochster v. De La Tour

Courier (P) v. Employer (D)

Q. B., 2 El. & Bl. 678, 118 Eng. Rep. 922 (1853).

NATURE OF CASE: Action for breach of contract.

FACT SUMMARY: De La Tour (D), who had engaged Hochster (P) for a three-month period of employment beginning on a future date, renounced the contract prior to the date employment was to begin.

🏛 RULE OF LAW
A plaintiff may bring suit for breach of contract prior to the time for performance of the contract if the defendant has repudiated the contract.

FACTS: De La Tour (D) contracted with Hochster (P) to engage Hochster's (P) services as a courier for a three-month tour of Europe to begin at a future date. Prior to the date for the tour to begin, De La Tour (D) renounced the contract. Hochster (P) then sued for breach of contract. De La Tour (D) moved for arrest of judgment on the basis that Hochster (P) had brought suit prematurely, as the time for performance had not yet come, and De La Tour (D) should be given the opportunity to change his mind.

ISSUE: May a plaintiff bring suit for breach of contract prior to the time for performance of the contract if the defendant has repudiated?

HOLDING AND DECISION: (Lord Campbell, C.J.) Yes. A plaintiff may bring suit for breach of contract prior to the time for performance of the contract if the defendant has repudiated the contract. One who wrongfully renounces a contract into which he has entered cannot justly complain if he is immediately sued for damages by the injured party. The injured party may either sue immediately, or wait until the time for the performance of the contract. In this case, it would not be reasonable to require Hochster (P) to remain ready to perform, refraining from entering into any other employment which might interfere with his promise to travel with De La Tour (D) for the specified time, and to equip himself for a three-month tour of Europe, so that he might be ready to perform on the day in question, as a prerequisite to bringing suit. It is much more rational, and more to the benefit of both parties, that, after De La Tour's (D) renunciation of the agreement, Hochster (P) should consider himself absolved from any future performance of it, retaining his right to sue for any damage he has suffered. De La Tour (D) argues that the suit should not be allowed prior to the time for performance of the contract, because of the difficulty of calculating damages. However, if this rationale were applied, no action could ever be brought until the time for the completion of the contract. The calculation of damage is a matter for the jury. Judgment entered for Hochster (P).

▶ ANALYSIS

This case was the first to recognize an anticipatory repudiation; classical contract analysis had previously viewed a promise for performance, which could only be breached after the deadline for performance had passed. Cases involving anticipatory repudiation often also give rise to the issue of mitigation, or "cover." Cover provisions seek to ensure that an aggrieved party is fully compensated, while the breaching party pays no more than necessary to achieve that result.

━■━

Quicknotes

ANTICIPATORY REPUDIATION Breach of a contract subsequent to formation but prior to the time performance is due.

COVER The purchase of an alternate supply of goods by a buyer, after a seller has breached a contract for sale, for which the buyer may recover the difference between the cost of the substituted goods and the price of the original goods pursuant to the contract, so long as the buyer purchases the alternate goods in good faith and without unreasonable delay.

MITIGATION Reduction in penalty.

━■━

Hope's Architectural Products v. Lundy's Construction

Custom window maker (P) v. Construction company (D)

781 F. Supp. 711 (D. Kansas 1991).

NATURE OF CASE: Action for damages for breach of contract.

FACT SUMMARY: When Hope's Architectural Products (Hope's) (P) was late in delivering windows to Lundy's Construction (Lundy's) (D), Lundy's threatened to withhold partial payment as damages, prompting Hope's (P) to demand payment in full before delivery.

🏛 RULE OF LAW
A party who has breached the contract may not demand assurances of performance from the other party.

FACTS: Lundy's Construction (Lundy's) (D) contracted with Hope's Architectural Products (Hope's) (P) for the manufacture of custom window fixtures on June 13, 1988. Delivery was to take place no later than October 24, 1988, and Hope's (P) was to be paid $55,000. There were production delays in the intervening period, and on October 14, 1988, Lundy's (D) wrote to Hope's (P) threatening to withhold partial payment as damages if the deadline was not met. Hope's (P) did not reply to this letter and shipped the windows for delivery on November 4, 1988. As the windows were being shipped, Lundy's (D) again threatened to withhold damages from the $55,000 payment owed Hope's (P). Hope's (P) wrote Lundy's (D) on November 2, 1988, stating that it would not deliver the windows unless it received assurances from Lundy's (D) that the whole contract price would be paid. On November 3, 1988, Hope's (P) demanded that the full payment be made in advance of delivery. Lundy's (D) refused, canceled the contract, and obtained the windows elsewhere. Hope's (P) filed suit to recover the contract price.

ISSUE: May a party who has breached the contract demand assurances of performance from the other party?

HOLDING AND DECISION: (Lungstrum, J.) No. A party who has breached the contract may not demand assurances of performance from the other party. Uniform Commercial Code (UCC) § 2-609 governs the demand for assurances and states that a written demand for adequate assurances may be made after there is reasonable grounds for insecurity regarding performance by the other party. Hope's (P) first made a written demand for assurances on November 2, but at this time Hope's (P) had already breached the contract since delivery was due on October 24. Hope's (P) could not coerce Lundy's (D) into giving up its rights to damages for Hope's (P) breach by demanding assurances under § 2-609. Furthermore, Hope's (P) demands that full payment be made in advance of

delivery were excessive since Lundy's (D) never gave any indication that it was unwilling to pay the amount owed under the payment schedule of the contract. Finally, Hope's (P) cannot prevail on quantum meruit because Hope's (P) never conferred a benefit on Lundy's (D) as its windows were not used in the project. Judgment for Lundy's (D).

▶ ANALYSIS

The court noted in its decision that Hope's (P) may have been justified in demanding assurances following the October 14 letter from Lundy's (D), but it failed to make any demand at that time. The Restatement (Second) of Contracts view of assurances is similar to UCC § 2-609. Under § 251 of the Restatement, the assurances need to be given within 30 days as under § 2-609, and the demand for assurances need not be in writing.

■==■

Quicknotes

ANTICIPATORY REPUDIATION Breach of a contract subsequent to formation but prior to the time performance is due.

ASSURANCES Guarantees; security.

■==■

Greguhn v. Mutual of Omaha Insurance Co.

Disabled worker (P) v. Insurance company (D)

Utah Sup. Ct., 23 Utah 2d 214, 461 P.2d 285 (1969).

NATURE OF CASE: Appeal of judgment awarding benefits under insurance policies.

FACT SUMMARY: Greguhn (P), a disabled worker who sought to collect benefits under policies with Mutual of Omaha Insurance Co. (D) and with another insurer after these insurers discontinued the benefits, was awarded by the trial court future benefits as well as past payments.

🏛 **RULE OF LAW**
The doctrine of anticipatory breach does not extend to unilateral contracts.

FACTS: Greguhn (P), who had health and accident policies with Mutual of Omaha Insurance Co. (Mutual of Omaha) (D) and another insurer, suffered an accident on his job as a bricklayer and thereafter felt back pain. A medical exam showed that Greguhn (P) had the pre-existing condition of spondylolisthesis. The insurers (D), who had been making payments to Greguhn (P), subsequently discontinued them, and Greguhn (P) sued. At trial, it was generally agreed that Greguhn (P) would be unable to continue in his occupation as a brick mason, a trade he had followed for some 30 years. The jury found for Greguhn (P), and the court awarded him not only past benefits, but future benefits as well, on the theory that the insurers (D) had repudiated their contracts. Accordingly, based on Greguhn's life expectancy, the trial court awarded him a lump sum for the future benefits. The insurers (D) appealed, arguing that the trial court had erred in granting future benefits on a theory of anticipatory breach. The state's highest court granted review.

ISSUE: Does the doctrine of anticipatory breach extend to unilateral contracts?

HOLDING AND DECISION: (Tuckett, J.) No. The doctrine of anticipatory breach does not extend to unilateral contracts. The issue is one of first impression in this jurisdiction, but the majority rule is that a plaintiff may only recover accrued and unpaid installments under a disability policy. In a unilateral contract for payment of installments, one of more defaults will not amount to an anticipatory breach of the rest of the installments. As the doctrine of anticipatory breach did not apply to Greguhn's (P) contracts with the insurance companies, it was inappropriate for the trial court to award Greguhn (P) future benefits. Remanded so the trial court can eliminate the part of its judgment pertaining to future benefits.

DISSENT: (Ellett, J.) Where there is a repudiation of all contractual obligations, the better policy is to allow full recovery in one action. Some of the cases that limit recovery to past-due installments do so because of a provision in the policy requiring the insured to furnish proof of continued disability as a condition of liability to pay. This should not be necessary where, as here, there has been a determination in court that the disability is total and permanent.

▶ **ANALYSIS**

The dissent stated that the majority's holding confuses a suit for specific performance with an action for damages for breach of contract. Corbin addresses such confusion: "In the case of an express contract for the payment of money...a judgment for money damages may appear...to be a judgment for specific performance. This it certainly is not if the judgment is not for the full sum promised, but merely for its present value, after making proper discount for advance collection." A. Corbin, *Contracts*, § 965 (1962). Here, the action was for damages, not specific performance. Accordingly, the dissent reasoned that the majority's ruling would compel Greguhn (P) to abide by terms of the contract when neither party requested such a ruling.

■=■

Quicknotes

ANTICIPATORY REPUDIATION Breach of a contract subsequent to formation but prior to the time performance is due.

SPECIFIC PERFORMANCE An equitable remedy whereby the court requires the parties to perform their obligations pursuant to a contract.

UNILATERAL CONTRACT An agreement pursuant to which a party agrees to act, or to forbear from acting, in exchange for performance on the part of the other party.

■=■

Third Party Beneficiaries

Quick Reference Rules of Law

Lawrence v. Fox

Lender (P) v. Friend of borrower (D)

N.Y. Ct. App., 20 N.Y. 268 (1859).

NATURE OF CASE: Appeal from affirmance of verdict for plaintiff third party in action to recover damages for breach of contract made for his benefit.

FACT SUMMARY: Fox (D) promised Holly for consideration that he would pay Holly's debt to Lawrence (P).

🏛 RULE OF LAW
A third party for whose benefit a contract is made may bring an action for its breach notwithstanding a lack of privity with the promisor.

FACTS: Holly owed Lawrence (P) $300. Holly loaned $300 to Fox (D) in consideration of Fox's (D) promise to pay the same amount to Lawrence (P), thereby erasing Holly's debts to Lawrence (P). Fox (D) did not pay Lawrence (P), and Lawrence (P) brought suit for breach of Fox's (D) promise to Holly. The trial court rejected the defense, inter alia, of lack of privity, and the jury returned a verdict for Lawrence (P). The state's intermediate appellate court affirmed, and the state's highest court granted review.

ISSUE: May a third party for whose benefit a contract is made bring an action for its breach notwithstanding a lack of privity with the promisor?

HOLDING AND DECISION: (Gray, J.) Yes. A third party for whose benefit a contract is made may bring an action for its breach notwithstanding a lack of privity with the promisor. "[In the case of] a promise made to one for the benefit of another, he for whose benefit it is made may bring an action for its breach." This principle, which has been long applied in trust cases, is in fact a general principle of law that is not limited to such cases and that may be applied here. Affirmed.

CONCURRENCE: (Johnson, C.J.) It should be presumed the promise was made to the plaintiff through the medium of his agent whose action he could approve when it became known to him, notwithstanding the lack of prvity.

DISSENT: (Comstock, J.) Lawrence (P) should not be allowed to sue. There is no privity of contract. The plaintiff must either be the promisee, or have a legal interest in the contract through a trust or agency relationship. Lawrence (P) was not the promisee and had no control over the contract. At any time, Holly could have told Fox (D) to pay the money to someone other than Lawrence (P) and Lawrence (P) would have had no right to demand the money. Nor did Holly give the money to Fox (D) in trust for Lawrence (P). In all cases where a third party has been allowed to sue, the third party was a trust beneficiary. A trust beneficiary has a specific interest in the trust money. Additionally, Fox (D) was not Holly's agent.

▶ ANALYSIS

This is the leading case which started the general doctrine of "third-party beneficiaries." In the parlance of the original Restatement of Contracts, Lawrence (P) was a "creditor" beneficiary. Restatement (Second) of Contracts § 133 has eliminated the creditor/donee distinction which the original Restatement fostered and has lumped both under the label of "intended" beneficiary. Although the court in the present case went to some effort to discuss trusts and agency, ultimately the court allowed Lawrence (P) to recover because it was manifestly "just" that he should recover. Such has been the creation of many a new legal doctrine. The dissenting justices were primarily worried about freedom of contract and the continuing ability of promisor and promisee to rescind or modify their contract. As the doctrine has developed, various rules have arisen to handle these situations.

■=■

Quicknotes

AGENCY RELATIONSHIP A fiduciary relationship whereby authority is granted to an agent to act on behalf of the principal in order to effectuate the principal's objective.

CREDITOR BENEFICIARY A creditor who receives the benefits of a contract between a debtor and another party, pursuant to which the other party is obligated to tender payment to the creditor.

PRIVITY OF CONTRACT A relationship between the parties to a contract which is required in order to bring an action for breach.

THIRD-PARTY BENEFICIARY A party who benefits from a promise made pursuant to a contract although he is not a party to the agreement.

■=■

Seaver v. Ransom

Niece (P) v. Executor of uncle's estate (D)

N.Y. Ct. App., 224 N.Y. 233, 120 N.E. 639 (1918).

NATURE OF CASE: Appeal from affirmance of judgment for a third party in action to recover damages for breach of a contract related to a will.

FACT SUMMARY: Beman made a promise to his wife for the benefit of their niece, Seaver (P), who then sued Beman's executor (D) for breach of that promise.

🏛 RULE OF LAW
A third party for whose benefit a promise is made to a testator has an action for breach of that promise by the promisee.

FACTS: Mrs. Beman, on her death bed, wished to leave some property to her niece, Seaver (P). Her husband induced her, as she was dying, to sign a will leaving use of the house to him for his life, even though she wanted to leave the house to Seaver (P), by promising that he would leave a certain amount in his own will to Seaver (P). Mr. Beman died without making such a provision for Seaver (P). Seaver (P) brought suit against Ransom (D), as executor of Beman's estate, for Beman's breach of his promise to his dying wife, on the theory that a trust of Mr. Beman's property had been created for her. The trial court returned a judgment for Seaver (P) on this theory, and the state's intermediate appellate court affirmed, but on the theory that Seaver (P) could recover as a third-party beneficiary of the promise Mr. Beman had made to Mrs. Beman. The state's highest court granted review.

ISSUE: Does a third party for whose benefit a promise is made to a testator have an action for breach of that promise by the promisee?

HOLDING AND DECISION: (Pound, J.) Yes. A third party for whose benefit a promise is made to a testator has an action for breach of that promise by the promisee. First, where a legatee (here, Mr. Beman) promises the testator (here, Mrs. Beman) that he will use property given him by the will for a particular purpose, a trust arises. Here, however, all that Mr. Beman received was use of the house for his life, so equity cannot impose a trust on his property, but Mr. Beman remains bound by his promise. Therefore, the intermediate appellate court affirmed on the correct ground. The core issue is whether Ransom (D) can be liable for damages arising out of Mr. Beman's promise, or can be held to be a trustee for performance of that promise. Although a general rule requires privity between a plaintiff and a defendant as necessary to the maintenance of an action on the contract, one of several exceptions to the rule is the case where a contract is made for the benefit of another member of the

family. Here Mrs. Beman was childless and Seaver (P) was a beloved niece. However, "the constraining power of conscience is not regulated by the degree of relationship alone. The dependent or faithful niece may have a stronger claim than the affluent or unworthy son. No sensible theory of moral obligation denies arbitrarily to the former what would be conceded to the latter." The reason for this "family" exception (and other exceptions) to the rule is that it is just and practical to permit the person for whose benefit a contract is made to enforce it against one whose duty it is to pay. "The doctrine of *Lawrence v. Fox*, 20 N.Y. 268 (1859) is progressive, not retrograde." Finally, in this particular case, the "equities" are with Seaver (P). Affirmed.

▶ ANALYSIS

In this case, the court (as does the original Restatement of Contracts) uses the term "donee beneficiary" to describe Seaver (P). The Restatement (Second) of Contracts erases the creditor/donee distinction and labels both types of beneficiaries as "intended." Although the court here is very insistent on the close family relationship, subsequent New York cases have erased that requirement for donee beneficiaries as the doctrine governing third-party beneficiaries has expanded. These subsequent cases represent the now-prevailing view in the country.

■━■

Quicknotes

DONEE BENEFICIARY A third party, not a party to a contract, but for whose benefit the contract is entered with the intention that the benefits derived therefrom be bestowed upon the person as a gift.

PRIVITY Commonality of rights or interests between parties.

■━■

H.R. Moch Co. v. Rensselaer Water Co.

Owner of premises (P) v. Water company (D)

N.Y. Ct. App., 247 N.Y. 160, 159 N.E. 896 (1928).

NATURE OF CASE: Appeal from reversal of denial of dismissal of action for damages for breach of contract.

FACT SUMMARY: H.R. Moch Co. (P) contended that it was a third party beneficiary to a contract involving a municipality by virtue of its being a resident of that municipality.

🏛 RULE OF LAW
One cannot claim to be a third party beneficiary of a contract involving a municipality merely by virtue of being a resident of that municipality.

FACTS: Rensselaer Water Co. (D) contracted with the City of Rensselaer to furnish the city with water. During a fire on the premises owned by H.R. Moch Co. (P), Rensselaer Water (D) did not supply sufficient water to save the building. H.R. Moch (P) sued under the contract, contending that it was a third party beneficiary. The trial court denied Rensselaer Water's (D) motion to dismiss, but the state's intermediate appellate court reversed. H.R. Moch Co. (P) appealed. The state's highest court granted review.

ISSUE: Can one claim to be a third party beneficiary of a contract involving a municipality merely by virtue of being a resident of that municipality?

HOLDING AND DECISION: (Cardozo, C.J.) No. One cannot claim to be a third party beneficiary of a contract involving a municipality merely by virtue of being a resident of that municipality. Before one can claim to be a third party beneficiary of a contract involving a municipality, the benefits to the claiming party must be immediate and primary. Every contract involving a city should be for the benefit of the public, and such incidental benefits are not sufficient to confer third party benefit status. To hold otherwise would extend limitless liability to city contractors. Here, the benefit to H.R. Moch (P) was no greater than benefit to the public at large, so H.R. Moch (P) was not a third party beneficiary. Because there was no specific intent to benefit any particular member of the public, including H.R. Moch (P), Rensselaer Water (D) is liable on the contract only to the city. Affirmed.

▌ ANALYSIS

H.R. Moch (P) also sued on a tort theory. The casebook excerpt omitted most discussion of this issue. However, it was noted that the city was under no legal duty to provide fire protection, so such a duty ought not to be imposed on a city contractor.

■━■

Quicknotes

THIRD-PARTY BENEFICIARY A party who benefits from a promise made pursuant to a contract although he is not a party to the agreement.

■━■

Blair v. Anderson

Federal convict (P) v. State prison official (D)

Del. Sup. Ct., 325 A.2d 94 (1974).

NATURE OF CASE: Appeal of dismissal of action for damages for personal injury and breach of contract.

FACT SUMMARY: An ex-prisoner (P) sued the state of Delaware (D) for injuries he sustained in prison from an attack by another prisoner.

 RULE OF LAW
(1) State sovereign immunity is not a defense to a contract claim.
(2) A federal convict in a state prison is a third-party creditor beneficiary of the federal-state contract which provides for his incarceration.

FACTS: Under a contract, the federal government paid the state of Delaware (D) to hold federal convicts in Delaware (D) prisons. Delaware (D) was to provide for the convicts' "safekeeping, care and subsistence." Blair (P) was a federal convict in a Delaware (D) prison. He was attacked by another prisoner. After his release, he sued Delaware (D) on tort and contract theories for injuries he sustained in the attack. Blair (P) argued that Delaware (D) breached its duty under its federal-state contract by not protecting him, that he was a third-party beneficiary of the contract, and, thus, that he could sue for Delaware's (D) breach. The trial court dismissed all claims, holding Delaware (D) was protected from the suit by sovereign immunity. The court also found that Blair (P) was a donee or incidental beneficiary, not a creditor beneficiary, and, thus, not entitled to sue to enforce the contract. Blair (P) appealed. The state's highest court granted review.

ISSUE:
(1) Is state sovereign immunity a defense to a contract claim?
(2) Is a federal convict in a state prison a third-party creditor beneficiary of the federal-state contract which provides for his incarceration?

HOLDING AND DECISION: (Duffy, J.)
(1) No. State sovereign immunity is not a defense to a contract claim. The Delaware Constitution provides the state may not be sued unless the legislature waives sovereign immunity. Where, as here, the state assembly authorizes a contract to be made, the state implicitly waives immunity to a suit for breach of that contract. Blair's (P) tort claims, however, are barred by sovereign immunity.
(2) Yes. A federal convict in a state prison is a third-party creditor beneficiary of the federal-state contract which provides for his incarceration. If performance of a contract will satisfy a legal duty owed by the promisee to the beneficiary, then the beneficiary is a creditor beneficiary with standing to sue. The federal government owed a duty under federal law to care for Blair (P). Delaware's (D) performance of its duties under the federal-state contract would have satisfied the federal government's duty to Blair (P). Thus, Blair (P) may sue to enforce the federal-state contract. Reversed as to the contract claim.

▶ ANALYSIS

Creative third-party beneficiary claims often are asserted to pursue what is basically a tort claim. The facts of *Blair* make out a standard tort claim for personal injury caused by a defendant's breach of a duty of care. Blair (P) likely predicted his tort claim would not survive a sovereign immunity defense. So, he asserted a third-party beneficiary claim to circumvent sovereign immunity and pursue essentially the same claim. Note, however, that the punitive damages are generally unavailable in breach of contract actions.

■▬■

Quicknotes

CREDITOR BENEFICIARY A creditor who receives the benefits of a contract between a debtor and another party, pursuant to which the other party is obligated to tender payment to the creditor.

THIRD-PARTY BENEFICIARY A party who benefits from a promise made pursuant to a contract although he is not a party to the agreement.

■▬■

Bain v. Gillispie

Referee (P) v. T-shirt manufacturer (D)

Iowa Ct. App., 357 N.W.2d 47 (1984).

NATURE OF CASE: Appeal from grant of summary judgment in a suit requesting injunctive relief.

FACT SUMMARY: In Bain's (P) action against Gillispie (D) for injunctive relief, actual and punitive damages, Gillispie (D) contended, in his counterclaim, that Bain's (P) conduct as a referee in officiating a basketball game between the University of Iowa and Purdue University was below the standard of competence required of a professional referee and constituted malpractice which entitled Gillispie (D) to $175,000 plus exemplary damages as a beneficiary under Bain's (P) contract with the Big 10 college basketball division.

🏛 RULE OF LAW
The real test as to whether a party is a beneficiary under a contract is whether the contracting parties intended that a third person should receive a benefit which might be enforced in the courts.

FACTS: Bain (P), who was a referee employed by the Big 10 college basketball division to officiate college basketball games, made a call during a University of Iowa-Purdue University game, which some University of Iowa fans asserted caused Purdue to win the game. Gillispie (D), who operated a novelty store near the University of Iowa, marketed, after the game, a T-shirt which was deprecatory of Bain (P). Bain (P) sued Gillispie (D) for injunctive relief and actual and punitive damages. Gillispie (D) counterclaimed, contending that Bain's (P) conduct, in officiating the game, was below the standard of competence required of a professional referee and constituted malpractice which entitled Gillispie (D) to $175,000 plus exemplary damages as a beneficiary under Bain's (P) contract with the Big 10. The trial court found that Gillispie (D) had no rights and sustained a motion for summary judgment dismissing Gillespie's (D) counterclaim. Gillispie (D) appealed.

ISSUE: Is the real test as to whether a party is a beneficiary under a contract whether the contracting parties intended that a third person should receive a benefit which might be enforced in the courts?

HOLDING AND DECISION: (Snell, J.) Yes. The real test as to whether a party is a beneficiary under a contract is whether the contracting parties intended that a third person should receive a benefit which might be enforced in the courts. Here, because Gillispie (D) was not privy to the contract between Bain (P) and the Big 10, Gillispie (D) must be a direct beneficiary to maintain a cause of action against Bain (P). A direct beneficiary is either a donee or a creditor beneficiary. Gillispie (D) makes no claim that he is a creditor beneficiary, and he does not come within the definition of a donee beneficiary. A donee beneficiary is one, other than the promisor or promisee, who will benefit from performance of a promise. The purpose of the promisee in obtaining such a promise from a promisor must be to make a gift to the beneficiary. It is clear that, here, any promise which Bain (P) might have made was not to confer a gift on Gillispie (D). Likewise, the Big 10 did not owe Gillispie (D) any duty. If a contract did exist between Bain (P) and the Big 10, Gillispie (D) can be considered nothing more than an incidental beneficiary, and, as such, unable to maintain a cause of action. Affirmed.

▌ ANALYSIS

Beneficiaries, who can claim under a contract, have been divided into donee or creditor beneficiaries. A promisee's intent to benefit the beneficiary named by her in a contract is clear in the case of the donee beneficiary. A creditor beneficiary is one for whom performance of a promise will satisfy an actual or supposed duty of the promisee to the beneficiary.

■═■

Quicknotes

CREDITOR BENEFICIARY A creditor who receives the benefits of a contract between a debtor and another party, pursuant to which the other party is obligated to tender payment to the creditor.

DONEE BENEFICIARY A third party, not a party to a contract, but for whose benefit the contract is entered with the intention that the benefits derived therefrom be bestowed upon the person as a gift.

INCIDENTAL BENEFICIARY A person for whom a trust is not specifically created and who has no right to assert an interest in the trust, yet derives incidental benefits therefrom.

INTENDED BENEFICIARY A third party who is the recipient of the benefit of a transaction undertaken by another.

■═■

Board of Education of Community School District No. 220 v. Village of Hoffman Estates

Board (P) v. Village (D)

Ill. App. Ct., 126 Ill. App. 3d 625, 467 N.E.2d 1064 (1984).

NATURE OF CASE: Appeal from summary judgment awarding damages to a third party beneficiary.

FACT SUMMARY: The Village of Hoffman Estates (the Village) (D) entered into annexation agreements with a group of developers whereby the developers would pay the Village (D) an amount of money to be held in escrow for five years during which the parties would try to have the area annexed included in School District 15, but if this effort were unsuccessful, the money would be paid to District 220 (P). Prior to the expiration of the five-year period, the parties amended their agreement to extend the period to nine years, and District 220 (P) sued for the escrowed funds.

> 🏛 **RULE OF LAW**
> A third party beneficiary does not have a vested right under a contract if it has not been specifically identified as the beneficiary.

FACTS: Two groups of developers (Owners) who wanted to have certain tracts of land annexed to the Village of Hoffman Estates (D) (the Village) agreed to pay $135 to the Village (D) for each residential unit developed "for the benefit of education" in return for the Village's (D) annexing the areas. The funds were to be kept in escrow during the following five years while the parties used their best efforts to cause the annexed area to be included within the boundaries of School District 15. If the parties were successful, the escrowed funds would be paid to District 15, but if their efforts were unsuccessful, at the end of the five-year period, the money would be paid to District 220 (P). The owners and the Village (D) were unsuccessful in attempting to have the area included in District 15. Shortly before the expiration of the five-year period, they amended their agreement, extending the period to nine years, and providing that the parties would use their best efforts to cause the area to be included in either School District 15 or 54, but that if the parties were unsuccessful, at the end of the nine-year period, the money would be paid to District 220 (P). At the end of the five-year period (during which the area had been included in District 220 (P), which had been providing education to the children residing in the area) District 220 (P) sought a declaratory judgment that it was entitled to the funds, on the basis that it was a donee beneficiary of the contract between the Owners and the Village (D). The trial court granted summary judgment to District 220 (P), holding that execution of the agreement

created a vested right in District 220 (P). The state's intermediate appellate court granted review.

ISSUE: Does a third-party beneficiary have a vested right under a contract if it has not been specifically identified as the beneficiary?

HOLDING AND DECISION: (Sullivan, J.) No. A third-party beneficiary does not have a vested right under a contract if it has not been specifically identified as the beneficiary. Here, District 220 (P) was merely a potential beneficiary of the promise to pay certain sums for the benefit of education. At the time the Owners and the Village (D) modified their contract, the actual beneficiary had not been identified, as it could have been either District 220 (P) or District 15. Since neither School District was identified as the beneficiary, neither has a vested right under the contract. Therefore, the Owners and the Village (D) were free to modify the contract. Reversed and remanded.

▶ ANALYSIS

The Restatement (Second) of Contracts states that in the absence of language in the contract making the rights of a third-party beneficiary irrevocable, "the promisor and promisee retain power to discharge or modify the duty by subsequent agreement" until such time as the beneficiary, without notice of the discharge or modifications "materially changes his position in justifiable reliance on the promise or brings suit on it or manifests assent to it at the request of the promisor or promisee." Restatement (Second) Contracts § 373. A majority of jurisdictions have adopted the Restatement rule.

■■■

Quicknotes

THIRD-PARTY BENEFICIARY A party who benefits from a promise made pursuant to a contract although he is not a party to the agreement.

VESTED RIGHT Rights in pension or other retirement benefits that are attained when the employee satisfies the minimum requirements necessary in order to be entitled to the receipt of such benefits in the future.

■■■

CHAPTER 10

Assignment and Delegation

Quick Reference Rules of Law

Macke Co. v. Pizza of Gaithersburg, Inc.

Drink machine supplier (P) v. Pizza shops (D)

Md. Ct. App., 259 Md. 479, 270 A.2d 645 (1970).

NATURE OF CASE: Suit for damages for breach of contract.

FACT SUMMARY: In 1967, Pizza of Gaithersburg, Inc. (D) entered into a contract under which Virginia Coffee Service, Inc. was to install and maintain cold drink vending machines in their pizza shops. Shortly thereafter, Macke Co. (P) bought Virginia Coffee, and Virginia Coffee assigned the contract to Macke (P).

🏛 **RULE OF LAW**
Where there is no contrary provision, rights and duties under an executory bilateral contract may be assigned or delegated except that duties under a personal service contract may not be assigned nor rights delegated where performance by the delegee would vary substantially from the performance of the original party.

FACTS: Pizza of Gaithersburg, Inc. (Pizza) (D) and five other pizza shops owned by the same individuals entered into separate contracts with Virginia Coffee Service (Virginia) under which Virginia was to install, maintain, and supply drink vending machines at the pizza shops. The contract was for a period of one year, automatically renewable in the absence of 30 days' notice to the contrary. After Virginia sold its assets to Macke Co. (P) and assigned the pizza contract to them (P), Pizza (D) attempted to terminate all the contracts. Macke (P) brought suit against Pizza (D) for breach of contract and, from a judgment in favor of Pizza (D), appealed. The state's highest court granted review.

ISSUE: Where there is no contrary provision, rights and duties under an executory bilateral contract may be assigned or delegated except that duties under a personal service contract may not be assigned nor rights delegated where performance by the delegee would vary substantially from the performance of the original party?

HOLDING AND DECISION: (Singley, J.) Yes. Where there is no contrary provision, rights and duties under an executory bilateral contract may be assigned or delegated except that duties under a personal service contract may not be assigned nor rights delegated where performance by the delegee would vary substantially from the performance of the original party. The agreement for the supply and maintenance of drink vending machines cannot be regarded as a personal service contract because the duties required do not involve genius or unique abilities on the part of the supplier. Pizza (D) argued, however, that they originally contracted with Virginia rather than with Macke (P) because of their prior experience with Macke (P) and their preference for Virginia's more individualized services and

that performance of the contract by Macke (P) would vary from the performance bargained for with Virginia. The actual details of Virginia's additional services were not included in the contract, however, and the difference in service which Pizza (D) expected does not constitute so material a change in the performance of the contract as to justify Pizza's (D) refusal to recognize the assignment of the contract. Since Pizza (D) was not entitled to rescind the agreements, Macke (P) has an action for damages in the form of anticipated profits lost as a result of the breach. Although such damages were formerly not permitted by courts because of the inherent uncertainty of calculation, they are now permitted where the amount involved can be shown with reasonable certainty. In the instant case, the evidence presented did not enable the court to determine the loss of profits with reasonable certainty and therefore the case must be remanded for further evidence on this issue. The judgment in favor of Pizza (D) must therefore be reversed with costs awarded to Macke (P) and the cause remanded for a new trial on damages.

▶ **ANALYSIS**

The general rule that prohibits the delegation of duties where the contract is one for personal services is reasonable and protects the party who contracts for a unique, special, or particular service by another. In contracts involving the provision of common goods and services where there are no express provisions against assignment or delegation, assignment should be permitted as a matter of commercial convenience. The Uniform Commercial Code specifically makes ineffective any provision of a contract which forbids the assignment of a contract right. And where the performance involved does not involve a unique service, there should be no barrier to the delegation of duties in the absence of an express provision to that effect.

■═■

Quicknotes

ASSIGNMENT A transaction in which a party conveys his or her entire interest in property to another.

DELEGATION The authorization of one person to act on another's behalf.

EXECUTORY BILATERAL CONTRACT An agreement pursuant to which each party promises to undertake an obligation, or to forbear from acting, at some time in the future and whose terms have yet to be performed.

■═■

Herzog v. Irace

Physician (P) v. Attorneys (D)

Me. Sup. Jud. Ct., 594 A.2d 1106 (1991).

NATURE OF CASE: Appeal of affirmance of an award of damages for breach of assignment.

FACT SUMMARY: Although Jones assigned a personal injury claim to Herzog (P) and so notified his attorneys, Irace (D) and Lowry (D), they failed to pay the settlement to Herzog (P).

🏛 RULE OF LAW
An assignment is binding upon the obligor when the obligor is notified of the intent to relinquish the right to the assignee.

FACTS: Jones, who was injured in a motorcycle accident, hired attorneys Irace (D) and Lowry (D) to represent him in a personal injury action. Jones required surgery for his injuries, which was performed by Herzog (P), a physician. Since Jones was unable to pay for this treatment, he signed a letter stating that he requested "that payment be made directly . . . to John Herzog [P]" of money received in settlement for his claim. Herzog (P) notified Irace (D) and Lowry (D) of the assignment in 1988. The following year, Jones received a $20,000 settlement for his claim. Jones instructed Irace (D) and Lowry (D) to pay the money to him rather than to Herzog (P). Irace (D) and Lowry (D) followed this instruction, and Jones failed to pay Herzog (P) for the medical treatment. Herzog (P) brought a breach of assignment action against Irace (D) and Lowry (D), and the trial court ruled in favor of Herzog (P). The state's intermediate appellate court affirmed, and Irace (D) and Lowry (D) appealed to the state's highest court.

ISSUE: Is an assignment binding upon the obligor where the assignor has intended to relinquish the right and the obligor has been notified?

HOLDING AND DECISION: (Brody, J.) Yes. An assignment is binding upon an obligor when the assignor has intended to relinquish his rights and the obligor has been notified. The letter directing payment to be made directly to Herzog (P) clearly and unequivocally showed Jones's intent to relinquish his control over any money received for his personal injury claim. Irace (D) and Lowry (D) were duly notified of this assignment, and therefore the settlement money should have been paid to Herzog (P). Also, the assignment did not interfere with the ethical obligations that Irace (D) and Lowry (D) owed to Jones, since he had already assigned the proceeds to Herzog (P) and he, not the lawyers, was the one who had encumbered those proceeds. Affirmed.

▶ ANALYSIS

Limitations on the right of assignment exist in many situations. Most states have a statute which restricts the assignment of wages. Also, public policy considerations protect assignors who attempt to assign future rights. The Restatement (Second) of Contracts § 317(2) does not allow assignment where the duty to the obligor would be materially changed.

■■■■

Quicknotes

ASSIGNMENT A transaction in which a party conveys his or her entire interest in property to another.

ASSIGNOR A party who assigns his interest or rights to another.

OBLIGOR Promisor; a party who has promised or is obligated to perform.

■■■■

Cheney v. Jemmett

Seller of real estate (P) v. Buyer (D)

Idaho Sup. Ct., 107 Idaho 829, 693 P.2d 1031 (1984).

NATURE OF CASE: Appeal from grant of defense motion for involuntary dismissal of action for breach of a non-assignment provision.

FACT SUMMARY: After Jemmett (D) agreed when buying real estate from Cheney (P) that he would not assign the purchase agreement without Cheney's (P) consent, Cheney (P) withheld such consent when Jemmett (D) proposed to resell the property.

> ## 🏛 RULE OF LAW
> When a contract for sale of property grants the purchaser the right to assign it conditioned upon the seller's consent, the seller must act reasonably and in good faith in withholding his consent to the proposed assignment.

FACTS: The Cheneys (P) sold real estate to the Jemmetts (D) for a purchase price of $32,500, $5,000 down and $27,500 through Treasure Valley Bank at the close of escrow. The Jemmetts (D) also agreed that they would not assign the purchase agreement without first obtaining the written consent of the Cheneys (P). The Jemmetts (D) subsequently decided to move and to sell the property to Honn, and accordingly requested the Cheneys' (P) consent, but the Cheneys (P) refused to consent. Upon the advice of an attorney, the Jemmetts (D) then rented the property to Honn until the escrow at Treasure Valley Bank was paid in full, when Honn would purchase it. The Cheneys (P) declared a default due to the assignment and sued to recover the balance on the contract. Their case was involuntarily dismissed upon motion of the Jemmetts (D), the trial court finding that the agreement between the Jemmetts (D) and Honn was not an assignment, and that, in any event, the Cheneys (P) had unreasonably withheld their consent when first asked for it. The state's highest court granted review.

ISSUE: When a contract for sale of property grants the purchaser the right to assign it conditioned upon the seller's consent, must the seller act reasonably and in good faith in withholding his consent to the proposed assignment?

HOLDING AND DECISION: (Donaldson, C.J.) Yes. When a contract for sale of property grants the purchaser the right to assign it conditioned upon the seller's consent, the seller must act reasonably and in good faith in withholding his consent to the proposed assignment. The issue of whether the Jemmett (D)-Honn agreement was an assignment does not need to be reached because the Cheneys (P) unreasonably withheld their consent in the first place. Although clauses which forbid assignment are valid, the non-assignment clause at issue was not absolute, since it allowed the Jemmetts (D) to obtain the consent of the Cheneys (P) to assign the property.

However, the seller must nevertheless act reasonably and in good faith in withholding such consent. Here, the Cheneys (P) had no objection to the proposed assignee's credit or reputation yet still refused consent. This was unreasonable and in bad faith. As prevailing parties, the Jemmetts (D) are entitled to recover attorneys' fees. Affirmed.

CONCURRENCE: (Bistline, J.) Interpreting such a restricted assignment clause as requiring good faith by the obligor allows modern society to avoid penalizing an increasingly transient population. However, attorneys' fees should not have been awarded because they were not in the language of the contract.

DISSENT: (Bakes, J.) This court cannot make for the parties better agreements than they can make for themselves; in reading a "good faith" requirement into the restricted assignment clause, it ignores the express provisions of the contract.

▶ ANALYSIS

On denial of petition for rehearing, the court aligned itself with the concurrence and struck its award of attorneys' fees. The law on assignability of contracts has been expanded still further under the Uniform Commercial Code (UCC), which expressly allows assignments in future contracts. Under UCC § 9-204, a party can perfect a security interest in "after-acquired" property which the debtor will acquire after he first transacts with the creditor.

■=■

Quicknotes

ASSIGNMENT A transaction in which a party conveys his or her entire interest in property to another.

OBLIGOR Promisor; a party who has promised or is obligated to perform.

■=■

Ford Motor Credit Co. v. Morgan

Credit division (D) v. Car buyers (P)

Mass. Sup. Jud. Ct., 404 Mass. 537, 536 N.E.2d 587 (1989).

NATURE OF CASE: Appeal of denial of damages on counterclaims for unfair and deceptive practices and breach of warranty.

FACT SUMMARY: The Morgans (P), whose car payments were assigned to Ford Motor Credit Co. (Ford Credit) (D) by a car dealer, sought to recover damages from Ford Credit (D) for the actions of the dealer.

🏛 RULE OF LAW
An affirmative recovery of damages by a consumer is not available against an assignee-creditor of an installment contract.

FACTS: The Morgans (P) purchased a car from Neponsit Lincoln Mercury, Inc. in 1978. To finance the purchase, the Morgans (P) signed an installment contract prepared by Ford Motor Credit (Ford Credit) (D). The contract assigned the credit payments to Ford Credit (D) and contained language that stated that the creditor-assignee, Ford Credit (D), was subject to all claims and defenses which the debtor, the Morgans (P), could assert against the seller, Neponsit (D). It also stated that recovery could not exceed the amounts paid by the Morgans (P) under the contract. During 1979, the Morgans (P), because of problems they were having with the car, stopped making payments. They refused to surrender the car after defaulting on the contract; they also let the insurance lapse. Following a contempt order, the Morgans (P) returned the car to Ford Credit (D), which attempted to sell it, but it was vandalized before it could be sold. Ford Credit (D) sued the Morgans (P) for damages because their failure to procure insurance made the vandalism loss unrecoverable. The Morgans (P) filed three counterclaims: (1) for fraud by Neponsit (D), (2) for unfair and deceptive practices by Neponsit (D), and (3) for breach of warranty. The jury decided for the Morgans (P) on the fraud action, and the trial court ruled that this verdict provided the Morgans (P) with a defense to Ford Credit's (D) claim. The trial court dismissed the other two claims, reasoning the Morgans (P) were not entitled to any affirmative recovery from Ford Credit (D). The Morgans (P) appealed this ruling. The state's highest court granted review.

ISSUE: Is an affirmative recovery of damages by a consumer available against an assignee-creditor of an installment contract?

HOLDING AND DECISION: (O'Connor, J.) No. An affirmative recovery of damages by a consumer is not available against an assignee-creditor of an installment contract. The contractual provision stating that the debtor can assert all claims against the creditor-assignee was required by the Federal Trade Commission (FTC). The FTC regulations state that a consumer-debtor may not obtain an affirmative recovery from an assignee-creditor unless payments have been made and the goods have not been delivered. Policy considerations also favor denying affirmative recovery to consumers because it would make the assignee-creditor an insurer of the seller's performance. Moreover, there is nothing in Chapter 9 of the Uniform Commercial Code (UCC) that supports the Morgans' (P) claimed entitlement to affirmative recovery against Ford Credit (D). The Morgans (P) may use claims which they have against Neponsit (D) to defend, but they may not use these claims to make an affirmative recovery against Ford Credit (D). Affirmed.

▶ ANALYSIS

The court's decision is in accord with the majority view when the transaction has a commercial purpose. Other cases have found that the FTC language permits affirmative recovery in consumer credit transactions. See *Eachen v. Scott Housing Systems*, 630 F. Supp. 162 (M.D. Alabama 1986).

■=■

Quicknotes

CONTEMPT An act of omission that interferes with a court's proper administration of justice.

COUNTERCLAIM An independent cause of action brought by a defendant to a lawsuit in order to oppose or deduct from the plaintiff's claim.

■=■

Seattle-First National Bank v. Oregon Pacific Industries

Assignee of invoice (P) v. Plywood purchaser (D)

Or. Sup. Ct., 262 Or. 578, 500 P.2d 1033 (1972).

NATURE OF CASE: Appeal from judgment for plaintiff in action to collect a debt.

FACT SUMMARY: Oregon Pacific Industries (Oregon Pacific) (D) owed money to Centralia Plywood, which assigned its invoice to Seattle-First National Bank (Bank) (P). When Bank (P) filed suit to collect on the invoice, Oregon Pacific (D) attempted to set off claims it had against Centralia, but which had accrued after Oregon Pacific (D) received notice of the assignment.

🏛 RULE OF LAW
An assignee of a right to collect money is not subject to claims of the obligor arising out of other transactions with the assignor where those claims did not accrue before notice of the assignment was given.

FACTS: Oregon Pacific Industries, Inc. (Oregon Pacific) (D) purchased plywood from Centralia Plywood. The next day, Centralia assigned the invoice evidencing the sale to Seattle-First National Bank (Bank) (P), which notified Oregon Pacific (D) of the assignment. Oregon Pacific (D) refused to tender payment, whereupon Bank (P) brought suit. Prior to the assignment, Oregon Pacific (D) had placed two separate orders with Centralia which that company had failed to fill, allegedly to the injury of Oregon Pacific (D). Citing those orders, Oregon Pacific (D) claimed a setoff against Bank (P). Such a setoff could be asserted, Oregon Pacific (D) contended, because Centralia had been insolvent at the time of the assignment and both Centralia and Bank (P) were nonresidents. Judgment was rendered in favor of Bank (P), but Oregon Pacific (D) appealed. The state's highest court granted review.

ISSUE: Is an assignee of a right to collect money subject to claims of the obligor arising out of other transactions with the assignor where those claims did not accrue before notice of the assignment was given?

HOLDING AND DECISION: (Denecke, J.) No. An assignee of a right to collect money is not subject to claims of the obligor arising out of other transactions with the assignor where those claims did not accrue before notice of the assignment was given. The circumstances cited by Oregon Pacific (D) were deemed sufficient to entitle the obligor to set off claims in *Pearson v. Richards*, 211 P. 167 (1922). But that case predated the Uniform Commercial Code and was not incorporated into the Code. According to § 9-318 of the Code, terms and defenses included in the contract between the obligor and the assignor may be asserted against the assignee. However, claims not arising from that contract may be asserted only if they accrued prior to notification of the assignment. A claim may be said to accrue when it ripens into a cause of action, which in this case occurred when Centralia failed to deliver the materials requested. This was after notification of the assignment. Therefore, since the claims arose independently of the transaction which was the subject of the assignment, Oregon Pacific (D) was not entitled to set off the claims in the action by the bank (P). Therefore, the judgment in the Bank's (P) favor is affirmed.

▶ ANALYSIS

The court in this case rejected the notion that pre-Code law which is not inconsistent with the Code should be retained and applied as a supplement to the Code's provisions. But § 9-318, upon which the court based its decision, theoretically is applicable only to assignments involving assets used for security, e.g., to obtain financing. Since § 9-318 technically has no relevance to assignments in other settings, it would seem that pre-Code law is still important to fill interstices which remain despite the care with which the Code was drafted.

■▬■

Quicknotes

ASSIGNEE A party to whom another party assigns his interest or rights.

ASSIGNOR A party who assigns his interest or rights to another.

OBLIGOR Promisor; a party who has promised or is obligated to perform.

■▬■

Langel v. Betz

Seller of land (P) v. Assignee of buyer (D)

N.Y. Ct. App., 250 N.Y. 159, 164 N.E. 890 (1928).

NATURE OF CASE: Appeal from judgment for plaintiff in action for specific performance of an assigned land sale contract.

FACT SUMMARY: Langel (P) made a contract with Betz's (D) assignor for the sale of certain land. The assignment contract contained no delegation to Betz (D) as assignee of the performance of the assignor's duties. Betz (D) refused to perform on the contract with Langel (P).

🏛 RULE OF LAW
A promise of the assignee to assume the assignor's duties cannot be inferred from the assignee's mere acceptance of an assignment of a bilateral contract absent circumstances surrounding the assignment that indicate a contrary intention.

FACTS: Langel (P) made a contract with Hurwitz for the sale of certain real property. Hurwitz, the vendee, assigned the contract to Benedict, who in turn assigned it to Betz (D). The assignment contract contained no delegation to Betz (D), as assignee, of the performance of the assignor's duties. Betz (D) requested and obtained an extension of the time in which to close title. Betz (D) then refused to perform. Langel (P) sued for specific performance and obtained judgment in his favor in the trial court. The state's intermediate appellate court affirmed, and the state's highest court granted review.

ISSUE: Can a promise of the assignee to assume the assignor's duties be inferred from the assignee's mere acceptance of an assignment of a bilateral contract absent circumstances surrounding the assignment that indicate a contrary intention?

HOLDING AND DECISION: (Pound, J.) No. A promise of the assignee to assume the assignor's duties cannot be inferred from the assignee's mere acceptance of an assignment of a bilateral contract absent circumstances surrounding the assignment that indicate a contrary intention. The mere assignment of a bilateral executory contract may not be interpreted as a promise by the assignee to the assignor to assume the performance of the assignor's duties, so as to have the effect of creating a new liability on the part of the assignee to the other party to the contract assigned. The assignee may, however, expressly or impliedly, bind himself to perform the assignor's duties. But a promise to do so will not be inferred in the absence of circumstances surrounding the assignment which indicate an intention on the part of the assignee to so bind himself. Here, there were no such circumstances. Betz's (D) request for and obtaining an extension of the performance date was not such an assertion of a right under the contract as to make it enforceable against him here. Reversed.

▶ ANALYSIS

It is a general principle that an assignment of a contract does not operate to cast upon the assignee the duties and obligations or the liabilities imposed by the contract on the assignor in the absence of the assignee's express assumption of such liabilities. The Uniform Commercial Code provides, in § 2-210(4), that "assignment of 'the contract' or an assignment in similar terms is an assignment of rights and unless the language or the circumstances indicate the contrary, it is a delegation of performance of the duties of the assignor and acceptance by the assignee constitutes a promise by him to perform those duties. This promise is enforceable by either the assignor or the other party to the original contract."

Quicknotes

ASSIGNMENT A transaction in which a party conveys his or her entire interest in property to another.

BILATERAL CONTRACT An agreement pursuant to which each party promises to undertake an obligation, or to forbear from acting, at some time in the future.

DELEGATION The authorization of one person to act on another's behalf.

EXECUTORY Something that has not been fully completed or performed.

Rouse v. United States

Buyer of real estate (D) v. Assignee of note (P)

215 F.2d 872 (D.C. Cir. 1954).

NATURE OF CASE: Appeal from summary judgment for plaintiff in action for payment of a debt.

FACT SUMMARY: When Rouse (D) bought Winston's house, he agreed to assume payment of a debt secured by a note, but was not informed that the note had been assigned to the United States (P), which paid the debt and sought to collect on the debt from Rouse (D) after Winston defaulted on it. Rouse (D) asserted as defenses Winston's fraud and claims he had against the original creditor.

🏛 RULE OF LAW
(1) One who promises to make a payment to the promisee's creditor can assert against the creditor, and against the creditor's assignee, any defense that the promisor could assert against the promisee.
(2) A promisor may not assert against a third-party beneficiary a defense which the promisee would have against the beneficiary.

FACTS: Associated Contractors, Inc. (Associated) installed a heating plant in Winston's house. Winston gave Associated a promissory note for $1,008.37 payable in monthly installments of $28.01. Associated assigned the note to the United States (P), which paid the note. Winston later sold her house to Rouse (D), who agreed in the contract of sale "to assume payment of $850 for the heating plant payable $28 per Mo." Winston defaulted on her note, and the United States (P) sued Rouse (D) for payment of $850 and interest. Rouse (D) defended by alleging (1) that Winston fraudulently misrepresented the condition of the heating plant and (2) that Associated didn't install the heater properly in the first place. The district court granted summary judgment for the United States (P). The court of appeals granted review.

ISSUE:
(1) Can one who promises to make a payment to the promisee's creditor assert against the creditor, and against the creditor's assignee, any defense that the promisor could assert against the promisee?
(2) Can one who promises to make a payment of a sum certain to the promisee's creditor assert against the creditor and the creditor's assignee a defense that the promisee would have against the creditor?

HOLDING AND DECISION: (Edgerton, J.)
(1) Yes. One who promises to make a payment to the promisee's creditor can assert against the creditor, and against the creditor's assignee, any defense that the

promisor could assert against the promisee. Thus, Rouse's (D) defense of fraud, which he would certainly have been entitled to show against Winston, is equally effective against Winston's creditor, Associated, and, in turn, against Associated's assignee, the United States (P). Therefore, the district court erroneously dismissed this defense. Reversed as to this issue.

(2) No. One who promises to make a payment of a sum certain to the promisee's creditor cannot assert against the creditor and the creditor's assignee a defense that the promisee would have against the creditor. Here Rouse's (D) promise was to pay a specified sum of money to the beneficiary (P), and it is irrelevant whether or not the promisee (Winston) was actually indebted in that amount. "Where the promise is to pay a specific debt . . . this interpretation will generally be the true one." 2 Williston, *Contracts* § 399. The result would be different if Rouse (D) had merely promised to discharge whatever liability Winston was under. In that case, the promisor must certainly be allowed to show that the promisee was under no enforceable liability, so in such a case, Rouse (D) would have been able to assert the defense that Associated failed to adequately perform its services and therefore was not entitled to payment. The district court was correct to dismiss this defense. Affirmed as to this issue. Reversed and remanded.

▶ ANALYSIS

This well-known case clearly lays out what defenses are, and are not, available to a promisor in an action by a promisee's creditor—and the creditor's assignee. While the promisor usually may assert against the creditor any defense which he could assert against the promisee, he usually may not assert defenses which the promisee might have raised against the creditor. In support of its denial of Rouse's (D) second defense, the court rests on Williston's presumption as to the nature of the promisor's promise. Unless it is clearly indicated that a promisor is only undertaking to pay "the debt" of the promisee (whatever it may turn out to be), it will be presumed that the promise is to pay the specific amount, regardless of whether it is actually owed. Whether this "presumption" necessarily effects a "just" result in all (or even most) ambiguous cases is open to some question.

■▬■

Continued on next page.

Quicknotes

ASSIGNOR A party who assigns his interest or rights to another.

PROMISOR Party who promises to render an obligation to another in the future.

THIRD-PARTY BENEFICIARY A party who benefits from a promise made pursuant to a contract although he is not a party to the agreement.

■═■

Glossary

Common Latin Words and Phrases Encountered in the Law

A FORTIORI: Because one fact exists or has been proven, therefore a second fact that is related to the first fact must also exist.

A PRIORI: From the cause to the effect. A term of logic used to denote that when one generally accepted truth is shown to be a cause, another particular effect must necessarily follow.

AB INITIO: From the beginning; a condition which has existed throughout, as in a marriage which was void ab initio.

ACTUS REUS: The wrongful act; in criminal law, such action sufficient to trigger criminal liability.

AD VALOREM: According to value; an ad valorem tax is imposed upon an item located within the taxing jurisdiction calculated by the value of such item.

AMICUS CURIAE: Friend of the court. Its most common usage takes the form of an amicus curiae brief, filed by a person who is not a party to an action but is nonetheless allowed to offer an argument supporting his legal interests.

ARGUENDO: In arguing. A statement, possibly hypothetical, made for the purpose of argument, is one made arguendo.

BILL QUIA TIMET: A bill to quiet title (establish ownership) to real property.

BONA FIDE: True, honest, or genuine. May refer to a person's legal position based on good faith or lacking notice of fraud (such as a bona fide purchaser for value) or to the authenticity of a particular document (such as a bona fide last will and testament).

CAUSA MORTIS: With approaching death in mind. A gift causa mortis is a gift given by a party who feels certain that death is imminent.

CAVEAT EMPTOR: Let the buyer beware. This maxim is reflected in the rule of law that a buyer purchases at his own risk because it is his responsibility to examine, judge, test, and otherwise inspect what he is buying.

CERTIORARI: A writ of review. Petitions for review of a case by the United States Supreme Court are most often done by means of a writ of certiorari.

CONTRA: On the other hand. Opposite. Contrary to.

CORAM NOBIS: Before us; writs of error directed to the court that originally rendered the judgment.

CORAM VOBIS: Before you; writs of error directed by an appellate court to a lower court to correct a factual error.

CORPUS DELICTI: The body of the crime; the requisite elements of a crime amounting to objective proof that a crime has been committed.

CUM TESTAMENTO ANNEXO, ADMINISTRATOR (ADMINISTRATOR C.T.A.): With will annexed; an administrator c.t.a. settles an estate pursuant to a will in which he is not appointed.

DE BONIS NON, ADMINISTRATOR (ADMINISTRATOR D.B.N.): Of goods not administered; an administrator d.b.n. settles a partially settled estate.

DE FACTO: In fact; in reality; actually. Existing in fact but not officially approved or engendered.

DE JURE: By right; lawful. Describes a condition that is legitimate "as a matter of law," in contrast to the term "de facto," which connotes something existing in fact but not legally sanctioned or authorized. For example, de facto segregation refers to segregation brought about by housing patterns, etc., whereas de jure segregation refers to segregation created by law.

DE MINIMIS: Of minimal importance; insignificant; a trifle; not worth bothering about.

DE NOVO: Anew; a second time; afresh. A trial de novo is a new trial held at the appellate level as if the case originated there and the trial at a lower level had not taken place.

DICTA: Generally used as an abbreviated form of obiter dicta, a term describing those portions of a judicial opinion incidental or not necessary to resolution of the specific question before the court. Such nonessential statements and remarks are not considered to be binding precedent.

DUCES TECUM: Refers to a particular type of writ or subpoena requesting a party or organization to produce certain documents in their possession.

EN BANC: Full bench. Where a court sits with all justices present rather than the usual quorum.

EX PARTE: For one side or one party only. An ex parte proceeding is one undertaken for the benefit of only one party, without notice to, or an appearance by, an adverse party.

EX POST FACTO: After the fact. An ex post facto law is a law that retroactively changes the consequences of a prior act.

EX REL.: Abbreviated form of the term "ex relatione," meaning upon relation or information. When the state brings an action in which it has no interest against an individual at the instigation of one who has a private interest in the matter.

FORUM NON CONVENIENS: Inconvenient forum. Although a court may have jurisdiction over the case, the action should be tried in a more conveniently located court, one to which parties and witnesses may more easily travel, for example.

GUARDIAN AD LITEM: A guardian of an infant as to litigation, appointed to represent the infant and pursue his/her rights.

HABEAS CORPUS: You have the body. The modern writ of habeas corpus is a writ directing that a person (body) being detained (such as a prisoner) be brought before the court so that the legality of his detention can be judicially ascertained.

IN CAMERA: In private, in chambers. When a hearing is held before a judge in his chambers or when all spectators are excluded from the courtroom.

IN FORMA PAUPERIS: In the manner of a pauper. A party who proceeds in forma pauperis because of his poverty is one who is allowed to bring suit without liability for costs.

INFRA: Below, under. A word referring the reader to a later part of a book. (The opposite of supra.)

IN LOCO PARENTIS: In the place of a parent.

IN PARI DELICTO: Equally wrong; a court of equity will not grant requested relief to an applicant who is in pari delicto, or as much at fault in the transactions giving rise to the controversy as is the opponent of the applicant.

IN PARI MATERIA: On like subject matter or upon the same matter. Statutes relating to the same person or things are said to be in pari materia. It is a general rule of statutory construction that such statutes should be construed together, i.e., looked at as if they together constituted one law.

IN PERSONAM: Against the person. Jurisdiction over the person of an individual.

IN RE: In the matter of. Used to designate a proceeding involving an estate or other property.

IN REM: A term that signifies an action against the res, or thing. An action in rem is basically one that is taken directly against property, as distinguished from an action in personam, i.e., against the person.

INTER ALIA: Among other things. Used to show that the whole of a statement, pleading, list, statute, etc., has not been set forth in its entirety.

INTER PARTES: Between the parties. May refer to contracts, conveyances or other transactions having legal significance.

INTER VIVOS: Between the living. An inter vivos gift is a gift made by a living grantor, as distinguished from bequests contained in a will, which pass upon the death of the testator.

IPSO FACTO: By the mere fact itself.

JUS: Law or the entire body of law.

LEX LOCI: The law of the place; the notion that the rights of parties to a legal proceeding are governed by the law of the place where those rights arose.

MALUM IN SE: Evil or wrong in and of itself; inherently wrong. This term describes an act that is wrong by its very nature, as opposed to one which would not be wrong but for the fact that there is a specific legal prohibition against it (malum prohibitum).

MALUM PROHIBITUM: Wrong because prohibited, but not inherently evil. Used to describe something that is wrong because it is expressly forbidden by law but that is not in and of itself evil, e.g., speeding.

MANDAMUS: We command. A writ directing an official to take a certain action.

MENS REA: A guilty mind; a criminal intent. A term used to signify the mental state that accompanies a crime or other prohibited act. Some crimes require only a general mens rea (general intent to do the prohibited act), but others, like assault with intent to murder, require the existence of a specific mens rea.

MODUS OPERANDI: Method of operating; generally refers to the manner or style of a criminal in committing crimes, admissible in appropriate cases as evidence of the identity of a defendant.

NEXUS: A connection to.

NISI PRIUS: A court of first impression. A nisi prius court is one where issues of fact are tried before a judge or jury.

N.O.V. (NON OBSTANTE VEREDICTO): Notwithstanding the verdict. A judgment n.o.v. is a judgment given in favor of one party despite the fact that a verdict was returned in favor of the other party, the justification being that the verdict either had no reasonable support in fact or was contrary to law.

NUNC PRO TUNC: Now for then. This phrase refers to actions that may be taken and will then have full retroactive effect.

PENDENTE LITE: Pending the suit; pending litigation under way.

PER CAPITA: By head; beneficiaries of an estate, if they take in equal shares, take per capita.

PER CURIAM: By the court; signifies an opinion ostensibly written "by the whole court" and with no identified author.

PER SE: By itself, in itself; inherently.

PER STIRPES: By representation. Used primarily in the law of wills to describe the method of distribution where a person, generally because of death, is unable to take that which is left to him by the will of another, and therefore his heirs divide such property between them rather than take under the will individually.

PRIMA FACIE: On its face, at first sight. A prima facie case is one that is sufficient on its face, meaning that the evidence supporting it is adequate to establish the case until contradicted or overcome by other evidence.

PRO TANTO: For so much; as far as it goes. Often used in eminent domain cases when a property owner receives partial payment for his land without prejudice to his right to bring suit for the full amount he claims his land to be worth.

QUANTUM MERUIT: As much as he deserves. Refers to recovery based on the doctrine of unjust enrichment in those cases in which a party has rendered valuable services or furnished materials that were accepted and enjoyed by another under circumstances that would reasonably notify the recipient that the rendering party expected to be paid. In essence, the law implies a contract to pay the reasonable value of the services or materials furnished.

QUASI: Almost like; as if; nearly. This term is essentially used to signify that one subject or thing is almost analogous to another but that material differences between them do exist. For example, a quasi-criminal proceeding is one that is not strictly criminal but shares enough of the same characteristics to require some of the same safeguards (e.g., procedural due process must be followed in a parole hearing).

QUID PRO QUO: Something for something. In contract law, the consideration, something of value, passed between the parties to render the contract binding.

RES GESTAE: Things done; in evidence law, this principle justifies the admission of a statement that would otherwise be hearsay when it is made so closely to the event in question as to be said to be a part of it, or with such spontaneity as not to have the possibility of falsehood.

RES IPSA LOQUITUR: The thing speaks for itself. This doctrine gives rise to a rebuttable presumption of negligence when the instrumentality causing the injury was within the exclusive control of the defendant, and the injury was one that does not normally occur unless a person has been negligent.

RES JUDICATA: A matter adjudged. Doctrine which provides that once a court of competent jurisdiction has rendered a final judgment or decree on the merits, that judgment or decree is conclusive upon the parties to the case and prevents them from engaging in any other litigation on the points and issues determined therein.

RESPONDEAT SUPERIOR: Let the master reply. This doctrine holds the master liable for the wrongful acts of his servant (or the principal for his agent) in those cases in which the servant (or agent) was acting within the scope of his authority at the time of the injury.

STARE DECISIS: To stand by or adhere to that which has been decided. The common law doctrine of stare decisis attempts to give security and certainty to the law by following the policy that once a principle of law as applicable to a certain set of facts has been set forth in a decision, it forms a precedent which will subsequently be followed, even though a different decision might be made were it the first time the question had arisen. Of course, stare decisis is not an inviolable principle and is departed from in instances where there is good cause (e.g., considerations of public policy led the Supreme Court to disregard prior decisions sanctioning segregation).

SUPRA: Above. A word referring a reader to an earlier part of a book.

ULTRA VIRES: Beyond the power. This phrase is most commonly used to refer to actions taken by a corporation that are beyond the power or legal authority of the corporation.

Addendum of French Derivatives

IN PAIS: Not pursuant to legal proceedings.

CHATTEL: Tangible personal property.

CY PRES: Doctrine permitting courts to apply trust funds to purposes not expressed in the trust but necessary to carry out the settlor's intent.

PER AUTRE VIE: For another's life; during another's life. In property law, an estate may be granted that will terminate upon the death of someone other than the grantee.

PROFIT A PRENDRE: A license to remove minerals or other produce from land.

VOIR DIRE: Process of questioning jurors as to their predispositions about the case or parties to a proceeding in order to identify those jurors displaying bias or prejudice.

Casenote® Legal Briefs